T0183556

Communications in Computer and Information Science 973

Commenced Publication in 2007
Founding and Former Series Editors:
Phoebe Chen, Alfredo Cuzzocrea, Xiaoyong Du, Orhun Kara, Ting Liu,
Dominik Ślęzak, and Xiaokang Yang

More information about this series at http://www.springer.com/series/7899

Hein Venter · Marianne Loock
Marijke Coetzee · Mariki Eloff
Jan Eloff (Eds.)

Information Security

17th International Conference, ISSA 2018
Pretoria, South Africa, August 15–16, 2018
Revised Selected Papers

 Springer

Editors
Hein Venter ⓘ
University of Pretoria
Pretoria, Gauteng, South Africa

Mariki Eloff ⓘ
University of South Africa
Pretoria, Gauteng, South Africa

Marianne Loock ⓘ
University of South Africa
Florida, Gauteng, South Africa

Jan Eloff ⓘ
University of Pretoria
Pretoria, Gauteng, South Africa

Marijke Coetzee ⓘ
University of Johannesburg
Auckland Park, Gauteng, South Africa

ISSN 1865-0929   ISSN 1865-0937 (electronic)
Communications in Computer and Information Science
ISBN 978-3-030-11406-0   ISBN 978-3-030-11407-7 (eBook)
https://doi.org/10.1007/978-3-030-11407-7

Library of Congress Control Number: 2018967049

This Springer imprint is published by the registered company Springer Nature Switzerland AG
The registered company address is: Gewerbestrasse 11, 6330 Cham, Switzerland

Preface

ISSA is the annual conference for the information security community that continues with the successful recipe established in 2001. The conference is held under the auspices of the Academy for Computer Science and Software Engineering at the University of Johannesburg, the School of Computing at the University of South Africa, and the Department of Computer Science at the University of Pretoria.

The ISSA 2018 Conference was held during August 15–16, 2018. The conference has evolved each year in various ways. For the first time the conference was hosted at the premises of the University of Pretoria. We believe that the quality and relevance of the information presented by industry practitioners and academics have also evolved over the years, as have the opportunities for senior research students to present their research to a critical and representative audience. This year university students were allowed to register for the conference for an unprecedented ZAR200 per person in order to make the conference extremely accessible to students.

Conferences have become a major focus area – and often a money spinner – in many industries, so at any time a number of conferences are advertised in similar fields such as information or cyber security. What sets the ISSA conference apart is that it is not intended to generate profit for an organization, and it does not encourage marketing of products and services through presentations. Instead, the proceeds from registration fees are reinvested to ensure that the conference evolves each year. In exchange for their investment in the conference, sponsors are afforded an opportunity to present company-specific information that has a bearing on the conference themes, and presentations submitted by potential speakers go through a vigorous double-blind review process, managed by a team of respected international experts in information security.

We trust that the annual ISSA conference will continue to be recognized as a platform for professionals from industry as well as researchers to share their knowledge, experience, and research results in the field of information security on a South African but also on an international level.

To ensure ongoing improvement, every year we encourage input from all those interested in the field of information security, particularly those who are actively seeking to advance the field, to take part and share their knowledge and experience.

On behalf of the general conference chairs, we would like to extend our heartfelt appreciation to all the conference committee members and chairs for their hard work in organizing ISSA 2018! Without your continuous hard work and efforts, ISSA 2018 would not have been possible. Again, we thank you!

www.infosecsa.co.za

August 2018

Hein Venter
Marianne Loock
Marijke Coetzee
Mariki Eloff
Jan Eloff

Conference Focus

Information security has evolved and in the past few years there has been renewed interest in the subject worldwide. This is evident from the many standards and certifications now available to guide security strategy. This has led to a clearer career path for security professionals.

The Internet of Things (IoT) together with advances in wireless communications has brought new security challenges for the information security fraternity. As these IoT devices become more available, and more organizations attempt to rid their offices of "spaghetti," the protection of data in these environments becomes a more important consideration. It is this fraternity that organizations, governments, and communities in general look to for guidance on best practice in this converging world.

Identity theft and phishing are ongoing concerns. What we are now finding is that security mechanisms have become so good and are generally implemented by companies wanting to adhere to good corporate governance, attackers are now looking to the weak link in the chain, namely, the individual user. It is far easier to attack them than attempt to penetrate sophisticated and secure corporate systems. A spate of ransomware is also doing the rounds, with waves of viruses still striking periodically. Software suppliers have started stepping up to protect their users and take some responsibility for security in general and not just for their own products.

The conference therefore focused on all aspects of information and cyber security and invited participation across the information security spectrum including but not being limited to functional, business, managerial, theoretical, and technological issues.

Invited speakers talked about the international trends in information security products, methodologies, and management issues. In the past, ISSA has secured many highly acclaimed international speakers, including:

- Pieter Geldenhuys, Vice-chair of the Innovation Focus Group at the International Communications Union, Geneva, Switzerland. Topic: "BUSINESS UNUSUAL: Strategic Insight in Creating the Future. Leveraging the Value of the Hyper-connected World"
- Wayne Kearney, Manager: Risk & Assurance at Water Corporation. Topic: "Why Are Management Shocked with all the 'PHISH' Caught? A Case Study in Perspective"
- Prof. Sylvia Osborn, Associate Professor of Computer Science, The University of Western Ontario, Ontario, Canada. Topic: "Role-Based Access Control: Is it Still Relevant?"
- Prof. Steve Marsh, Associate Professor at the University of Ontario, Institute of Technology. Topic: "Trust and Security - Links, Relationships, and Family Feuds"
- Alice Sturgeon manages the area that is accountable for identifying and architecting horizontal requirements across the Government of Canada. Her topic made reference to "An Identity Management Architecture for the Government of Canada"

- Dr. Alf Zugenmaier, DoCoMo Lab, Germany. His topic was based on "Security and Privacy"
- William List, WM List and Co., UK. His topic was: "Beyond the Seventh Layer Live the Users"
- Prof. Dennis Longley, Queensland University of Technology, Australia. His topic was: "IS Governance: Will It Be effective?"
- Prof. TC Ting: University of Connecticut, and fellow of the Computing Re-search Association, United States
- Prof. Dr. Stephanie Teufel: Director of the International Institute of Management in Telecommunications (iimt). Fribourg University, Switzerland
- Rich Schiesser, Senior Technical Planner at Option One Mortgage, USA Rick Cudworth, Partner, KPMG LLP, International Service Leader, Security and Business Continuity - Europe, Middle East and Africa
- Dario Forte - CISM, CFE, Founder, DFLabs Italy and Adj. Faculty University of Milan
- Reijo Savola - Network and Information Security Research Coordinator, VTT Technical Research Centre of Finland
- Mark Pollitt - Ex Special Agent of the Federal Bureau of Investigation (FBI) and professor at the Daytona State College, Daytona Beach, Florida, USA
- Prof. Joachim Biskup - Professor of Computer Science, Technische Universität Dortmund, Germany
- Dr. Andreas Schaad - Research Program Manager, SAP Research Security & Trust Group, Germany
- Prof. Steven Furnell - Head of School, School of Computing and Mathematics (Faculty of Science and Technology), University of Plymouth, UK
- Prof. Matt Warren - School of Information and Business Analytics, Deakin University, Australia
- Christian Damsgaard Jensen - Associate Professor, Institute for Mathematics and Computer Science, Technical University of Denmark
- Prof. Rebecca Wright - Director of DIMACS, Rutgers University, USA

The purpose of the conference was to provide information security practitioners and researchers worldwide with the opportunity to share their knowledge and research results with their peers. The objectives of the conference are defined as follows:

- Sharing of knowledge, experience, and best practice
- Promoting networking and business opportunities
- Encouraging the research and study of information security
- Supporting the development of a professional information security community
- Assisting self-development
- Providing a forum for education, knowledge transfer, professional development, and development of new skills
- Promoting best practice in information security and its application in Southern Africa
- Facilitating the meeting of diverse cultures to share and learn from each other in the quest for safer information system

Organization

Conference General Chairs

Hein Venter — Department of Computer Science, University of Pretoria, South Africa

Marijke Coetzee — Academy for Computer Science and Software Engineering, University of Johannesburg, South Africa

Marianne Loock — School of Computing, University of South Africa

Mariki Eloff — Institute for Corporate Citizenship, University of South Africa

Jan Eloff — Department of Computer Science, University of Pretoria, South Africa

Organizing Committee

Mariki Eloff — Institute for Corporate Citizenship, University of South Africa

Marijke Coetzee — Academy for Computer Science and Software Engineering, University of Johannesburg, South Africa

Marianne Loock — School of Computing, University of South Africa

Hein Venter — Department of Computer Science, University of Pretoria, South Africa

Jan Eloff — Department of Computer Science, University of Pretoria, South Africa

Program Committee

Reinhardt Botha — Nelson Mandela University, South Africa

Marianne Loock — School of Computing, University of South Africa

Mariki Eloff — Institute for Corporate Citizenship, University of South Africa

Publication Chair

Hein Venter — Department of Computer Science, University of Pretoria, South Africa

Honorary Committee

The following member is an honorary committee member of the ISSA conference. This committee member is honored for his effort as one of the founding members of the ISSA conference in 2001. The current conference committee feels obliged to honor him as such.

Les Labuschagne — University of South Africa

Review Committee

A rigorous double-blind refereeing process was undertaken by an international panel of referees to ensure the quality of submissions before acceptance. Authors initially submit abstracts to determine if the paper meets the goals and fits into the theme of the conference. The ISSA Program Committee assesses each submission for relevance and fit. Authors are then notified whether their abstracts were accepted, and if so, invited to submit a full paper for peer review. The task of a reviewer is often a thankless task; however, without them this conference would not be possible. The ISSA Organizing Committee would like to extend their heartfelt thanks to the list of reviewers including leading information security experts from around the world.

On the due date, authors submit full papers, anonymized by the authors for the double-blind review process. Each paper goes through an administrative review and is assigned to at least three reviewers selected from an international panel of reviewers, in order to confirm that the paper conforms to the specifications and quality for the conference. If a paper does not meet the requirements, the author is asked to make the required changes as indicated by reviewers and asked to resubmit the paper, or to consider submitting the paper to another conference.

A review committee is invited to participate, consisting of both local and international experts in the field of information security. A process is followed by the Program Committee to allocate papers to reviewers based on their area of expertise. Reviewers are subject matter experts, of whom over 50% are international. Reviewers usually have five or six categories that they are willing to review in. Each reviewer will establish the number of papers they can review in a specific time period and are allowed to bid on the papers they want to review. An automated process allocated papers to each reviewer according to their preferences.

Each paper is reviewed by a minimum of two reviewers (but mostly by three reviewers) in a double-blind review process. Papers are reviewed and rated on a 5-point system with 1 being poor and 5 being excellent as follows:

- Originality (1 to 5)
- Contribution (1 to 5)
- Overall quality (1 to 5)
- Reviewer's confidence (1 to 5)
- Overall evaluation (calculated by an algorithm as a number in the range −5 to 5, where a negative score of −5 would indicate an extremely strong reject, 0 would indicate a borderline paper and 5 would indicate an extremely strong accept)

The reviewers' confidence in their own rating is also taken into account by the algorithm that calculates the overall evaluation. Reviewers are also encouraged to make anonymous suggestions to the author(s) of the paper.

Based on the overall evaluation (−5 to 5), a paper with 0 or below points can be recommended for a poster/research-in-progress session and a 3–5-point paper can be put in the "best paper" category. An acceptance rate of between 25% and 35% is maintained for the conference. In 2018 the acceptance rate was 30%.

Authors are notified of the outcome of the review process, which includes the anonymous suggestions and recommendations of the reviewers. Authors then have to submit the final version of the paper that will then be included in the formal conference proceedings. This volume is the official version of the proceedings. An unofficial version of the proceedings was distributed on USB flash drives during the conference. All USB proceedings from all previous ISSA conferences are also available at www.infosecsa.co.za/past.

Name	Company/Affiliation	Country	
Hanifa Abdullah	University of South Africa	South Africa	
Mary Adedayo	University of Pretoria	South Africa	
Ikuesan Adeyemi	University of Pretoria	South Africa	
Alapan Arnab	Private	South Africa	
Sampson Asare	University of Botswana	Botswana	
Hettie Booysen	Private	South Africa	
Reinhardt Botha	Nelson Mandela Metropolitan University	South Africa	
Rachelle Bosua	University of Melbourne	Australia	
K. P. Chow	University of Hong Kong	Hong Kong, SAR China	
Nathan Clarke	University of Plymouth	UK	
Evan Dembsky	University of South Africa	South Africa	
Moses Dlamini	University of Pretoria	South Africa	
Lynette Drevin	North-West University	South Africa	
David Ellefsen	University of Johannesburg	South Africa	

Eduardo Fernandez	Florida Atlantic University	USA	
Stephen Flowerday	University of Fort Hare	South Africa	
Evangelos Frangopoulos	University of South Africa	Greece	
Steven Furnell	University of Plymouth	UK	
Lynn Futcher	Nelson Mandela Metropolitan University	South Africa	
Stefanos Gritzalis	University of the Aegean	Greece	
Marthie Grobler	CSIRO's Data61	South Africa	
Paul Haskell-Dowland	Edith Cowan University	Australia	
Bertram Haskins	Nelson Mandela University	South Africa	
Barry Irwin	Rhodes University	South Africa	
Christian Damsgaard Jensen	Technical University of Denmark	Denmark	
Jason Jordaan		South Africa	
Hennie Kruger	North-West University	South Africa	
Grace Leung	University of Johannesburg	South Africa	
Buks Louwrens	Nedbank/University of Johannesburg	South Africa	
Tayana Morkel	University of Pretoria	South Africa	
Francois Mouton	Council for Scientific and Industrial Research	South Africa	
Rolf Oppliger	eSECURITY Technologies	Switzerland	

Jacques Ophoff	University of Cape Town	South Africa	
Mauricio Papa	University of Tulsa	USA	
Guenther Pernul	University of Regensburg	Germany	
Rayne Reid	Nelson Mandela Metropolitan University	South Africa	
Karen Renaud	University of Glasgow	UK	
Jill Slay	La Trobe University	Australia	
Bobby Tait	University of South Africa	South Africa	
Barend Taute	CSIR	South Africa	
Stephanie Teufel	University of Fribourg	Switzerland	
Kerry-Lynn Thomson	Nelson Mandela Metropolitan University	South Africa	
Aleksandar Valjarevic	Vlatacom Research and Development Institute	Serbia	
Dustin van der Haar	University of Johannesburg	South Africa	
Johan Van Niekerk	Nelson Mandela Metropolitan University	South Africa	
Brett van Niekerk	University of Kwazulu Natal	South Africa	
Alf Zugenmaier	Munich University	Germany	

Additional Reviewers

Deon Cotterell	University of Johannesburg	South Africa	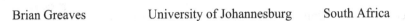
Brian Greaves	University of Johannesburg	South Africa	
Mathias Mujinga	University of Pretoria	South Africa	
Carl van der Westhuizen	University of Johannesburg	South Africa	

Contents

Distributed Ledger Technology to Support Digital Evidence Integrity Verification Processes

William Thomas Weilbach[(✉)] and Yusuf Moosa Motara[(✉)]

Rhodes University, Grahamstown 6140, South Africa
thomas.weilbach@gmail.com, y.motara@ru.ac.za

Abstract. This paper examines the way in which blockchain technology can be used to improve the integrity of the chain of evidence in digital forensics. A particular scalable method of verifying point-in-time existence of a piece of digital evidence, using the OpenTimestamps (OTS) service, is described, and tests are carried out to independently validate the claims made by the service. The results demonstrate that the OTS service is highly reliable, but not suitable for time-sensitive digital timestamping.

Keywords: Digital forensics · Blockchain · Evidence integrity

1 Introduction

In the face of an impending financial crisis, an anonymous researcher, going by the pseudonym Satoshi Nakamoto, proposed a cryptographic solution to the problem of distributed trust, also known as "The Byzantine Generals Problem" [8]. This solution, in the form of blockchain technology, was presented in a paper titled: "Bitcoin: A Peer-to-Peer Electronic Cash System" [11]. Blockchain technology has emerged as a significant and potentially revolutionary technology inspiring a new class of solutions to problems all but forgotten.

The potential applications of blockchain technology are vast and continue to diversify every day with the emergence of smart contract platforms such as Ethereum [4] and digital currencies such as Zcash [22]. However, despite its widespread adoption, blockchain technology remains relatively unexplored in areas that extend beyond payments and currency. Blockchains solve a few fundamental issues of trust by operationally incorporating the properties of immutability and transparency, and when applied to other problem domains, these exact properties are equally valuable. One of those problem domains is the domain of digital forensics: "the discipline that combines elements of law and computer science to collect and analyse data from computer systems, networks, wireless communications, and storage devices in a way that is admissible as evidence in a court of law" [16].

© Springer Nature Switzerland AG 2019
H. Venter et al. (Eds.): ISSA 2018, CCIS 973, pp. 1–15, 2019.
https://doi.org/10.1007/978-3-030-11407-7_1

This paper examines the application of blockchain technology to the field of digital forensics. More specifically, it identifies a particular requirement – proof of existence – within the field, and independently assesses its application and relevance in the context of the OpenTimestamps (OTS) system which could meet this requirement. Given the criticality of digital forensics in the broader space of cyber crime, is essential that software such as OTS be tested to provide assurances as to its reliability and accuracy since it must be assumed that these aspects of digital forensics technology will at some point be called into question as part of an investigation. It is therefore necessary to provide a conclusive and vetted explanation of the proof mechanism to pass peer review.

The paper is structured as follows. Section 2 describes the field of digital forensics and argues strongly for the importance of trustworthy and independently verifiable digital evidence. Section 3 then describes blockchain technology and the properties thereof. Section 4 considers the proof-of-existence problem and is followed by a section that specifically focuses on OpenTimestamps. Independent testing of this software follows, and the paper concludes with some discussion and conclusions.

2   Digital Forensics

The digital forensic process, can, at a high level, be described by three basic practices: acquisition, analysis, and presentation [18]. The act of acquiring evidence is the first step in any digital forensic investigation and can be a non-trivial task at the best of times [2]. The acquisition phase is also arguably the most critical in any investigation, as any error here will naturally propagate to the following phases and potentially affect the integrity and admissibility of the evidence as a whole: any issue that adversely affects the admissibility of digital evidence can cast doubt on entire investigations [20].

The analysis phase can be subdivided into activities such as identification, collection and transportation. With digital evidence, as with physical evidence, the collection and transportation activities pose the greatest threat to the chain of custody, and to the overall integrity of the evidence. Particularly relevant with regard to digital evidence, though, is the inherent need for the evidence to be moved or replicated from its (potentially volatile) source to another system. Moving, replication, or analysis of evidence cannot alter the evidence itself. If such alteration occurs, the evidence is inadmissible in a court of law. Completeness and accuracy are the two critical measurable attributes of the acquisition phase, and there is a complex hierarchy of trust at play during a typical acquisition phase [2]. Trust is essential to ensure evidence is free from accidental or intentional tampering [2], and many tools, techniques and frameworks have been developed solely for this purpose: see, for example, [3,6,18].

A common, and sometimes mandated, practice during the acquisition phase is the act of hashing evidence [2]. A cryptographic hash, also referred to as a digest, is a unique, fixed-length value, generated from any evidentiary artefact of variable length (the pre-image), that can serve to identify that piece of evidence.

A cryptographic hash is the product of a one-way deterministic mathematical function through which data of arbitrary length can be passed to produce a collision-resistant fixed length representation of that data [21]. A key property of a hash function is that a minor change in the input will result in a significant change in the fixed length output [12]. A second key property is that cryptographic hashes are computationally infeasible to reverse to determine a pre-image of a given hash [10]. Hashes are most commonly used to determine if the evidence has been tampered with between the time the hash was generated and when the evidence is scrutinised.

The concepts of integrity and the chain of custody are as relevant in the analysis phase as in the acquisition phase as there is interaction with the evidence. In an ideal scenario, analysis would not be performed on the original artefacts but rather on a validated copy thereof, and an investigator would ideally receive non-volatile evidence under controlled circumstances and as part of a defined process. In a non-ideal scenario, there would be some level of interaction with the original evidentiary artefact; i.e., where interaction with volatile evidence like memory, is required in the field. It is during these non-ideal types of interaction that there exists the greatest chance of intentionally or accidentally modifying the evidence in question.

The presentation phase of the digital forensic process involves sharing or presenting the results to a selected audience, and includes showcasing and explaining the information concluded from the previous phases.

The presentation phase of an investigation can be, and most likely will be, subjected to intense scrutiny regarding the integrity of evidence [7]. This is especially relevant if the investigation forms part of a criminal case. It is, therefore, of paramount importance that any observations presented be irrefutably backed up by facts derived from evidence of which the integrity can be proved without a doubt.

3 Blockchain

Satoshi Nakamoto proposed the Bitcoin blockchain upon which all subsequent blockchain implementations to date are based [11]. Figure 1 is a simplified visual representation of a blockchain-type system.

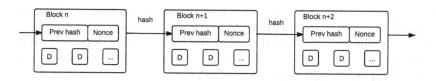

Fig. 1. A visual illustration of a blockchain

In Fig. 1, there is no starting, or genesis, block, but rather a sequence of blocks at some point after the genesis block. It can be seen that one input into a block is the hash of the previous block. To further improve security, this hash is combined with a nonce and some arbitrary data items before it is once again hashed and provided as input to the following block. A nonce is simply a value used once for a particular message or operation [14], and is usually a random value [15]. By chaining blocks together like this, it is possible to verify the data in them, as any change in the data will result in a change of the hash which will necessarily cascade up the chain, changing all subsequent block hash values.

To explain general blockchain functionality further, the first implementation of a blockchain-driven system – Bitcoin – will be used. Although not all blockchains follow this exact model, they are all based on the same basic principles.

Blocks are collections of structured data that form a fundamental part of the ledger. A "miner" within the system can "mine" a block – thus obtaining a new block to append to the chain – by solving a computationally difficult puzzle that is associated with the latest block in the chain.

The *chain* is a series of connected blocks. Each block in the chain contains a collection of transactions, each of which contains a series of inputs and outputs. Figure 2 is a high level view of blocks in the Bitcoin blockchain.

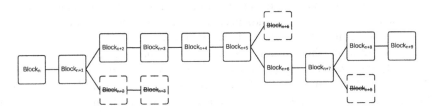

Fig. 2. Example of a Bitcoin blockchain with forks

A block can be separated into two main components: a header and a body. The head of a block contains some reference data, including the block structure version, a reference to the previous block, and a timestamp, while the body of a block contains transaction data. The larger the body, the greater the cost of adding it to the blockchain. Once a puzzle is solved, the miner broadcasts the proof-of-work (PoW) along with the block, and other miners then proceed to verify that proof. If the proof is accepted, the block is added to the chain as the most recent block and the miner is rewarded for the work it has completed. Once a new block is added to the chain, the hash of the block header is used by the miners in the network to create a new block, add waiting transactions to that block structure, and repeat the whole process.

This ongoing work results in the chain as depicted in Fig. 2. Due to the distributed nature of the system where many nodes compete to solve the PoW puzzle, it occasionally happens that more than one miner solves the PoW for different blocks at the same time. When this happens, it results in a *fork* in the chain; and each node will then accept the first proof it receives as the correct one and build the chain from that block. When this happens, the rejected block is called an orphaned block, depicted in Fig. 2 as the block with dotted borders. However, transactions that were part of these orphaned blocks are not lost but are instead rebroadcast to the network for later inclusion. Miners always work on the longest chain, which implies the chain on which the most computational effort was exerted. This is to ensure that there is consensus around which chain is the correct chain, and to prevent malicious nodes from altering previous blocks to create an alternative chain.

An *induced fork* occurs when the majority of nodes agree to reprocess a previous block to create an alternative chain, invalidating the previous chain. Induced forks are not a common occurrence but are usually the subject of controversy in a blockchain community [13].

There are economic incentives that explain why miners choose to mine blocks; there is more to be said about the exact structure of a block; there is more complexity to be understood around the increasing difficulty of PoW puzzles; and there is more depth to be examined relating to the mechanics of block verification. However, these topics are not directly relevant to this work and have been elided. Instead, from a digital forensics perspective, what has been said is sufficient to understand four key properties of a blockchain: immutability, chronology, redundancy, and transparency.

Immutability, the lack of ability to be changed, is arguably one of the most important properties of blockchain systems. Immutability is not a property on the macro level - as the chain is constantly changing and expanding when new blocks are added - but rather on a more granular level as data and transactions that are embedded in the blocks are unchangeable. This immutability is conditional and strengthens over time as a consequence of the design of the system [21]. As newer blocks form on top of older blocks, the block depth increases and the ability to change data embedded in that block diminishes. Any entity that wishes to change some data within a block would have to change the data in that block and recompute that block and all subsequent blocks faster than all the other nodes in the network can. It would therefore be theoretically possible for multiple nodes to collude to change some data, but this type of collusion is unlikely and inherently detectable. In the Bitcoin blockchain, the current block depth to guarantee a permanent and unchangeable transaction is six-blocks deep [21]. This immutability means that the public ledger record cannot be altered to reflect a record that represents a false or fabricated transaction, and can thus be trusted. The immutability of the information embedded in the blockchain means that, to any observer or participant, all information can be considered an unchangeable and a true record of data over time.

Chronology – the sequential arrangement of events or transactions over time – is another property of blockchain design that gives it immense value and utility. Timestamping is the ability to associate the existence of a certain piece of information with a specific moment in time [5], and all blocks contain timestamps [11]. A mining node can reject a timestamp that is deemed to be too old or in the future, and timestamps are thus validated by distributed consensus.

By combining immutability in the form of an append-only chain and chronology in the form of trusted timestamping, blockchains give the unique ability to store and verify the existence of data at a point in time with accuracy.

Redundancy is a further significant property of a blockchain-based system, and was a key design consideration in the Bitcoin blockchain [11]. Not only would the system need to be fault-tolerant to be widely used, but it would also necessitate the participation of many entities to safeguard the decentralisation that lies at the core principle of the concept: trust. Decentralised trust, or the lack of trust in a single entity, implies that trust is the responsibility all participants and not that of a governing entity or a subset of privileged entities. Most blockchain-based systems therefore have incentive systems and each differ slightly in terms of reward. By having a completely distributed system with decentralised trust, the resiliency of the system can be guaranteed for as long as there is an incentive to participate in the system.

Transparency is the final of the four core blockchain properties and is more of a functional requirement and not a design consequence. All transactions need to be broadcast openly to any entity willing to listen. Furthermore, the information embedded inside the ledger must be open for all to see and verify. This is necessary for the Bitcoin system to work as a distributed financial ledger since transactions are stored instead of balances. Therefore, to calculate the balance of a specific address, all the transactions to and from that address need to be visible.

By combining immutability, chronology, redundancy, and transparency, blockchain-based systems are uniquely equipped to address many of the problems associated with trust and decentralised processing.

4   Proof of Existence of Digital Evidence

It is useful, at this point, to summarise the requirements of the digital forensics community and tie those to properties of the blockchain.

– **Existence**. It is important to verify the existence of digital evidence. The blockchain allows arbitrary data, including digital evidence, to be embedded within it. The transparency and immutability of the blockchain can ensure that the evidence is preserved for as long as the blockchain itself exists, and that the evidence can be examined by any party at any time.
– **Chronology**. It is important to verify that digital evidence existed at a particular point in time. The chronology of a blockchain, and the digital consensus around timestamps, can be used to show this.
– **Non-repudiation**. It is important that the digital forensics analyst cannot change a claim that is made. If this were the case, then the trust that is placed in digital evidence would rest solely on the reputation of the digital forensics analyst. The blockchain's immutability, transparency and redundancy makes it easy to make a claim that cannot be repudiated at a later date. This, in turn, ensures that the claim made before the analysis stage begins cannot be changed at the analyst's discretion.

The existence requirement is complicated by two issues: firstly, the evidence may sometimes be of a private nature, and may therefore not be revealed to the public; and, secondly, the evidence may be very large. The second issue ties in directly with the already-mentioned fact that a larger block payload is correspondingly more expensive to store in a blockchain. Both of these issues are addressed by a blockchain timestamping services such as Chainpoint [19], proof-of-existence (PoE) [1] and OpenTimestamps [17].

PoE or blockchain timestamping services embed the hash of arbitrary data – and not the data itself – into a block. By using this method, it is possible to permanently embed a small amount of data into the Bitcoin blockchain; the embedded data may also be prepended with some marker bytes that makes searching for such proofs in the blockchain easier. Of the various PoE services, OpenTimestamps (OTS) is the only one which is completely open source and transparent, and therefore the only one which is open to public examination and testing – both of which are very important for a service of this nature in the context of digital forensics.

5   OpenTimestamps

The OTS service consists of server-side and client-side components that inter-act, using an open protocol, to perform the timestamping of data as well as validate existing timestamps for which proofs have been received. The client-side component takes some arbitrary data as input, hashes it, incorporates that hash into a predefined structure and submits it to the server-side component via remote procedure call (RPC). The server-side components then takes the data and incorporates it into a Bitcoin transaction and submits that transaction to be processed into the Bitcoin blockchain. The server then sends a OTS proof back to the client and the client can, from that point onward, use that proof to verify the timestamp and the integrity of the data by performing another RPC call.

In the OTS system, the Bitcoin blockchain acts as notary as it affords users thereof the ability to create and verify both the integrity of a document and the approximate date at which it must have existed. OTS allows any participant to submit the hash of an arbitrary piece of data to be embedded in a transaction in the Bitcoin blockchain and to timestamp that document hash on the blockchain. The accuracy of such a time stamp is estimated by to be within two to three hours of the submission date and time [17].

OTS uses "commitment operations" [17] which simply is a function that alters the function input to produce a deterministic output. A simple concate-nation function such as $a\|b = ab$ is an example of a commitment operation. In OTS, the verification of an OTS timestamp is the execution of the sequence of commitment operations and the comparison of the output to the value stored on the Bitcoin blockchain. OTS timestamps can therefore be said to be trees of operations with the root being the message, the edges (also known as nodes) being the commitments, and leaves being the attestations. The usage of these terms is not coincidence but rather as a result of the heavy reliance on Merkle Hash Trees (MHTs) [9] to support OTS functionality.

A MHT is a data structure that relies heavily on cryptographic hashing for its function and value. The broad purpose of a MHT is to make the validation of data more efficient, by providing a way for large amounts of data to be validated against a single hash value without having to rehash all the data. It is often used in peer-to-peer protocols to facilitate the validation of data without having to transfer vast amounts of data between peers on a bandwidth-restricted network. In this sense, the purpose of a MHT is to provide a mechanism for validating large sets of data in a distributed environment with reduced capacity for data storage, transfer and computation. Its application in blockchain technology is for this exact same purpose; and, in fact, it is used by the Bitcoin blockchain itself, as well as by the OTS application that is built upon the blockchain.

MHT consist of three basic components:

1. The root, also called the Merkle Root (MR), of which there is only one per tree
2. The nodes, also referred to as Child Nodes (H), of which there must be at least two; theoretical there is no maximum number of Child Nodes per tree
3. The leaves (L) of which there must be at least two; theoretical there is no maximum number of leaves per tree

Figure 3 shows a basic example of a MHT with four leaves, six nodes and a root. For the purpose of explanation, the four leaves would be the raw data needing to be verified. This data is not included in the tree but serves as the basis of its creation. Theoretically, there can be an infinite number of leaves, but the number of leaves is usually limited to avoid long running computation. One level up (level MR-2) are the nodes, H_1 to H_4, which are hashes of the respective leaves (L_1 to L_4). It is essential to note that these nodes are hashes (one-way functions) of the leaves but that the actual hash algorithm is not stipulated. Each use case may call for different hash algorithms, based on the preference for speed over security, or vice versa. In the Bitcoin implementation and other implementations where security of the hash values (their resistance to collision) is important, hash algorithms, like SHA256, are used. One level up (MR-1) are the secondary nodes, which each consists of the hash of the concatenation ($Hxy = H_x \| H_y$) of its children on MR-2. Finally, on the very top level is the MR which, like the nodes below it, is a hash of its concatenated children. It is considered the root as it is a single hash that incorporates elements of all the leaves. In this way, a seemingly insignificant change in a single leaf will propagate up the tree and result in a changed MR. It is clear that MR can be used to verify the integrity of all of the leaves independently or as a whole; therein lies the power of MHT as a mechanism for verification.

By using MHTs, a large amount of arbitrary data can be hashed into a single MR hash. To verify any leaf on the tree, its original data, the hashes on its path, and the root hash needs to be known. This means that not all the leaves need to be present to be able to validate the integrity of a single leaf, thereby allowing MHT preserve space.

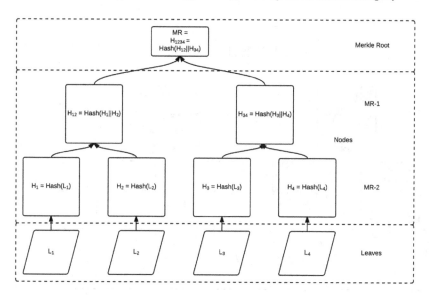

Fig. 3. A symmetric binary Merkle Hash Tree

OTS primarily makes use of MHTs to address the problem of scalability. By using MHTs, OTS can compress large amounts of data into a single hash by adding individual hashes as leaves of a MHT. These leaves would then be collapsed into the MHT root which, in turn, is embedded into a Bitcoin transaction. This aggregation occurs on OTS aggregation servers when the OTS client sends the hash of the desired data to at least two OTS aggregation servers. These aggregation servers collect all of the different hashes from different OTS clients, uses them as leaves of a MHT and computes the MR. This MR is in turn embedded into a single Bitcoin transaction.

Once a MR for a given set of leaves has been embedded in the Bitcoin blockchain, verifying any single leaf can be accomplished by simply replaying a subset of commitment operations with efficiency $O(log2(n))$. Figure 4 serves as a visual example of a series of relevant commitments to be able to prove the integrity and existence of data in L_2.

Note how, to verify the integrity or the timestamp associated with the data in L_2, only a subset of leaves or nodes need to be known. This means that many hashes representing large datasets can be stored within the bounds of a small amount of blockchain data by aggregating these leaves into a MHT. The root of that tree is then stored in a block, and returns only the commitments necessary to follow the commitment path up the tree and to the MR.

The OTS timestamp, or proof, is at the core of the OTS protocol. It is the artefact that enables the verification of a given attestation. To understand what a timestamp does, it is necessary to first understand what a timestamp is and what an attestation is. An attestation, in the context of OTS, is a statement that some information - a logical file in the case of the current OTS design -

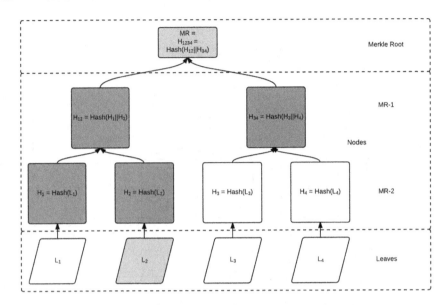

Fig. 4. A series of relevant OTS commitment operations to verify leaf $L2$

existed in a certain state at a certain point in time. An attestation is, therefore, time-bound and content-specific. An attestation is not a proof in any form but rather a claim, the authenticity of which is proven by an OTS timestamp.

The timestamp is a series of operations that, when replayed, provides evidence that the attestation is true for a particular source file. The source of truth for OTS is the Bitcoin blockchain, which is demonstrably immutable and chronological, as discussed in Sect. 3. Since a timestamp is essentially just a collection of commitment operations that are applied to an input message in a specified sequence, replaying those commitment operations in order is all that is necessary to verify the timestamp.

An OTS proof thus allows any person or entity in possession of the original file or an exact bit-by-bit replica thereof, and the timestamp generated from it, to verify two things without having to trust a third party: that the file existed in a specific time window in the past, and that the file's content remains unmodified from the time the timestamp was created.

When requested to timestamp a file, the OTS client will create a hash of the file and submit it to one or more *calendar servers*. A calendar server adds the file hash as a node in a MHT and provides the MR to the client; it thus *aggregates* hashes into the MHT. A client can also optionally "upgrade" their local proof by requesting the relevant MHT path from the calendar server, thus locally obtaining all the information that is necessary to verify the data; recall that, for a MHT to be verified, the user requires the original data, the MR, and the path through the MHT. After submission the calendar server submits a binary blob representing the MHT to the Bitcoin blockchain; after this point, a client can use the verify operation to verify that the data exists in the blockchain, and obtain the timestamp of that data. The end result is that a large number of hashes can be embedded within the blockchain without incurring a high cost.

6   Testing

Testing of two aspects of OTS was conducted in order to verify its usefulness in a digital forensics context: the timing and accuracy of the timestamping, and the failure rate of OTS. Data on the former was obtained by using the OTS client to stamp, submit, upgrade, and verify timestamps, and noting how long each of these operations took. The failure rate was obtained by intentionally tampering with OTS artefacts to create invalid files and timestamps, and attempting to verify them using OTS.

Data gathering lasted for 34 days, from 5 September 2017 up to and including 8 October 2017. OTS timestamps were created, upgraded, and verified every 10 min, resulting in a data set of 4,702 unique files, their timestamps, timestamp results, and some metadata. Data gathering was performed programmatically and involved a script that generated data files consisting of arbitrary binary data followed by the execution discrete OTS operations, all of which were recorded in a database for further evaluation. Table 1 shows the detailed descriptions of the main data fields recorded.

Table 1. Description of data fields recorded by script

Field name	Description
name	The name of the file which was created
size	The size in bytes of the file that was created
fileCreatedTime	The time (UNIX timestamp) the CreateFile event occurred
proofCreatedTime	The time (UNIX timestamp) the StampFile event occurred
proofUpgradedTime	The time (UNIX timestamp) the UpgradeFile event occurred
proofVerifiedTime	The time (UNIX timestamp) the VerifyFile event occurred
dataExistedTime	The time (UNIX timestamp) as of which OpenTimestamps can attest the data existed

Figure 5 shows the results of the timing and accuracy tests. Timestamp accuracy was defined as the difference in seconds between the point the timestamp was created (the known time at which data existed and was committed), and the time that verification can attest that the data first existed. This shows how precise OTS attestations are for a sample with a known creation time. A moving average over 144 data points (i.e. one day) is also calculated and shown in Fig. 5 to account for outliers, with the overall average accuracy being 2,687.64 s.

The verification function is the most critical of all OTS operations as it is the mechanism by which OTS delivers the attestation result. It is also likely that timestamping and upgrading may only be executed once for any particular file, but that verify might be executed many times throughout the relevant life of the file. Table 2 summarises the results.

Table 2. Error rate of verify function

Number of files tested	Pre-modification result		Modify action	Post-modification result		False positive result	False negative result
	True	False		True	False		
2,351	2,351	0	Modify file	0	2,351	0	0
2351	2,351	0	Modify timestamp	0	2,351	0	0

7 Discussion

The timestamp accuracy measures the difference between the time the initial timestamp commitment was received from a remote calendar server (the date and time the attestation was requested), to the time the Bitcoin blockchain can attest the data existed. The shorter the time span, the more accurate the timestamp attestation can be considered. Accuracy is very closely tied to the block confirmation time, and thus heavily influenced by Bitcoin network performance. Average accuracy is 2,687.64 s, with the maximum being 24,568.47 s and the minimum being 21.90 s. The minimum is an example of where a timestamp was requested from the remote calendar server close to the end of its aggregation cycle and transaction creation in the Bitcoin blockchain.

In Fig. 5, there is an instance between the dates 05/10/17 00:00:00 and 06/10/17 00:00:00 of an apparent cascading effect from very high y-axis values to lower values, with fixed intervals on the Y-axis. This cascading effect, along with others on Fig. 5, can be explained by slow block confirmation times during those dates. Regardless, the script that created the file and submitted the timestamp executed every 10 min irrespective of the Bitcoin network performance. This means that as the calendar server aggregates timestamp and waits for a block to be confirmed, multiple timestamps could have been submitted to it. Since the calendar server timing is subject to the block confirmation and the testing script is not, there is a backlog of timestamps being created on the calendar server when block confirmation is delayed. When the block confirmation finally occurs, all of these backlogged timestamps, created over a long time span, are included in the next block. Since this block now contains timestamps created over a matter of hours, ten minutes apart, but has a single confirmation time, the time difference between submission and attestation of the first timestamp submitted is very high and gradually gets smaller for each subsequent timestamp. Looking at Fig. 5, it can be seen that the y-axis values cascade down at intervals

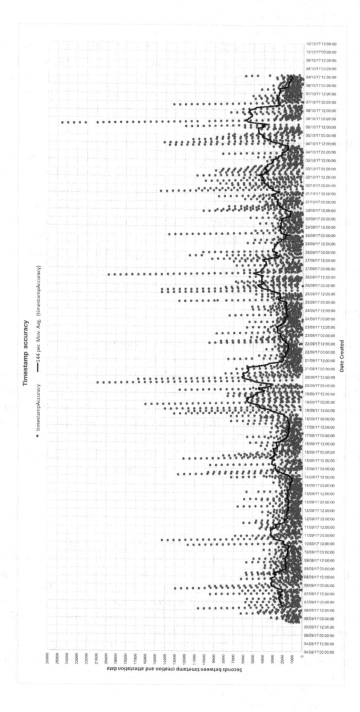

Fig. 5. Accuracy of a timestamp, in seconds, relative to the date and time the timestamp was created.

of approximately 600 s (10 min) is indicative of the testing script executing and submitting a new timestamp every 10 min.

Verification errors are the most serious of potential OTS errors, as they indicate that the verification operation does not return a truthful or accurate result. Since the use case for OTS is to reliably get accurate attestations as to the integrity and timestamp of a particular file, any error in this process should be considered critical. Errors in the verification process undermine the fundamental purpose of OTS, and even low error rates would indicate that OTS cannot be trusted.

OTS verification was tested extensively over the entire test sample. Exactly half of the test sample (2,351), previously validated, was modified by appending a few fixed bytes to the original file. The other half were modified by appending the same fixed bytes to the timestamp associated to the file. In this way, the error rates for invalid files or invalid timestamps, both of which should result in an outright failure to verify, were tested. There were no instances of false positive OTS verifications for the tested sample and, similarly, there were also no false negative OTS verification results in the tested sample. With zero errors in the tested sample, it is clear that the verification mechanism is robust.

8   Conclusion

This paper has described the field of digital forensics, its requirements, blockchain technology, the interaction between these, and independently analysed promising open source software in this niche. The results have been impressive, and certainly merit a great deal of discussion in the field of digital forensics. Blockchain technology, coupled with the design of OTS, has the potential to take one more human factor out of the digital forensics equation and increase trust in digital evidence as a whole. One caveat, however, is that timestamp accuracy is not to be taken for granted. The blockchain may therefore not be appropriate for digital evidence that must be independently timestamped with great accuracy.

References

1. Araoz, M., Ordano, E.: Proof of Existence (2013). http://proofofexistence.com/
2. Dykstra, J., Sherman, A.T.: Acquiring forensic evidence from infrastructure-as-a-service cloud computing: exploring and evaluating tools, trust, and techniques. Digital Invest. **9**, 90–98 (2012). https://doi.org/10.1016/j.diin.2012.05.001
3. Dykstra, J., Sherman, A.T.: Design and implementation of frost: digital forensic tools for the openstack cloud computing platform. Digit. Invest. **10**, S87–S95 (2013). https://doi.org/10.1016/j.diin.2013.06.010
4. Ethereum Foundation: Ethereum (2016). https://www.ethereum.org/
5. Gipp, B., Meuschke, N., Gernandt, A.: Decentralized trusted timestamping using the crypto currency bitcoin. In: iConference 2015, pp. 1–6 (2015)
6. InfoSec Institute: 22 Popular Computer Forensics Tools (2017). http://resources.infosecinstitute.com/computer-forensics-tools/

7. Kessler, G.C.: Anti-forensics and the digital investigator. In: Proceedings of the 2014 47th Hawaii International Conference on System Sciences, pp. 1–7 (2006). https://doi.org/10.4225/75/57ad39ee7ff25
8. Lamport, L., Shostak, R., Pease, M.: The byzantine generals problem. ACM Trans. Program. Lang. Syst. **4**(3), 382–401 (1982). https://doi.org/10.1145/357172.357176
9. Merkle, R.C.: Protocols for public key cryptography. In: Synopsis on Security and Privacy, pp. 122–134 (1980)
10. Motara, Y.M.: Preimages for SHA-1. Ph.D. thesis, Rhodes University (2017)
11. Nakamoto, S.: Bitcoin: A Peer-to-Peer Eelectronic Cash System (2008). https://bitcoin.org/bitcoin.pdf
12. Preneel, B.: Cryptographic hash functions. Eur. Trans. Telecommun. **5**(4), 431–448 (1994). https://doi.org/10.1002/ett.4460050406
13. Redman, J.: Popular Bitcoin Exchanges Reveal Controversial Hard Fork Contingency Plan (2017). https://news.bitcoin.com/popular-bitcoin-exchanges-reveal-controversial-hard-fork-contingency-plan/
14. Rogaway, P.: Nonce-Based Symmetric Encryption. In: Roy, B., Meier, W. (eds.) FSE 2004. LNCS, vol. 3017, pp. 348–358. Springer, Heidelberg (2004). https://doi.org/10.1007/978-3-540-25937-4_22
15. Schneier, B.: Applied Cryptography: Protocols, Algorithms, and Source Code in C. John Wiley & Sons Inc., New York (1993)
16. Nelson, B., Phillips, A., Steuart, C.: Guide to Computer Forensics and Investigations. Delmar Learning, 5th edn. (2015)
17. Todd, P.: OpenTimestamps: Scalable, Trustless, Distributed Timestamping with Bitcoin (2016). https://petertodd.org/2016/opentimestamps-announcement
18. Valjarevic, A., Venter, H.S.: Implementation guidelines for a harmonised digital forensic investigation readiness process model. In: 2013 Information Security for South Africa - Proceedings of the ISSA 2013 Conference, pp. 1–9, August 2013. https://doi.org/10.1109/ISSA.2013.6641041
19. Wayne, V., Wilkinson, S., Bukowski, J.: Chainpoint: a scalable protocol for recording data in the blockchain and generating blockchain receipts (2016). https://tierion.com/chainpoint
20. Wilson, C.: Digital evidence discrepancies: Casey Anthony Trial (2011). http://www.digital-detective.net/digital-evidence-discrepancies-casey-anthony-trial/
21. Witte, J.H.: The Blockchain: A Gentle Introduction, pp. 1–5 (2016). https://doi.org/10.2139/ssrn.2887567
22. Zerocoin Electric Coin Company: About Us (2016). https://z.cash/about.html

Real-Time Face Antispoofing Using Shearlets

Dustin Terence van der Haar[(✉)]

Academy of Computer Science and Software Engineering,
University of Johannesburg, Johannesburg, South Africa
dvanderhaar@uj.ac.za

Abstract. Face recognition. A promise made to the modern technologists as the ultimate access control or surveillance technology. However, it is still vulnerable to inexpensive spoofing attacks, which pose a threat to security. Basic face spoofing attacks that use photographs and video are still not addressed appropriately, especially in real-time applications, thereby making security in these environments a difficult task to achieve. Although methods have improved over the last decade, a robust solution that can accommodate changing environments is still out of reach. Face spoofing attacks introduce an object into the scene, which presents curvilinear singularities that are not necessarily portrayed in the same way in different lighting conditions. We present a solution that addresses this problem by using a discrete shearlet transform as an alternative descriptor that can differentiate between a real and a fake face without user-cooperation. We have found the approach can successfully detect blurred edges, texture changes and other noise found in various face spoof attacks. Our benchmarks on the publicly available CASIA-FASD, MSU-MFSD, and OULU-NPU data sets, show that our approach portrays good results and improves on the most popular methods found in the field on modest computer hardware, but requires further improvement to beat the current state of the art. The approach also achieves real-time face spoof discrimination, which makes it a practical solution in real-time applications and a viable augmentation to current face recognition methods.

Keywords: Face recognition · Face antispoofing
Presentation attack detection

1 Introduction

We are entering the age of automation. Machines can replace people with repetitive tasks and differentiate between people using face recognition. By giving machines the ability to identify or authenticate people automatically, it can prevent unauthorized users from accessing secure areas or provide a tailored user experience. Face recognition is already being used in public spaces for surveillance monitoring of citizens and to maintain watch-lists in airports, malls, border

© Springer Nature Switzerland AG 2019
H. Venter et al. (Eds.): ISSA 2018, CCIS 973, pp. 16–29, 2019.
https://doi.org/10.1007/978-3-030-11407-7_2

gates, and casinos. Other similar applications include its use in mobile computing for face tracking and in affective computing to detect the emotion of users [2].

However, as technology and methods have progressed for face recognition, so have the attacks to subvert face recognition systems. Attacks, such as using photos, modifying them in some way and video attacks [25], have become common in various subversion scenarios. Technology has also assisted attackers through the advent of cheaper 3D printing and increased computational resources. These combined with higher quality screens, which have improved resolutions and colour ranges, allow them to facilitate better replay attacks.

In order to keep up with these developments more liveness and antispoofing research and systems have been introduced to combat these attacks [3,5–7,9–11,17,18]. These approaches either determine liveness, analyze movement or perform image quality assessment. Both sides of technology improvements have resulted in an ebb and flow of attacks and defenses. However, a robust generic solution without significant computational resource overhead, which performs well under various conditions is yet to be realized. The work discussed here poses another defense in the war against face spoofing. It provides an alternative real-time presentation attack detection (PAD) method for describing the facial region of interest, which can tolerate blur, texture changes, and low-quality frames in order to achieve improved face antispoofing.

The article begins by unpacking the problem at hand and face antispoofing related work. The proposed approach is then discussed by outlining the method with an appropriate discussion. The experiment methodology followed by the researcher to validate the approach is then described for all three data sets, followed by the achieved results. The paper is then concluded, along with future work.

2   Related Work

The prevalence of face recognition systems in society has motivated criminals to find ways of subverting these systems to avoid identification. The ideal method for achieving this is for them to undergo facial plastic surgery that changes fundamental components of their face. Technology has also made it possible to achieve these attacks at a lower cost. Although plastic surgery is a pressing concern, there have been attacks that prove it is not necessary to go to that extent to subvert a face recognition system [15].

However, there are more simple, non-intrusive attacks that can be used to spoof face recognition systems. These attacks include (and examples can also be seen in the top row of Fig. 1 for most of them):

1. A *photo attack* where a printed image of a legitimate user is presented in front of the user's face.
2. The *warped photo attack* where the photo attack is extended to include movements and minor folding of the photo.

3. A *cut photo attack* where holes are cut out by the eyes are in the photo to fool blink-based liveness systems.
4. The *video replay attack* where a user places a video of a legitimate user in front of their head using a tablet or similar device [5,25].
5. A *mask attack* where the attacker wears a 3D mask of a legitimate user [10].

Thankfully researchers have become cognizant of these attacks and research has been pursued to address them appropriately. There have also been face antispoofing competitions to promote more novel solutions within the research community, as seen in the International Joint Conference on Biometrics (IJCB) 2011, 2013 and 2017. Data sets have been created that emulate these attacks, such the NUAA Photograph Impostor Database (which only contains photographs) [20], the REPLAY-ATTACK Database [5], the CBSR database [25], the CASIA-FASD [7], the MSU Mobile Face Spoofing Database (MFSD) [22] and more recently OULU-NP [4] (used in one of the2017 IJCB competitions) to serve as a benchmark for any proposed methods.

In the last decade, there has been significant progress in face antispoofing methods. Earlier methods used Gabor wavelets [20] or eye blinking in order to determine whether there was potential face spoofing occurring [18]. The approach had basic liveness detection with minimal computational overhead. However, blink detection still fell victim to the cut photo attack and poor accuracy. One of the major breakthroughs in the field was the use of micro-texture analysis with local binary patterns (LBP) [5]. It encapsulated the change of texture in the scene attributed to the foreign object, was also computationally fast and did not require cooperation from the user to blink. However, fine detail that can be used for discriminating between real and fake faces is lost when using LBP-based histograms around larger areas of the face. As shown by [17], there is value in dividing it into overlapping sub-regions (such as 3 by 3 pixels) and calculating sub region-based LBP histograms. However, it comes at the cost of a more sparse feature space, additional resources and is affected by blur present in the region of interest.

Another improvement uses LBP from Three Orthogonal Planes (TOP) to achieve face antispoofing [6]. The improvement increases accuracy, by leveraging the power of dynamic textures, analyzing motion and texture, along with a score level fusion-based framework. However, the approach showed incremental improvement and it struggled with lower quality frames found in the CASIA-FASD data set.

The latter part of the decade was then spent on mostly building on existing methods, performing more image quality assessments and combining multiple methods. In [7] a score fusion framework was proposed and provided additional insights into data set quality. However, only methods that are statistically independent can be used in the score fusion framework, so any potential methods would need to be statistically vetted before it can be included. The work in [11] proposes a context-based antispoofing method. It showed that scene cues detected with Histogram of Oriented Gradients (HOG) descriptors and upper body analysis could be used for face antispoofing. The results show

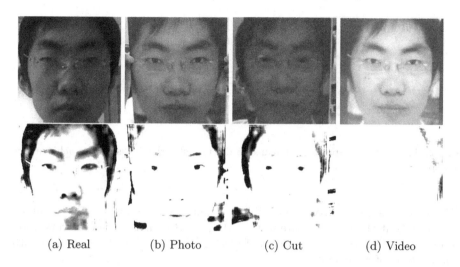

|(a) Real|(b) Photo|(c) Cut|(d) Video|

Fig. 1. Examples of various attack scenarios and their mean shearlet representation for the region of interest.

an improvement in other methods, especially in video replay attacks. However, it is constrained by very specific attack scenarios and is limited to close-up environments.

In [24] multiple feature vectors are created from twelve different components that form what they call their holistic face (or H-Face). The H-Face-based approach performs well, but there are many measures to calculate, thereby limiting its potential in real-time applications. Another approach by [10] uses general image quality assessment to achieve face antispoofing, by using a combination of different image quality measures, such as measures used to determine pixel difference, correlation and edges. These features, such as signal to noise ratio (SNR), average distance (AD) and total edge different (TED) present a low degree of complexity and can potentially be used for real-time applications. However, the approach exhibits only a marginal improvement over other methods.

Antispoofing based on color texture analysis is achieved in [3] by analyzing LBPs in various colour spaces, such as HSV, RGB and YC_bC_r. The approach shows promising results but suffers in varying lighting and environmental conditions. Patel et al. shows in [19] that Moiré pattern aliasing present in spoof face videos can be used for face antispoofing. The approach worked well on video but lacks results for photo-based spoofing methods. Agarwal also proposes in [1], the use of Haralick features to achieve face antispoofing with good accuracy, but it comes at the cost of very large feature space and computational overhead, which results from the subsequent dimensional reduction required.

More recently in [9], a fusion of various approaches is used to achieve face antispoofing. Face and scene optical flow-based motion features coupled with an image quality feature are used to train an artificial neural network for spoof discrimination. It results in very good accuracy, but at the cost of significant computational and memory resources. The use of convolutional neural networks

Fig. 2. The proposed approach that uses a discrete shearlet transform to achieve face anitspoofing.

(CNN) has also been shown to exhibit excellent accuracy for face antispoofing, which make it the current state of the art [16]. Although it achieves very good results, it too consumes a great deal of memory and is slower than methods with a lower level of complexity.

Methods in face antispoofing have improved, but it is still clear that there is still no robust solution that performs consistently under various changes (such as a change in camera, resolution or lighting) without incurring significant computational and memory overhead. Little attention is paid to the resource usage of methods, its potential use in real-time applications and its performance under varying environmental conditions. The approach discussed in the next section remains cognizant of these requirements (especially the real-time application aspect) and attempts to address them appropriately.

3   Face Antispoofing Using Shearlets

In a spoof scenario, there are certain elements in a video frame present, which will help with face-based spoof discrimination. Attacks introduce a rigid object within the scene to mimic a legitimate object. Much of the work done so far attempts to differentiate between these rigid objects from a non-rigid face by deriving a feature space that can classify for anomalies. However, in many of them rely on color space-based and are greatly affected by lighting changes. However, there is value in analyzing curvature and significant edges found in the scene that is more robust to lighting changes. Our approach uses a discrete shearlet transform-based (DST) descriptor to achieve this.

3.1   DST for Face Antispoofing

Shearlets were introduced to overcome the traditional wavelet limitation of describing directionality. They are a natural extension to wavelets that can efficiently represent anisotropic features, such as edges in images, and serve as a good sparse approximation of multidimensional data. These properties make it an excellent candidate for face antispoofing because the rigid objects introduced in the scene exhibit anomalies in the form of curvilinear singularities in a compact and computationally efficient form. A discrete shearlet transform (DST) is defined as [14]:

$$SH_\psi f(j, k, m) = \langle f, \psi_{j,k,m} \rangle, j > 0, k \in \mathbb{Z}, m \in \mathbb{Z}^2 \qquad (1)$$

where SH_ψ maps the function f to the shearlet coefficients, j is associated with the scale index, k the orientation index and m the positional index. Shearlets have been used for edge detection [12] and non-reference image quality assessment [13], but we believe it has the potential for face antispoofing. The DST can highlight blurred edges, texture changes and other noise found in the frame, which can be attributed to the rigid object used in a typical face spoofing attack.

When applied to a video frame captured in the scene that contains a face, it allows us to perform face spoof discrimination. As seen in Fig. 1, the DST results can be seen for each attack scenario. In Fig. 1a the sharp outline of significant curvature found on the real face can be seen, along with subtle details of the face. Whereas in Fig. 1b and c key details of the face are missing, which can be attributed to the lack of detail portrayed in the photograph and cut attack. Lastly, it can also be seen there is a significant detail lost in the video attack portrayed in Fig. 1d. These examples show that there is clear value in using DST for face antispoofing.

3.2   The Proposed Method

In order to use DST within the context of face antispoofing (as seen in the process found in Fig. 2) there are specific steps that need to be made to perform face antispoofing that maximizes performance and make it tolerant of environmental changes. Each captured video frame undergoes face region of interest (ROI) segmentation. The Viola-Jones face detector [21] is used capture the face, but instead of using the method for every subsequent frame, a basic color histogram check is performed and if it passes the check, the coordinates of the previous ROI is used. In order to compensate for motion artifacts that cause ROI drift, minor translation smoothing is applied by analyzing prior ROI coordinates found in previous frames.

Once the face ROI is segmented, the DST is used to derive the features. It begins by going through a calibration phase, where the shearlet spectrum is derived for the ROI. The precomputed shearlet spectrum during the calibration phase is then used in subsequent frames for deriving the shearlet coefficients in a significantly faster manner. Frames that fail the previous color test trigger another shearlet spectrum derivation event. This optimization allows the approach to achieve face antispoofing in real-time. Further speed optimizations can be achieved on much higher resolutions (such as 4 k video) by using partial shearlet coefficients at a specific direction only, as seen in Fig. 3. Directionality present in the DST can also be leveraged further if details of the scene are known, such as subject pose and camera position. However, for this investigation the partial orientation coefficients are not explored, a combination of all the orientations are explored.

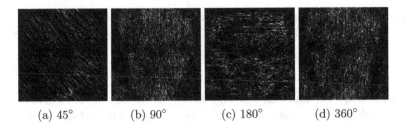

(a) 45°   (b) 90°   (c) 180°   (d) 360°

Fig. 3. Partial shearlet orientation coefficients.

In the last step before classification, the feature space is converted into a more succinct representation that can be compared. Unlike LBP-based systems, which lose specificity across large areas, the DST-based feature space is not changed into a histogram. Instead, a DST-based feature mean (as seen in Fig. 2) is calculated across the orientations for a defined window of video frames (the results use a 100 frame window) and fed into the classifier for assessment.

Once the DST-based features have been calculated, we investigate the classification accuracy using support vector machines (SVM). We first used a Linear SVM classifier and then similar to other methods [3,6,17] we use a Radial Basis Function (RBF)-based SVM for determining whether the DST features depict a real or fake face. The use of the SVM classifier instead of a neural network-based classifier allowed us to achieve the most memory and computational gains. The SVM classifier is first trained using a set of real and fake faces with ground truth labels according to each respective data set's assessment protocols.

4   Experiment Analysis

In order to validate the approach an experiment is used, which is cognizant of environmental changes and the real-time constraint. In order to ensure more robust results, unlike many other approaches which portray results for a favorable data set, the proposed approach was validated against 3 data sets. The experiment data and setup is discussed in the subsections that follow.

4.1   Experimental Data

In order to provide more robust, repeatable results public data sets available were used for the experiment. The CASIA-FASD, MSU-MFSD and OULU-NPU data sets were all selected for the experiment and compared because they exhibited the most common attacks under varying environmental conditions and portrayed a good range of quality for samples. Each of the data sets contains at least three types of videos used for face antispoofing assessment. At least one video with the subject's real face, which would constitute the true videos, along with videos that facilitate a print attack and video attack (with CASIA-FASD also containing the cut attack) to represent the spoofed video. By using various data

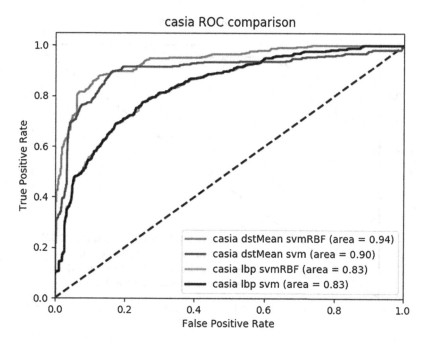

Fig. 4. The receiver operating characteristic (ROC) curves and Area Under Curves (AUC) for our various approaches for face antispoofing on the CASIA-FASD data set.

sets, it also allows us to assess results under varying lighting conditions with a diverse amount of subjects.

The CASIA-FASD data set contains 20 subjects for training and 30 subjects for testing. The base videos are captured at a resolution of 640 by 480 pixels, and their higher resolution videos are captured at a resolution of 720 by 1280. Both the standard and higher resolution videos were captured using a web camera at a frame rate of 25 frames per second under varying lighting conditions for at least 6 s. The MSU-MFSD data set contains 35 subjects (in the publicly available version) captured using two types of cameras (a Macbook Air camera at 640 by 480 pixels and Google Nexus 5 camera at 720 by 480 pixels) to capture video at 30 frames per second. The OULU-NP data set contains 20 subjects for training and 15 for development. The videos are captured at a resolution of 1080 by 1920 at a frame rate of 30 frames per second using multiple devices and under varying lighting conditions.

4.2   Experimental Setup

The videos of the subjects for each data set corresponding to the training and test sets were used to facilitate the benchmark. All the captured ROI images are normalized to 256 by 256 pixels before the DST-based mean for each window of samples is derived. The results of our approach are then compared against

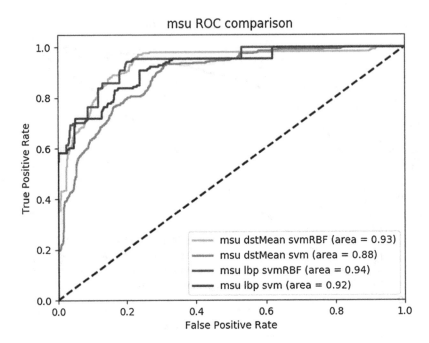

Fig. 5. The receiver operating characteristic (ROC) curves and Area Under Curves (AUC) for our various approaches for face antispoofing on the MSU-MFSD data set.

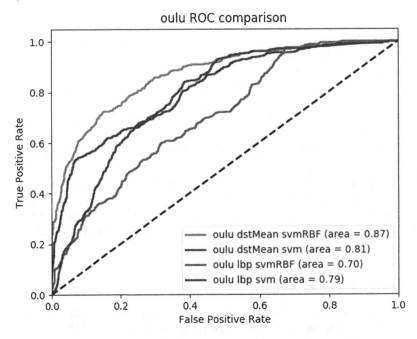

Fig. 6. The receiver operating characteristic (ROC) curves and Area Under Curves (AUC) for our various approaches for face antispoofing on the OULU-NPU data set.

a local binary pattern (LBP) approach under the same conditions (using both a linear and RBF-based SVM). Time traces and memory usage-based tests are performed between frames and an average is calculated on a modest computer with an i7 920 CPU with 2.67 GHz and 4 GB of RAM all using un-optimized python code. Each benchmark is done independently of each other and given the same resources to provide objective results.

4.3   Experiment Results

We evaluated the performance of our approach using three different data sets and compared its results with LBP. The performance of the approach is determined in terms of the receiver operating characteristic (ROC) curve to determine its accuracy for each respective data set (CASIA, MSU and OULU). The equal error rate (EER) is then calculated for each data set and compared with current approaches (as seen in Table 1) to provide perspective on the results.

As seen in Figs. 4, 5 and 6, our DST approach performs consistently across the low, medium and even high quality ranges. Interestingly enough, as seen in Figs. 5 and 6 the choice of linear and RBF-based SVM's exhibit different results for LBP and DST by a margin of 3–8%, thereby validating it as a better choice

Table 1. A table comparing the EER results of DST-based face antispoofing with other approaches on different data sets.

Approach	CASIA	MFSD	OULU
IQA+LDA [10]	32.4%	-	-
LBP+SVM	24.1%	17%	29.5%
LBP+SVM(RBF)	24.4%	14%	37.75%
Gabor Filters+LTVfused [20]	17.0%	-	-
LBP-TOP+SVM(RBF) [8]	10.0%	-	-
IDA+SVM [22]	-	8.58%	-
dstMEAN+SVM(RBF)	12.1%	14%	22%
Haralick+PCA+ SVM[1]	6.7%	2.9%	-
CNN [23]	7.34 %	-	-
Multi-cues integration+ NN [9]	5.83%	-	-

Table 2. A table comparing the average time trace results (excluding training time) for LBP (in ascending quality order) and DST on various face antispoofing data sets applied on the experiment computer.

Approach	Resolution	Frame rate	LBP	DST
CASIA	640 by 480	25 fps	0.03 ms	9 ms
MSU-MFSD	720 by 480	14–29 fps	0.03 ms	9 ms
OULU-NPU	1080 by 1920	30 fps	0.04 ms	9 ms

Table 3. A table comparing the average memory usage results (excluding training time) for LBP (in ascending quality order) and DST on various face antispoofing data sets applied on the experiment computer.

Approach	LBP	DST
CASIA	144 MB	290 MB
MSU-MFSD	76 MB	310 MB
OULU-NPU	189 MB	301 MB

for face antispoofing methods. The EER in Table 1 show that it outperforms many methods, but still needs further improvement to beat very recent methods. As higher quality video become more prevalent, it would be interesting to see how these recent methods tolerant high definition video, lighting differences and different camera artifacts. The performance can be attributed to DST's blur tolerance and much of the error can be attributed to significant over-exposed frames. These over-exposed frames show there is a limit to how tolerant methods can be with regards to lighting.

In Tables 2 and 3, we can also see that the timing and memory results on a modest computer are reasonable and the approach allows for real-time detection. As expected, when the quality of the video increases, so does the time it take to derive the results using LBP. As seen in Table 2 our DST approach achieves relatively stable timings irrespective of the image quality difference, thereby allowing it scale better at higher resolutions. When looking at the memory usage, LBP does use more memory for the OULU data set, but not for the MSU-MFSD data set. Interestingly, as seen in Table 3 when using LBP, the memory usage was not as consistent as the DST approach's memory usage. Upon further inspection, it was found that the MSU-MFSD dataset drop in memory usage can be attributed to a lack of textures derived when video capture occurs when using their specific mobile device cameras, thereby affecting accuracy and specificity. The resource usage shows that the DST approach works well considering the 4 GB memory and processing power constraint.

Alternatively, other quality measures can be included in order to improve accuracy. However, it comes at the cost of additional computational resources and more time required to achieve face antispoofing. Using the mean DST for a window of frames allowed us to break the real-time barrier at a minor cost to accuracy. We have also seen that it is also possible to improve accuracy by deriving shearlets at multiple scales (i.e. increasing the j index in Eq. 1). However, the scale reaches a saturation point that is directly proportional to the resolution of the video frame. Any increases to the scale after that point has diminishing returns on accuracy. Currently, the scale for the DST which maximizes accuracy and still maintains real-time (based on the hardware constraints) is at:

$$DST_s = \frac{log_2(max(width, height))}{2} \tag{2}$$

The various datasets used to test the approach allowed us to gage better performance across varying image qualities, population diversity, and lighting conditions. The CASIA low-quality data set with an average resolution of 640 by 480 covers the low-quality band. The MSU-MFSD data sets with 720 by 480 respectively for the medium quality range with different sensors. The OULU-NPU data set with 1080 by 1920 resolution to cover the high definition range with even more environmental changes. Thereby showing consistent DST's performance even in varying difficult conditions.

Overall, the DST-SVM(RBF)-based implemented system detected most of the spoofing videos under varying environmental conditions and video qualities with a minimal resource footprint. Deriving DST features on average consumed around 311MB of RAM on average took 9ms to complete. This provides proof that our proposed approach can potentially be used in a low resource environment and still achieve real-time detection. Whereas other methods would require a networked solution to offload computation to a server or require additional computation or memory resources.

5 Conclusion

The prevalence of face recognition systems has made face antispoofing research an important concern. As face recognition system remain vulnerable to face spoofing, a practical solution is in dire need. Part of making face antispoofing methods feasible in the real world is making sure that the results can be achieved in real-time. By achieving faster results, critical security environments can become more proactive in mitigating potential spoof attempts and prevent any potential attackers from entering a secure area or masquerading as another user. These results also need to be validated on varying image qualities to gain better insights into its robustness, as well as its applicability within different contexts.

By taking into account on how curvilinear singularities can be derived in shearlets, we found it to be a good solution for achieving face spoof discrimination. By precomputing the shearlet spectrum during a calibration phase, we achieved real-time performance for the full assessment process at a little cost to complexity and resources. The discrete shearlet transform-based mean features are fed into a linear or RBF SVM is very computationally efficient. The overall results from the three data sets are good in varying environmental conditions and also show that it can compete with existing methods, thereby showing that our approach is viable in practical real-time face antispoofing application.

Further preliminary results also show that our approach has great potential in higher quality video, such as 4 k video, without a significant computational footprint. We believe that further improvements to displays with higher resolutions and high dynamic range (HDR), along with cheaper 3D face masks are going to be the next challenge ahead for face antispoofing methods and we need to be ready for them.

References

1. Agarwal, A., Singh, R., Vatsa, M.: Face anti-spoofing using haralick features. In: 2016 IEEE 8th International Conference on Biometrics Theory, Applications and Systems (BTAS), pp. 1–6. IEEE (2016)
2. Bartlett, M.S., Littlewort, G., Fasel, I., Movellan, J.R.: Real time face detection and facial expression recognition: development and applications to human computer interaction. In: 2003 Conference on Computer Vision and Pattern Recognition Workshop, vol. 5, pp. 53–53, June 2003
3. Boulkenafet, Z., Komulainen, J., Hadid, A.: Face anti-spoofing based on color texture analysis. In: 2015 IEEE International Conference on Image Processing (ICIP), pp. 2636–2640. IEEE (2015)
4. Boulkenafet, Z., Komulainen, J., Li, L., Feng, X., Hadid, A.: OULU-NPU: a mobile face presentation attack database with real-world variations. In: 2017 12th IEEE International Conference on Automatic Face & Gesture Recognition (FG 2017), pp. 612–618. IEEE (2017)
5. Chingovska, I., Anjos, A., Marcel, S.: On the effectiveness of local binary patterns in face anti-spoofing. In: 2012 BIOSIG-Proceedings of the International Conference of the Biometrics Special Interest Group (BIOSIG), pp. 1–7. IEEE (2012)
6. de Freitas Pereira, T., Anjos, A., De Martino, J.M., Marcel, S.: LBP-TOP based countermeasure against face spoofing attacks. In: Park, J.-I., Kim, J. (eds.) ACCV 2012. LNCS, vol. 7728, pp. 121–132. Springer, Heidelberg (2013). https://doi.org/10.1007/978-3-642-37410-4_11
7. de Freitas Pereira, T., Anjos, A., De Martino, J.M., Marcel, S.: Can face anti-spoofing countermeasures work in a real world scenario? In: 2013 International Conference on Biometrics (ICB), pp. 1–8. IEEE (2013)
8. de Freitas Pereira, T., et al.: Face liveness detection using dynamic texture. EURASIP J. Image Video Process. **2014**(1), 2 (2014)
9. Feng, L., et al.: Integration of image quality and motion cues for face anti-spoofing: a neural network approach. J. Vis. Commun. Image Represent. **38**, 451–460 (2016)
10. Galbally, J., Marcel, S.: Face anti-spoofing based on general image quality assessment. In: 22nd International Conference on Pattern Recognition (ICPR), pp. 1173–1178. IEEE (2014)
11. Komulainen, J., Hadid, A., Pietikainen, A.: Context based face anti-spoofing. In: 2013 IEEE Sixth International Conference on Biometrics: Theory, Applications and Systems (BTAS), pp. 1–8. IEEE (2013)
12. Kutyniok, G., Petersen, P.: Classification of edges using compactly supported shearlets. Appl. Comput. Harmon. Anal. **42**(2), 245–293 (2017)
13. Li, Y., Po, L.-M., Xuyuan, X., Feng, L.: No-reference image quality assessment using statistical characterization in the shearlet domain. Signal Process. Image Commun. **29**(7), 748–759 (2014)
14. Lim, W.-Q.: The discrete shearlet transform: a new directional transform and compactly supported shearlet frames. IEEE Trans. Image Process. **19**(5), 1166–1180 (2010)
15. Liu, X., Shan, S., Chen, X.: Face recognition after plastic surgery: a comprehensive study. In: Lee, K.M., Matsushita, Y., Rehg, J.M., Hu, Z. (eds.) ACCV 2012. LNCS, vol. 7725, pp. 565–576. Springer, Heidelberg (2013). https://doi.org/10.1007/978-3-642-37444-9_44

16. Lucena, O., Junior, A., Moia, V., Souza, R., Valle, E., Lotufo, R.: Transfer learning using convolutional neural networks for face anti-spoofing. In: Karray, F., Campilho, A., Cheriet, F. (eds.) ICIAR 2017. LNCS, vol. 10317, pp. 27–34. Springer, Cham (2017). https://doi.org/10.1007/978-3-319-59876-5_4
17. Määttä, J., Hadid, A., Pietikäinen, M.: Face spoofing detection from single images using micro-texture analysis. In: 2011 international joint conference on Biometrics (IJCB), pp. 1–7. IEEE (2011)
18. Pan, G., Sun, L., Wu, Z., Lao, S.: Eyeblink-based anti-spoofing in face recognition from a generic webcamera. In: IEEE 11th International Conference on Computer Vision, 2007, ICCV 2007, pp. 1–8. IEEE (2007)
19. Patel, K., Han, H., Jain, A.K., Ott, G.: Live face video vs. spoof face video: use of moiré patterns to detect replay video attacks. In: 2015 International Conference on Biometrics (ICB), pp. 98–105. IEEE (2015)
20. Tan, X., Li, Y., Liu, J., Jiang, L.: Face liveness detection from a single image with sparse low rank bilinear discriminative model. In: Daniilidis, K., Maragos, P., Paragios, N. (eds.) ECCV 2010. LNCS, vol. 6316, pp. 504–517. Springer, Heidelberg (2010). https://doi.org/10.1007/978-3-642-15567-3_37
21. Viola, P., Jones, M.J.: Robust real-time face detection. Int. J. Comput. Vis. 57(2), 137–154 (2004)
22. Wen, D., Han, H., Jain, A.K.: Face spoof detection with image distortion analysis. IEEE Trans. Inf. Forensic Secur. 10(4), 746–761 (2015)
23. Xu, Z., Li, S., Deng, W.: Learning temporal features using LSTM-CNN architecture for face anti-spoofing. In: 2015 3rd IAPR Asian Conference on Pattern Recognition (ACPR), pp. 141–145, November 2015
24. Yang, J., Lei, Z., Liao, S., Li, S.Z.: Face liveness detection with component dependent descriptor. In: 2013 International Conference on Biometrics (ICB), pp. 1–6, June 2013
25. Zhang, Z., Yan, J., Liu, S., Lei, Z., Yi, D., Li, S.Z.: A face antispoofing database with diverse attacks. In: 2012 5th IAPR international conference on Biometrics (ICB), pp. 26–31. IEEE (2012)

Password Policies Adopted by South African Organizations: Influential Factors and Weaknesses

Pardon Blessings Maoneke[1]([⊠]) and Stephen Flowerday[2]

[1] Namibia University of Science and Technology,
13 Storch Street, Windhoek 9000, Namibia
blessings83@gmail.com
[2] Rhodes University, Prince Alfred Street, Grahamstown 6140, South Africa
s.flowerday@ru.ac.za

Abstract. Organizations worldwide are revisiting the design of their password policies. This is partly motivated by the security and usability limitations of user-generated passwords. While research on password policies has been ongoing, this has taken place in the Global North. Accordingly, little is known about the strengths and weaknesses of password policies deployed in the Global South, especially Africa. As such, this study researched password policies deployed on South African websites. Password policies of thirty frequently visited websites belonging to South African organizations were analyzed. Our observations show diverse password requirements. Even though the desire for strong passwords is the dominant motivator of complex password policies, South African organizations often adopt obsolete measures for attaining password security. The ten most common passwords in the literature were considered acceptable on most sites. In addition, some sites did not explicitly display password requirements and only a few sites adopted measures for providing real-time feedback and effective guidance during password generation.

Keywords: Password · Password usability · Password security
Password policy · Password strength meter

1 Introduction

Research findings from the analysis of more than 100 million English and Chinese passwords that were leaked into the public domain exposed various security limitations associated with user-generated passwords. In response, organizations are adjusting their password policies while institutions responsible for the promulgation of authentication guidelines are revising their perceptions on password strength and usability [1–3]. However, the literature reports inconsistency between the complexity of deployed password policies and prescribed best practices [1, 3]. For example, institutions that are expected to adopt complex password policies have simple policies and vice versa. In addition, passwords assumed strong by one password policy may be considered weak by another [3]. This is exacerbated by research that is focused on password policies (password strength meters and rule-based policies) deployed on Global North websites

© Springer Nature Switzerland AG 2019
H. Venter et al. (Eds.): ISSA 2018, CCIS 973, pp. 30–43, 2019.
https://doi.org/10.1007/978-3-030-11407-7_3

[3]. Little is known about password policy implementation in other countries, especially the Global South with a focus on Africa. As such, this study investigated password policies deployed by South African based organizations. The aim of this study was to identify factors motivating the adoption of password policies, as well as to evaluate the strengths and weaknesses of deployed password policies [4]. It was deemed important to establish the influence of international best practices and previous research findings on South African organizations' adoption of password policies. South Africa is Africa's most industrialized economy. It was therefore worth researching how the adoption of password policies is comparable to international trends. Such findings can play a leading role in informing authentication policy designs and implementation.

2   Background and Related Work

This study used the National Institute of Standards and Technology's (NIST) Digital Identity Guidelines and a study by Florêncio and Herley [1] to identify factors influencing the adoption of complex password policies. The NIST, a United States based research institute, has published various editions of Special Publications (SPs) on password guidelines that have been influential in shaping the design of password policies since 2006. In addition, guidelines in the NIST SPs complement propositions in prominent international electronic authentication frameworks for Australia, India and the European Union [5]. While the NIST SPs consider security to be the major factor influencing password policy design, Florêncio and Herley [1] propose a holistic approach for understanding the factors influencing the design of password requirements. Thus, the NIST SPs and Florêncio and Herley's [1] study give a balanced view on the factors that influence password policies.

2.1   NIST SP: 800-63-3 Digital Identity Guideline

The NIST SPs on electronic authentication guidelines have been influential in guiding password policies. Early versions of the NIST SP on electronic authentication guidelines were inspired by Shannon entropy to estimate password strength. It was assumed that the use of different character sets would enhance password strength. Studies conducted a few years later, starting with Wier et al. [6], proved that entropy was not a good measure of password strength. In response to these findings, NIST made modifications to its conceptualization of password strength and usability as reflected in the SP editions released in 2013 and 2017 [2, 7]. In 2017, NIST released an SP 800-63-3, which is considered a "suite of volumes" with the following three documentations for guiding user authentication:

- SP 800-63A Enrolment and Identity Proofing,
- SP 800-63B Authentication and Lifecycle Management
- SP 800-63C Federation and Assertions [2].

NIST indicated that the SP 800-63A and 800-63B could be used in the private sector while US federal agencies are required to also incorporate specifications in the SP 800-63C. This study focuses on authentication; hence, it is limited to the 800-63B of the SP 800-63-3 Digital Identity Guideline. According to NIST, service providers should evaluate the risks associated with their online transactions to establish assurance levels that will guide choices regarding authentication complexity [2]. Memorized secrets such as passwords are among the authentication measures considered by NIST. Propositions in SP 800-63B suggest a shift from NIST's view of password strength that was traditionally centered on the use of different character sets. Today, system designers are encouraged to make use of a blacklist with common passwords and dictionary words [2]. The use of keyboard patterns and personal information during password generation is strongly discouraged. In addition, user-generated passwords should be at least eight characters long. Password policies are to be designed in such a way that they provide feedback and guidance to users as they generate new passwords. These propositions to some extent concur with suggestions in the literature that are being advanced with the aim of enhancing password security and usability. For example, Dropbox's zxcvbn algorithm for guiding password generation makes use of a blacklist, guards against the use of keyboard patterns, personal information and gives real-time feedback on the reasons for password rejection [7]. Similarly, Shay et al. [8] found that using a blacklist promotes password strength even though it is less usable. Furnell [9] suggests a need to provide feedback and guidance during password generation. Password feedback make provisions for ratings on password strength, while password generation guidance goes on to provide "more explanatory detail about how well the resulting password would serve" users [10, p. 5].

2.2 Factors Influencing the Adoption of Complex Password Policies

Florêncio and Herley [1] researched factors influencing the adoption of different password policies. Their analysis of seventy-five websites found that websites are adopting diverse password policies. This finding was corroborated by research findings from studies conducted in the Global North [3, 4, 9]. Florêncio and Herley [1] observe that factors assumed to be of importance when deciding on the complexity of password policies were irrelevant. The "size of the site, the number of user accounts, the value of the resources protected, and the frequency of non-strength related attacks all correlate very poorly with the strength required by the site" [1, p. 1]. These findings suggest that security-related factors may not inspire the adoption of complex password policies. Other studies found the security requirements determined by potential risks not sufficient to motivate the adoption of complex password policies [3, 4]. Rather, these organizations are mainly influenced by the usability of adopted password policies with the aim of encouraging users to sign up irrespective of security implications [9].

3 Methodology

This study adapts and modifies an approach used by Florêncio and Herley [1] and Wang and Wang [3] in which sites are selected for analysis, measuring the strength of password policies. These are explained next.

3.1   Selecting Sites and Password Policy Analysis

Considerations of popular sites were based on online traffic ranking using Alexa's top sites list (www.alexa.com/topsites/countries/ZA). This approach is widely used in the literature [3, 9, 11]. Accordingly, South African websites that appeared among the first one hundred and fifty (150) on Alexa's list were considered. The focus was on websites owned by companies with headquarters based in South Africa. The idea was to establish the perception of South African organizations on password strength and usability. Besides, password requirements on websites of most multinational companies such as Dropbox, Google, YouTube and Yahoo have received wide research [1, 3, 5, 9, 11]. Limiting websites to those appearing among the top one hundred and fifty allows this study to base its conclusions on the most visited [11] South African sites. It is expected that these sites influence a number of end-users and may set a standard [9] on password requirements for South African sites. In addition, their popularity might inspire a desire to conform to international password requirement best practices.

Once the websites were identified, they were categorized according to different themes based on web services. For each site, password requirements were investigated focusing on "length limits, charset requirement, whether rules are explicitly stated, whether allowing special characters, whether using a blacklist, whether deterring the use of personal data" [3, p. 10], password creation guidance and the use of a password strength meter. An attempt to generate a password or create an account was made where possible to enhance the understanding of password requirements [1].

3.2   Password Policy Strength

The strength of passwords generated through the guidance of a password policy determines the strength of the policy [1, 3]. The literature suggests two common password strength measures, namely, entropy and password guessing [3, 6, 8]. This study adopts a formula in Florêncio and Herley [1] that is inclined towards ascertaining password entropy to measure password policy strength. The formula expresses password strength in terms of bits. The formula is stated as follows:

$$N_{min} Log_2 C_{min} \tag{1}$$

Where:

N_{min} is the minimum password length and

C_{min} is the cardinality of the minimum character set required [1, p. 2].

This study used a US standard keyboard with an ASCII character set that includes twenty-six letters (lower or upper case), ten digits, and thirty-three non-alphanumeric special characters [12]. For example, the bits of a password rule that requires at least six characters is computed as follows:

$$6. \log_2 26 = 28.2 \, bits$$

4   Findings and Results

This section reports on the findings from the reviewed sites.

4.1   Reviewed Sites

Alexa's top one hundred and fifty list shows that there are forty-seven websites matching this study's definition of websites owned by South African organizations. The remaining sites are owned by multinational organizations. However, seventeen of the selected forty-seven sites were not considered for further analysis in this study. The reason being that eight had no provisions for password generation, while two could not be opened as the Uniform Resource Locator was not found. The password generation requirements of the remaining sites (seven) could not be accessed as they were restricted to clients only. In the end, the password policies of thirty websites were analyzed. An attempt to create passwords was done on twenty-four of the thirty websites considered for this study. The reviewed sites were categorized according to themes based on web services as follows: e-Commerce (5), universities (4), news (4), banks (3), job vacancies (3), sites of Information and Technology (IT) corporations (2), television services (2), real estate (2), classified adverts (2), electronic mail (email) site (1), betting site (1) and an electronic government (e-Government) site for tax filing. Section 5 and the Appendix provides an overview of findings on the full set of the analyzed sites.

4.2   The Diversity of Password Policies and Strength

Data analysis shows that South African organizations deploy diverse password policies. These include password strength meters and rule-based password policies. Of all the sites analyzed, 10% used password strength meters and 90% used rule-based password policies. In addition, 85.2% of the sites using rule-based password policies had password composition rules requiring different character sets. Only 7.4% of sites of those assuming a rule-based password policy had a provision for a Single Sign-On (SSO), while the remaining 7.4% had provisions for users to either use a user-generated rule-based password or SSO. Findings in this study concur with the literature on the dominance of rule-based password policies and the diversity of password policies [1]. Table 1 shows the minimum password policy strength according to entropy that was computed using the formula in Sect. 3.2. Password policy strength varied across and within the analyzed categories, as shown by the entropy in the least and highest password policy strength columns.

Entropy was computed for sites with rule-based password policies. Table 1 reports on the lowest, median and highest minimum password policy strength observed for each password category analyzed. For example, the lowest password policy strength observed on all e-Commerce sites could encourage users to generate a password that is at least 23.5 bits. However, an e-Commerce site with the highest minimum password policy strength could see users generating passwords of at least 41.4 bits. Only the lowest password policy strength was reported in cases where the computed entropy was

Table 1. Password policy strength of researched categories of sites

Site Category	Minimum password policy strength (bits)		
	Least password policy strength	Median password policy strength	Highest password policy strength
*e-Commerce	23.5	31.03	41.4
Universities	28.2	55.3	78.8
*News site	23.5	33.1	47.6
Bank	37.6	46	52.7
*Job vacancies	4.7	4.7	4.7
IT corporations	47.6	47.6	47.6
Television services	28.2	28.2	28.2
*Real estate	28.2	32	35.7
Classified adverts	4.7	18.8	32.9
email	23.5	–	–
Betting site	31	–	–
e-Government	37.4	–	–

Note: *Some of the sites use SSO or a password strength meter, hence the strength of their policies was not computed.

for a single website, as shown in Table 1. Table 1 shows that sites of universities, IT corporations and banks had, on average, the strongest password policies.

It should be noted that there was a keen interest in testing the guessing resistance of candidate passwords generated under different policies. This study used an open source zxcvbn password-guessing algorithm. Zxcvbn is an outstanding password strength measure deployed today [4]. However, the majority of passwords that were found acceptable on researched policies have already been found weak and easy to guess in other studies. For example, passwords that were found acceptable by researched password policies include 1234567, password, qwerty, iloveyou and 12345678 and are, in fact, among the top ten of millions of leaked passwords [13]. These passwords were considered relevant on more than 60% of the researched sites to which the researchers had access to generate a candidate password. The Appendix shows candidate passwords found acceptable at each site researched.

4.3 Password Policies and Influential Factors

This section reports on the characteristics of researched password policies according to specifications in Sect. 3.1. An analysis of factors influencing the adoption of complex password policies is included. The analysis and findings are presented according themes based on web service:

University Sites. All the analyzed university websites had rule-based password policies together with a strict password minimum length requirement. All the sites clearly indicated password rules in advance. For example, one of the university websites required that passwords be at least six characters long with no additional requirements for character sets. Another university recommended passwords of at least eight characters with three additional character set requirements involving the use of lowercase and uppercase letters, a number and symbol. On the other hand, the other two university sites recommended long passwords of at least twelve and fourteen characters. The twelve-character password policy had additional requirements that users include upper and lowercase letters together with a number and special characters. However, the fourteen-character password policy does not require the inclusion of different character sets but the use of user identity details and keyboard patterns is restricted.

The analysis of password policies in this study was limited to university accounts for students. These accounts provided access to personal information including student results and emails. Accordingly, the Authentication Assurance Level (AAL) for university sites was considered to be AAL2 according to NIST. Our observations suggest that password policies on university sites are influenced by a desire to enhance password security. Florêncio and Herley [1] reason that, once enrolled at a university, students have no alternative source of services except from the institutions they are enrolled at. Hence, such institutions often have complex password requirements.

Bank Sites. The analyzed sites belong to commercial banks and had rule-based password policies. User-generated passwords are expected to be at least eight characters long, have a number and uppercase and lowercase letters. One of the three bank sites had additional requirements for users to include a special character in their passwords, as well as blacklisting passwords based on keyboard patterns. All the researched banks published their password rules for users to see during password generation. Researchers managed to generate a password under one of the researched bank site's password policy. While the bank had provisions for real-time feedback during password generation and blocking certain keyboard patterns, there was no provision for password guidance. In addition, none of the bank sites used a blacklist to prohibit passwords based on common dictionary words or personal information.

A review of the online banking services offered suggests that the AAL for the reviewed banks is at level three (AAL3) according to NIST [2]. Security breaches of passwords for accessing online banking services have potentially high financial loss and inconvenience. Hence, strong passwords should be used for accessing online services classed AAL3. Accordingly, complex password policies on bank sites reflect that the value of protected resources has an influence on password policy complexity.

e-Commerce Sites. One of the five researched e-Commerce sites had a password strength meter with the remaining sites using a rule-based password policy. In particular to the site with a password strength meter, the implemented meter appeared sensitive to the use of different character sets when determining password strength. For example, password *"passwo"* was considered very weak while *"Password12"* was considered better. The password *"P@55word"* was regarded as strong. Three e-Commerce sites with rule-based password policies insisted on the creation of passwords that are at least five or six or eight characters long. Only one e-Commerce site used a Facebook SSO. Diversity in rule-based password policies for this category saw some sites recommending a minimum password length without any other additional requirements. However, one of the researched e-Commerce sites using a rule-based password policy required that users mix numbers with any other character set. In addition, a small blacklist was included that blocked the use of the word *"password"* in user-generated passwords. Hence *"password1"* and *"pa55word"* were not acceptable. However, the policy succumbed to other practices of character replacement, use of common words, keyboard patterns and personal information. For instance, *"111111p"*, *"p@55word"* and *"iloveyou1"* were considered relevant passwords.

An analysis was carried out to establish the influence of password strength and usability on e-Commerce password policies. Given that there is a potential for financial loss and inconvenience as a result of compromised passwords, e-Commerce authentication assurance was classed AAL2 according to NIST. However, even though e-Commerce sites implemented password strength requirements, these requirements are fairly stringent, which points towards a need to maximize password usability. Florêncio and Herley [1] suggests that e-Commerce businesses thrive on the high volumes of clients that visit their sites; hence, password requirements are likely to be relaxed in order to reduce the chances of dissatisfaction.

News Site. All the news sites researched in this study use rule-based password policies. Only one site uses a Facebook SSO facility while the remaining sites make use of a password composition policy. Password composition policies require that users generate a password that comprises of at least five or six or eight characters. There are no character class restrictions on the five and six-character password sites, hence *"passw"* and *"password"* are seen as good passwords. However, the eight-character password policy insists that users include numbers, uppercase and lowercase letters. Attempts to generate a password showed that the inclusion of an uppercase letters in the password was not enforced despite it being one of the requirements.

Further analysis on news sites shows that users can log into these sites to make comments "and personalize news, weather and listings". Our evaluation of these websites suggests that there are very limited consequences for the organization and users as a result of password security breaches. Hence, an AAL for this category was set at AAL1. As suggested by Florêncio and Herley [1], the implementation of authentication on the news sites appears to be motivated by password usability. The news site accepts third-party adverts; hence, the need for increased readership and the presence of alternative online news sources further emphasize the need for usable authentications.

Television Service Sites. The companies involved in television broadcasting implement a password strength meter and a rule-based password policy for guiding password generation. The password strength meter has provisions for real-time feedback and password generation guidance. The password generation algorithm can warn users if the password is found among popular passwords and names or passwords are based on keyboard patterns and simple character replacement such as L33T. Password length has an effect on password strength as long as the phrases or words used are not among those blacklisted. It was observed that one could only fill the strength bar if the password was at least twelve characters long. The other television site required users to generate a password that is at least six characters long with no specific character class requirements. Users have an option for an SSO using Facebook account.

Our observations show that password breaches on the television service provider site may expose users' personal information and grant access to online television viewership. Accordingly, the authentication assurance requirements of this site were rated AAL2. Observations show that the password policies of the researched sites attempt to find a balance between usability and security. One of the sites implemented password generation requirements according to recent suggestions by NIST and zxcvbn.

Real Estate Sites. The real estate sites make use of a rule-based password policy: SSO using a Facebook or Google account and provisions for user-generated passwords of at least six characters. Of the two researched real estate sites, one has additional requirements for including upper and lowercase letters together with a special character or number in a password. However, these password rules are not displayed for users to see. Password rules only appear after one has failed to generate a password that meets any of the requirements upon clicking the register button. Further, some of the common passwords such as *"passwords"* or *"Password5@"* are blacklisted by one of the real estate sites while the other site found the passwords acceptable. However, the password policy with a blacklist succumbs to character replacement, passwords based on keyboard patterns and common words. For example, *"Ilove1995"*; *"P@s5word"* and *"Qwerty123"* were found acceptable.

Further analysis showed that there are limited consequences of password security breaches on the real estate sites. As such, real estate sites were classed AAL1 in terms of authentication assurance level. This explains the more usable password requirements employed on the researched sites.

IT Corporation Sites. The IT corporation sites researched in this study have rule-based password policies. Users are required to generate a password that is at least eight characters long with at least one upper or lowercase letter or a number. Password requirements are displayed prior to password generation. The password policy demonstrated good use of feedback during password generation. For example, one of the sites had ticks appearing after each password generation rule was met so that users are provided with instant feedback and are guided on their progress. However, no reason was given for including different character sets. Users create accounts for updating their profile, managing telecommunication services subscriptions, redeeming vouchers and purchasing data bundles. Based on these observations, we rated authentication assurance for these sites at AAL2.

Password requirements suggest that password security has a great influence. Further, there is a desire for usability, as reflected by real-time feedback on progress regarding the meeting of password requirements during password generation.

Sites for Job Vacancies. Password policies on three sites in this category were analyzed. These sites show that a password strength meter and rule-based password policies are in use. The implemented password strength meter recommends passwords that are at least six characters long using alphanumeric characters. However, the password strength meter does not seem to offer adequate feedback to guide users during password generation. During password generation attempts, the password strength meter identified the password "123456" as very weak. Moreover, changes in character classes and length to candidate passwords did not reflect any movement on the password strength meter suggesting improvements in password strength. Furthermore, the other two sites did not explicitly display password requirements. Password generation attempts show that a single character password such as "1" is accepted.

Further observations show that security breaches on job vacancy sites could expose personal information. As such, authentication assurance for these sites was rated AAL2. The password policies implemented suggest less caution in relation to password security. More interest is invested in designing simple and usable password policies, although the lack of adequate feedback may negatively affect usability. The desire for usable policies could be motivated by competition from other sites with vacancies.

Classified Adverts. The two researched sites make use of rule-based passwords. The password policy on one of the two sites recommends passwords of at least seven characters. Users could generate a password such as "1234567". However, the other researched site did not display password requirements. Password generation attempts revealed that a single character password was acceptable.

Further observations show that there is little risk that could affect users with compromised passwords. These sites make provision for subscriptions to the latest adverts and uploading adverts. As such, sites for classified adverts are classed AAL1 according to NIST. This rating is reflected by simple password policies implemented on the sites.

Betting Site. A single betting site was researched. The site recommends that users generate an alphanumeric password that is at least six characters long. One of the limitations of the site's password generation policy design is that password requirements only appear after a user has failed to generate a suitable password. In addition, the policy is open to weak passwords such as *"password123"*. Our observations show that the site gathers personal user data such as name, address and identity number. Password breaches could lead to the exposure of personal information; hence, this site is rated AAL2, suggesting relatively complex password requirements. However, the password policy on the betting site is more inclined towards usability. This could be explained by a need to attract more users.

E-Government Site. The password policy of the e-Government site recommends the generation of a password that is at least six characters long with upper and lowercase letters, a number and a symbol. Password requirements are displayed in advance for users to see. The use of special characters is limited to: ~!@#$%^&*()_+. Users are also warned against the use of personal information in passwords. Our observations suggest that security breaches could lead to the exposure of personal information. Hence, the researched e-Government site is classed AAL3 according to NIST. However, this suggestion is not in line with the site's implementation of a password policy which appears to be leaning towards usability rather than security.

5 Discussion

Popular South African sites have diverse password requirements even for institutions in the same type of industry. Rule-based password policies are the most popular policies when compared to the use of password strength meters. This study made the following key observations:

- There are cases where password policies are limited to a few permissible password characters.
- Password requirements are not always explicitly displayed for users to see.
- There is very limited use of effective guidance and feedback during password generation.
- The use of a blacklist is often poorly implemented. Most blacklists did not block the ten most common passwords in the public domain.
- Some password policies allow the generation of very short passwords (one-character password).
- There are instances where password requirements are not enforced.
- Sites that are expected to have strong password policies sometimes have weak policies.
- Most password policies are based on practices that were found to be obsolete in the literature – the use of different character sets and a limited use of blacklists.
- Sites with strict password policies are more likely to display their password rules explicitly.

However, there are some encouraging observations. For example, one of the deployed password strength meters appears to use the zxcvbn password generation algorithm coupled with a long blacklist and real-time interactive fear appeals such as *"names and surnames by themselves are easy to guess"* or *"this is a top-10 common password"*. The use of "interactive fear appeals" significantly increases password strength compared to simple password strength meters with bars that change in colour [14, p. 2988]. Similarly, a few sites that enforced a rule-based password policy gave real-time feedback and guidance during password generation. Password rule enforcement, real-time feedback and effective guidance are some of the most effective methods that have the potential to reduce password generation errors, inform and support users to generate strong passwords [8, 10, 15].

The study findings suggest an attempt to increase password security. However, the password strength measures implemented on most of the researched sites have since been rendered obsolete. Tremendous emphasis is placed on using different character sets to enhance password strength. Very few sites (four) appeared to have effectively implemented proposed best practices of using a blacklist, blocking keyboard patterns, or encouraging long passwords. This is also common in the literature [9]. In addition, there appears to be a general belief that short passwords are easy to generate. Little effort is made to explicitly display password requirements, feedback and guidance, something that could enhance usability [3, 10, 15].

A comparison of the findings of this study and those in the literature was done for each category researched, with a focus on categories that were previously researched in the literature. Frequently visited South African IT corporation sites had comparable password policies to their Chinese counterparts [3]. Irrespective of country, IT corporations encouraged passwords that are at least eight characters long with numbers, special characters, uppercase and lowercase letters. None of the sites were found to be using a blacklist. However, the majority of Chinese IT corporations restrict the use of personal information. On the other hand, Chinese email service providers explicitly show password rules and use a blacklist, with some restricting the use of personal information [3]. Interestingly, South Africa's popular email site does not use any of these measures in its password policy. Furthermore, password policies of frequently visited South African e-Commerce sites were found to be comparable to those reported in the literature [1, 3]. e-Commerce sites recommend nearly the same character sets and minimum password length but do not always restrict user information in passwords and do not use a blacklist. However, frequently visited South African university sites encourage longer passwords compared to their Chinese counterparts [3]. In addition, two frequently visited South African university sites recommend a longer minimum password length than those in the US [1]. However, South Africa's popular e-Government site was found to have a short minimum length (6) requirement that translated to a relatively weaker password policy compared to its American counterparts [1]. Popular South African banks encourage the use of more character sets compared to their US counterparts [1]. It should be noted that banks often use a two-factor authentication [1, 3, 5]. Both South African and US frequently visited sites for classified adverts and news do not seem to emphasize the use of different character sets.

6 Conclusion

The literature suggests that the failure to implement measures that could influence user behavior towards using the technology correctly is one of the reasons behind the generation of weak passwords [1, 9, 16]. This has seen studies investigating password generation rules in use with others recommending corrective measures [9, 10, 15]. This study researched password policies deployed by South African organizations. It was found that security and usability factors play an important role in influencing the extent of password requirement complexity. The value of protected resources appears important to banks, universities and television broadcasting companies. However, e-Commerce, email, news sites, classified adverts and job sites appear to emphasize usability. It should be noted that the desire for secure passwords on South African sites is hampered by the use of obsolete password strength measures. Despite Wier et al.'s [6] ground-breaking research finding that using different character sets alone may not enhance security, the practice remains popular in South Africa. There are suggestions that leading international sites too have implemented minimal changes to their password requirements policies since 2011 [9]. This is so despite the literature suggesting different measures to enhance password generation [9, 16]. In addition, while some South African institutions prefer the usability of password requirements, they often do not provide real-time interactive feedback and guidance to users during password generation. Nevertheless, the majority of password policies deployed on popular South African sites are comparable to their global counterparts.

Appendix

Researched Sites, Password Policies and Accepted Passwords

Category	Password strength meter	Rule-based password policy	Minimum length limits	Character set	Blacklist	Deter personal data	SSO	Explicitly display password rules	Accepted passwords
Bank site	No	Yes	8	ULNS	No	No	No	Yes	P@s$word5
Bank site	No	Yes	8	ULN	No	No	No	Yes	N/A
Bank site	No	Yes	8	UN/ LN	No	No	No	Yes	N/A
Betting site	No	Yes	6	UN/ LN	No	No	No	No	password123
Classified adverts	No	Yes	No	No	No	No	No	No	1, we, pass
Classified adverts	No	Yes	7	N/ L/S/U	No	No	No	Yes	1234567
e-Commerce	Yes	N/A	N/A	N/A	No	No	No	Yes	P@55word
e-Commerce	No	Yes	5	L/N/S/U	No	No	No	No	ilove
e-Commerce	No	Yes	N/A	N/A	No	No	Yes	N/A	N/A
e-Commerce	No	Yes	8	UN/LN	Yes	No	No	Yes	111111p; p@55word; iloveyou1
e-Commerce	No	Yes	6	U/L/N/S	No	No	No	No	password
E-Government	No	Yes	6	ULNS	No	No	No	Yes	N/A
E-mail	No	Yes	No	U/L/N/S	No	No	No	No	12345
Job vacancies	Yes	Yes	6	U/L/N/S	No	No	No	Yes	pa55word
Job vacancies	No	Yes	No	U/L/N/S	No	No	No	No	pass
Job vacancies	No	Yes	No	U/L/N/S	No	No	No	No	pass
News site	No	Yes	N/A	N/A	No	No	Yes	N/A	N/A
News site	No	Yes	6	U/L/N/S	No	No	No	No	password
News site	No	Yes	5	U/L/N/S	No	No	No	No	passw
News site	No	Yes	8	ULN	No	No	No	Yes	password1
Real estate	No	Yes	6	U/L/N/S	Yes	No	No	No	Pa$5word
Real estate	No	Yes	6	U/L/N/S	No	No	No	Yes	password
IT corporations	No	Yes	8	ULN	No	No	No	Yes	Password@1
IT corporations	No	Yes	8	ULN	No	No	No	Yes	Password1
TV services	Yes	N/A	N/A	N/A	Yes	No	No	Yes	
TV services	No	Yes	6	U/L/N/S	No	No	Yes	No	password
University	No	Yes	6	U/L/N/S	No	No	No	Yes	password
University	No	Yes	12	ULNS	No	No	No	Yes	N/A
University	No	Yes	14	U/L/N/S	Yes	Yes	No	Yes	N/A
University	No	Yes	8	ULN/ UNS/LNS	No	No	No	Yes	password1#

Key: U: Uppercase letters; L: Lowercase letters; N: Number; S: Symbol.
N/A: Not applicable

References

1. Florêncio, D., Herley, C.: Where do security policies come from? In: Proceedings of a Symposium on Usable Privacy and Security (SOUPS), pp. 1–14. ACM, Redmond (2010)
2. Grassi, P.A., Garcia, M.E., Fenton, J.L.: Digital Identity Guidelines. NIST Special Publication 800-63-3, pp. 1–62. NIST (2017)

3. Wang, D., Wang, P.: The emperor's new password creation policies: In: Pernul, G., Ryan, P. Y.A., Weippl, E. (eds.) ESORICS 2015. LNCS, vol. 9327, pp. 456–477. Springer, Cham (2015). https://doi.org/10.1007/978-3-319-24177-7_23
4. de Carnavalet, X., Mannan, M.: From very weak to very strong: analyzing password-strength meters. In: NDSS, vol. 14, pp. 23–26 (2014)
5. AlFayyadh, B., Thorsheim, P., Jøsang, A., Klevjer, H.: Improving usability of password management with standardized password policies. In: Proceedings of the Seventh Conference on Network and Information Systems Security (SAR-SSI), pp. 7983–7999. Kolkata, India (2012)
6. Weir, M., Aggarwal, S., de Medeiros, B., Glodek, B.: Password cracking using probabilistic context-free grammars. In: Proceedings of the 30th IEEE Symposium on Security and Privacy, pp. 391–405. IEEE, Washington (2009)
7. Wheeler, D.L.: zxcvbn: Low-Budget Password Strength Estimation. In: Proceedings of the 25th USENIX Security Symposium. pp. 157–173. USENIX Association, Austin (2016)
8. Shay, R., et al.: A spoonful of sugar? The impact of guidance and feedback on password-creation behavior. In: Proceedings of the Human Computer Interaction (HCI) Conference, pp. 2903–2912. ACM, Seoul (2015)
9. Furnell, S.: Password practices on leading websites – revisited. Comput. Fraud Secur. **12**, 5–11 (2014)
10. Furnell, S., Khern-am-nuai, W., Esmael, R., Yang, W., Li, N.: Enhancing security behaviour by supporting the user. Comput. Secur. **75**, 1–9 (2018)
11. Ur, B., et al.: How does your password measure up? The effect of strength meters on password creation. In: Proceedings of USENIX Security Symposium, pp. 65–80. USENIX, Bellevue (2012)
12. Yang, C., Hung, J.-L., Lin, Z.: An analysis view on password patterns of chinese internet users. Nankai Bus. Rev. Int. **4**, 66–77 (2013)
13. Wang, D., Cheng, H., Gu, Q., Wang, P.: Understanding Passwords of Chinese Users: Characteristics, Security and Implications. CACR Report, China (2015)
14. Vance, A., Eargle, D., Ouimet, K., Straub, D.: Enhancing password security through interactive fear appeals: a web-based field experiment. In: Proceedings of the 46th Hawaii International Conference on System Sciences, pp. 2988–2997. IEEE, Wailea (2013)
15. Furnell, S., Esmael, R.: Evaluating the effect of guidance and feedback upon password compliance. Comput. Fraud Secur. **1**, 5–10 (2017)
16. Althubaiti, S., Petrie, H.: Instructions for creating passwords: how do they help in password creation. In: Proceedings of the 31st British Computer Society Human Computer Interaction Conference, pp. 55–65. BCS Learning & Development Ltd, Sunderland (2017)

An Investigation into Students Responses to Various Phishing Emails and Other Phishing-Related Behaviours

Edwin Donald Frauenstein[(✉)]

Department of Information Technology, Walter Sisulu University,
East London, South Africa
efrauenstein@wsu.ac.za

Abstract. Reports continue to testify that the problem of phishing remains pertinent in many industries today. This descriptive study investigated 126 university students' responses to various forms of phishing emails and other security-related behaviours through a self-designed questionnaire. The majority of the participants reported having an average experience in using computers and the Internet. Most participants chose to respond to phishing emails purportedly originating from Facebook and university contexts thus supporting that users are more likely to fall victim to phishing if the message is of interest or has relevance to their context. However, susceptibility was significantly reduced when users were presented with emails that imitate well-known South African banking institutions. This may suggest that users are either aware of phishing schemes that impersonate banking institutions, or they feel uncomfortable giving up personal information when they feel more at risk to be affected financially. The results from this study offer insights on behavioural aspects that can assist the information security community in designing and implementing more efficient controls against phishing attacks. Furthermore, this study suggests that researchers should consider exploring the behaviour of social media users as they can be vulnerable to phishing.

Keywords: Phishing · Social phishing · Social engineering
Responses to phishing · Social network sites · Facebook · Human factors
Behavioural information security

1 Introduction

Phishing has been a research area of interest to information security scholars for over a decade [1, 2]. In 2016, phishing reduced from 1 in 1,846 emails to 1 in 2,596 emails [3]. On the contrary, the Anti-Phishing Working Group (APWG) reported that the total number of phishing attacks in 2016 was 1,220,523, a 65% increase over 2015 and was subsequently described as the worst year for phishing in history [4]. In the 3rd quarter of 2017, APWG [5] reported 296,208 unique cases of phishing, an increase over the previous quarter. More concerning, phishers were using https protection to fool their victims into thinking phishing sites are to be trusted [5]. The ProofPoint 2016 report [6] revealed that malicious emails were the preferred attack channel for a wide range of

© Springer Nature Switzerland AG 2019
H. Venter et al. (Eds.): ISSA 2018, CCIS 973, pp. 44–59, 2019.
https://doi.org/10.1007/978-3-030-11407-7_4

cyber-attacks during 2016 with one in 131 emails sent being malicious, the highest rate in five years. Scams involving the spoofing of CEO emails sent to CFOs fell by 28% in the final quarter while in the same year, email malware increased from 1 in 220 emails to 1 in 131 emails [3]. The latter poses an interesting dilemma in the statistics as phishing emails do not always contain links, but they may contain malware attachments.

Phishing cases occur almost daily and pose significant financial losses to organisations. Recently, two multi-billion dollar technology companies, Google and Facebook, were discovered to be the victims of a phishing scheme, losing a total of $100 million [7]. This is concerning as one would expect such reputable companies to have sound information security management practices in place. However, this exposes one of the key security challenges both organisations and individuals face today: the human factor. Organisations can implement effective network defences; however, techniques such as phishing are able to circumvent such controls as it exposes the vulnerability of humans. These vulnerabilities could include arrogance, urgency, fear, greed, compliance, desire to be helpful and generally a lack of awareness of security threats. As a result, researchers have focused on human behaviour [8], information processing [9] and personality traits [10] to help understand the phenomenon of decision-making in online environments. To ensure employees are aware of phishing, organisations typically implement computer-based awareness training, phishing simulation exercises, posters and newsletters [11]. Year-on-year, organisations have increasingly applied end-user security awareness training and measured their susceptibility to phishing [11].

However, phishers appear to be a step ahead as they constantly seek new methods by which to trick their victims. As social networking sites (SNSs) are popular worldwide with approximately 2.2 billion active Facebook users [12] and 16 million South Africans using Facebook [13], this has created various opportunities for phishers. Consequently, this adds another dimension towards addressing information security behaviour as users may be engaged in SNSs both at work and in their personal time. They may begin to develop certain bad habits and behaviours which might be brought into the organisation.

The most cited articles today and related to phishing, were published more than a decade ago [14–18]. These studies were conducted outside of South Africa and focused primarily on the user and how they would respond to either a phishing website, email or a browser warning. This study makes a similar contribution as it not only measures the frequency of potential susceptibility to phishing, but moreover includes the responses from the participants and may help researchers identify the reasons why they chose to respond in a certain way. The study also makes use of various forms of actual phishing emails that fit the context of South Africans. In instances where users were able to identify phishing correctly, their responses were further investigated to determine if their actions were based on emotion (i.e. feeling that it doesn't look right) or on existing knowledge of security threat agents.

The remainder of the paper is structured as follows: Sect. 2 briefly introduces SNSs as an opportunity for phishers, Sect. 3 describes the research instrument and the procedures on how data was collected, Sect. 4 presents the findings in detail while Sect. 5 reflects on the main findings and Sect. 6 formally concludes the paper.

2 New Opportunities for Phishers

Phishing is defined as "a criminal mechanism employing both social engineering and technical subterfuge to steal consumers' personal identity data and financial account credentials" [4]. Phishing effectively makes use of social engineering (SE) techniques that aim to exploit certain human vulnerabilities with the intent to lure people into performing certain actions such as opening attachments, following links, or disclosing their personal credentials. Phishers will take advantage of almost any opportunity, from religious holidays, tax seasons, enticing prize offers, elections campaigns, popular events and so on. South Africa is known to have a diverse culture, thus being referred to as the rainbow nation. With access to smartphones, popular SNSs such as Facebook have made it possible to close the digital divide in society as a whole as various cultural groupings can follow or join groups and pages. Ironically, the discussions, in the form of comments, taking place in these social network pages and groups can adversely divide users as arguments can arise on sensitive topics such as animal abuse, politics, religion and racial slurs. Phishers will take advantage, by creating clickbait links on SNSs or by creating crafty phishing emails that entice users to click on attachments or links to view the videos. For example, in Brazil, phishers are using both phishing emails and social media to commit fraud online [4].

Phishing, in the context of SNSs, is gaining interest amongst researchers. In [19] study found that due to contextual elements on SNSs, employees can be easily deceived on SNSs thus putting their organisations at risk. A taxonomy of SNSs attacks and controls to protect against these attacks was introduced by [20]. Researchers [21] investigated the relationship between the Big Five personality traits and email phishing response and how such can affect user behaviour on Facebook. A study by [22] found that users who habitually use Facebook are significantly more likely to fall victim to a SNS phishing attack. Users resorted to cognitive shortcuts when using Facebook on their smartphone [23].

3 Method

3.1 Research Setting and Demography

The study was conducted at a higher education institution located in South Africa. A convenience sample of 136 first-year students, registered in the Information Technology programme, took part in a questionnaire-based survey. Ten participants supplied partial responses to some questions and were, therefore, removed from the analysis. Thus, a total of 126 participants (58 male and 68 female) with a mean age of 20.4 years took part in the survey. The sample population is made up of Black African students, the majority of whom come from disadvantaged communities. The students speak English as a second language. Despite the students originating from disadvantaged backgrounds with little or no access to personal computers at home, the majority own smartphones and are engaged in popular SNSs such as Facebook.

3.2 Research Instrument

The entire questionnaire was developed by the researcher and consisted of 34 questions with the majority being closed-ended questions and was orientated towards smartphone and social network (SN) users. The layout was organised into four main sections: demographics, computer experience, online social networking behaviour and email behaviour. The email behaviour section, consisted of five screenshot images of actual phishing emails and a browser warning that the researcher personally received. Participants were required to respond to the phishing emails from a list of five predetermined options. Some questions followed up with open-ended questions. In comparison to other phishing studies, this study used screenshots of genuine phishing emails that fit more appropriately into the student context rather than the generic-type phishing emails of which the participants may already be more aware.

3.3 Procedures

To ensure a large enough sample was acquired, data was collected during the first month, as student attendance is usually higher in the first quarter. An online questionnaire would have been more desirable. However, computer lab space limitations and risks of network stability were factors that could hinder data collection. Paper-based questionnaires were distributed to the students in class as if it were a written examination. It took the students approximately 30–40 min to complete. The students had received no information security lessons at that point in time – that would have influenced them to identify scams more accurately. The students were able to ask questions for clarity if needed, and the students could be observed to ensure that they did not assist one another while answering the questionnaire. No incidents of misinterpretation of questions were reported to the researcher. The results of the survey were entered into a spreadsheet template for data analysis. Since English was a second language for all participants, open-ended responses had to be carefully interpreted and themed appropriately during analysis.

3.4 Ethics

Phishing-related experiments have been known to have relevant ethical concerns and requirements amongst information security researchers [24]. However, in this study the data collection process did not attempt to conduct any form of phishing attack against the participants, nor did it put them and the institution at any risk or loss – whether financially, emotionally and physically. Ethical clearance was granted by the Research Department. The researcher debriefed participants in the classroom, informing them that they are voluntarily participating in a survey. Furthermore, they were assured that their responses were to be treated as anonymous and confidential. In this regard, a statement had been declared on the cover page of the questionnaire.

4   Results

4.1   Computer and Internet Skills

A total of 61.9% participants reported that they had access to PCs or laptops during their secondary education, while 75.4% did not currently 'own' a PC or a laptop. Most participants rated their computer and Internet skills between those of a beginner and average level as reflected in Table 1.

Table 1. Participants rating of their abilities on computer skills and internet skills

Scale	Computer skill		Internet skill	
	n = 126	%	n = 126	%
Poor	17	13.5%	16	12.7%
Beginner/new	35	27.8%	28	22.2%
Average	49	38.9%	44	35%
Above average	14	11.1%	29	23%
Advanced	11	8.7%	9	7.1%

4.2   Most Used Social Applications

As mentioned earlier, SNSs provide a useful opportunity for phishers to exploit the vulnerability of users of these sites. The purpose of this question was to determine the most used social smartphone applications (apps). WhatsApp Messenger (94.4%), Facebook (87.3%), Facebook Messenger (59.5%), YouTube (53.2%) and Twitter (21.4%) was reported as some of the most used apps.

4.3   Rationale for Using Facebook

The purpose of this question was to determine if SN users are engaged in SNSs with a valid purpose, out of habit or for other forms of gratification. Recent research by Vishwanath [22] stated that habitual Facebook use can increase users' susceptibility to phishing attacks on SNSs. Participants' main reasons for using Facebook were reported as liking to see what their friends are doing with their posts and updates (67.5%), "liking" and/or following certain pages that could benefit them (61.1%), and using it to communicate with friends and family (60.3%). Interestingly, only 26.2% considered themselves hooked (i.e. addicted) to Facebook, while 3.2% used Facebook to seek new romantic relationships with 3.2% responding as not using Facebook.

4.4   Privacy of Personal Information on Facebook

The amount of personal information users are willing to share on SNSs can be used by phishers to launch spear phishing attacks on organisations [25]. In general, the participants appeared to be conservative in the type of personal information they are willing to divulge on Facebook. Using a multiple-answer question, a total of 52%

reported sharing only their full name, while 37.8% reported that they had never given out personal information unless they had met the person, and 27.6% reported that they had given out the university name and level at which they were in, while 16.5% had given out their home address. None of the participants reported giving out their bank details for money or airtime. Many Facebook users enjoy informing others on places they are visiting and with whom. Regarding the question if users check in to geographical locations and update SN posts or images, 51.6% participants stated 'Yes', while 48.4% do not. This lack of privacy to divulge where one is located can be advantageous to criminals who wish to conduct physical crime.

4.5   Responses to Visual Stimuli on Facebook

Participants were presented with a Facebook post depicting an image and a story of a four-month-old baby girl having survived after being found buried alive. The instruction embedded in the post requested the users to type Amen and share the post as "1 share will equal 100 prayers". This particular image was selected as the phisher's intention was to target the user's sympathy, and persuade users with strong religious beliefs. A majority (61.9%) chose to ignore the post while 23% would type Amen and share, and 15.1% would like the post.

Phishers can create fake social media accounts and use them to conduct other forms of cybercrime [26]. Thus, accepting friend requests from strangers can also pose security risks to SN users. When adding friends or accepting friend requests, the participants based their decisions on to whether they knew the person (83.5%) or had mutual friends (72.4%), while 40.9% considered whether they were comfortable in letting the person see their posts (i.e. updates). Interestingly, 11.8% based their decision on whether the individual had an attractive profile picture, while 15% were based on the person being successful and connected in industry. Participants were presented with the figure below and were requested to answer if they would consider opening the links if they saw this on Facebook.

Figure 1, is not video links but clickbait, which is content designed to attract users into clicking on it. A majority (88.9%) stated they would not open such links while the remainder would. Participants were further requested to state reasons why they would not open such links. Even though the links do not contain pornography, 38% of the participants who chose not to open the links considered it associated with nudity or pornography. This may indicate that users apply heuristic processing of messages as noted in other phishing studies [27]. As the majority of the students come from disadvantaged backgrounds, it is not unexpected that 15.9% would not open the link due to concerns of "wasting their data". Beliefs came up as another factor as some participants stated that they are "born again Christians" which may imply that they considered the images to be of a sexual nature thus going against their religious beliefs. Only 8% of the participants indicated that it may be spam, thus revealing that few students automatically understood the links to be malicious. Of the 13 participants (11%) who answered that they would open the links, their reasons given were that they were curious to see the video (38.5%), while others (23.1%) thought the video could be educational. For the latter, the participants may have paid closer attention to the descriptions stated in the links. One respondent stated "I'm an adult over 18 and have a right to view those things", while another stated "I don't like such videos but it may happen that I view them by mistake".

Fig. 1. Example of Clickbait on Facebook

4.6 Determining if a Webpage Is Safe

Participants were supplied with a screenshot of a legitimate Facebook login homepage using Google Chrome web browser. Without drawing much attention, the image displayed a security lock symbol on the address bar and an address beginning with https. Facebook logos and the login button were also present. Participants were requested to determine if it was a safe login. The majority (60.4%) responded that they did not know, 23% stated that it was not safe, while the remainder (16.6%) stated it is safe. Participants were required to supply reasons to further investigate why they regarded the webpage as safe.

For the participants who identified the webpage as safe (n = 21), 23.8% stated that the webpage required a username and password. This was followed by 19% who stated that it looks familiar from past experiences. From the security perspective, only 14.3% correctly identified the security padlock icon and 9.5% identified the "https" protocol reflected in the address bar. The 14.3% who stated that Facebook was safe because it did not keep their password, might indicate that these users might have experienced not logging out of their SNS and therefore might think that being presented with a login screen is a more secure option.

4.7 Responses to Phishing Emails from Various Sources

In this category, participants were presented with five various screenshots depicting actual emails that the researcher received. Participants had to respond by using the multiple-choice items. The phishing screenshots were: a Facebook phishing email (with attachment), University admin system update phishing email (with link), University HR request (non-phishing with link), Absa Bank phishing email (with link), and First National Bank phishing email (with attachment).

Facebook Phishing Email. In Fig. 2, participants were provided with this image of a phishing email purportedly originating from Facebook.

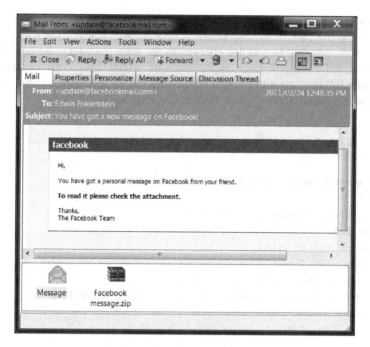

Fig. 2. Phishing email purportedly from Facebook

Since most students use Facebook, this email fits appropriately into the context of the students when compared to other frequently used phishing studies that request users to update their credit card details. Unlike most phishing emails that have a link leading to a spoofed website, this email preys on enticing the recipient into opening the attachment. Table 2 gives their responses to the Facebook email.

Table 2. Responses to Facebook phishing email

Responses to phishing email (Facebook)	n = 126	%
Check the attachment because I'm interested to know what my friend has to say	46	36.5%
Go to Facebook to read the message	27	21.4%
Do nothing/ignore	20	15.9%
Immediately delete the email	18	14.3%
I do not trust this email	15	11.9%
Reply to the email	0	0%

Concerningly, 36.5% of the participants would choose to open the attachment. Consequently, this action would most likely install malware on the user's device. However, 21.4% would choose to visit Facebook to view the message. Eight of the participants chose two actions (check the attachment, Go to Facebook to read the message) when the instrument required them to choose only one. In this regard, the researcher converted this to the response of "Check the attachment". The reason for this is because if the attachment was first checked by the user, it would make no difference to then visit the Facebook page as the malware would have been installed. The questionnaire followed up with an open-ended question for those that selected that they do not trust the email. Table 3 gives the detailed responses.

Table 3. Responses on why Facebook phishing email is not trusted

Reasons	n = 15
Facebook messages/notifications don't come via email	6
It's a scam	2
Facebook notifications would specify the friend	2
It's identity theft	1
The attachment could be a virus	1
Email not in a proper format	1
Anyone can pretend to be the Facebook team	1
My email does not have my Facebook details so impossible to receive Facebook notifications and I think its fake	1

For the participants (n = 15) who selected that they did not trust the email, six understood that Facebook did not typically notify users through email.

University Admin Phishing Email. It was expected that since the email address had the University's domain, users might trust it more. The typical phishing feature of not addressing the recipient by name was evident in the email. Furthermore, the email stated that a general system upgrade was required to fix bugs and provide web mail users with a better experience. Users were instructed to click on the link in order to update their account. Failure to do so might have resulted in disabled email access. From the multiple choice responses in Table 4, 46% of the participants would fall victim to the phishing email while only 10% did not trust the email.

Table 4. Responses to University Admin phishing email

Responses to phishing email (University Admin)	n = 126	%
Click on HERE so that I can update my account	58	46%
Do nothing/ignore	40	32%
Reply to the email	12	10%
I do not trust this email	12	10%
Immediately delete the email	4	3%

For the participants who selected that they did not trust the email (n = 12), the questionnaire followed up with an open-ended question to determine if they could give valid reasons why it should not be trusted. Some of the responses, with grammatical errors, could be grouped into themes as expressed in Table 5.

Table 5. Responses on why University Admin phishing email is not trusted

Reasons	n = 12
Its hackers	2
Its spam	2
Its viruses	1
Its phishing	1
I don't trust this and will further enquire with the admin	1
Notices and announcements would've been made instead	1
Admin should have a personal email address	1
I'm cautious - would rather go to university and ask them	1
My account should be automatically updated everytime I'm on a Wifi hotspot	1
Email doesn't have anything to do with the University's admin	1

The responses are somewhat different when compared to the previous phishing scenarios, as they reported with security terminology such as "hackers", "viruses" with one respondent correctly identifying the email as "phishing".

University Human Resources Email. Figure 3 depicts a screenshot of a valid email that was sent to all university employees. In the study, participants were instructed to respond as if the email was addressed to them (i.e. as an employee). The email possessed all the traits of a phishing email, namely not addressed to any specific person, spelling error "uptating", urgency to comply within a deadline, required to click on a link and vague email signature. The email was in the context appropriate for students as the domain of the email address was that recognisable of the University of study. Thus, recipients in this context might be more inclined to respond.

As indicated in Table 6, the participants (39.7%) would click on the link to update their details. Interestingly, a similar percentage of participants (31.7%) as in the previous question would also ignore this particular email. Although this was not a phishing email, it may indicate that users would likely comply with messages that impersonate entities of authority.

For the participants who selected that they did not trust the email (n = 10), the questionnaire followed up with an open-ended question to determine if they could give valid reasons on why it should not be trusted. They reported on some of the characteristics common to phishing emails. Their responses, with grammatical errors, are provided in Table 7.

Absa Bank Phishing Email. A phishing email purportedly originating from Absa Bank with the subject "Online Account Update" was given to the participants. The participants should have been familiar with the bank as it is local. The email originates

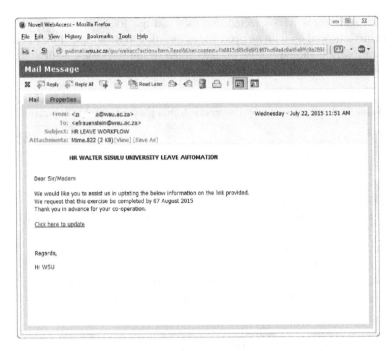

Fig. 3. Legitimate email from University Human Resources department

Table 6. Responses to legitimate email originating from University Human Resources Department

Responses to legitimate email (University HR)	n = 126	%
I will select "Click here to update"	50	39.7%
Do nothing/ignore	40	31.7%
Reply to the email	22	17.5%
I do not trust this email	10	7.9%
Immediately delete the email	4	3.2%

Table 7. Responses on why University Human Resources email is not trusted

Reasons
I think its identity theft
Don't know why I'm updating, there's spelling errors
I'm cautious of links in messages sent
It's not coming from HR dept. It should be more personal
Might be a scam should check it up before updating
The website does not state it's from the university, might be a trap
I don't see anybody who signed up for the email
I would ask HR directly at their office
Anyone can create a username as xxxxxx@wsu.ac.za
HR leave workflow has nothing to do with me as I am a student

from address ibsupport@absa.co.za. Within the email body, an Absa Bank logo is present and the email states that the Absa Online Banking Division is working on improving the online banking experience for their clients. It further states that they want to protect their clients against phishing attempts by fraudsters and to accomplish this they are migrating to a new TVN billing system. The user is requested to click on the link "Click here to update your account" which consequently leads them to a spoofed website. The email further stated that a minimal amount (unspecified) would be deducted from the client's account but would be refunded shortly after confirmation of the new system compatibility. The email concluded with the Security Department acknowledged in the signature details. Table 8 indicates the participants' responses.

Table 8. Responses to Absa Bank phishing email

Responses to phishing email (Absa Bank)	n = 126	%
Do nothing/ignore	49	38.9%
I do not trust this email	24	19%
I will select "Click here to update"	22	17.5%
Reply to the email	16	12.7%
Immediately delete the email	15	11.9%

The results are different when compared to the previous two email responses. The participants appeared to be more concerned as 38.9% selected to do nothing and 19% stated they do not trust the email. On further investigation into those that did not trust the email, most appeared to be aware of security threats as they were using terms such as "scams", "fraud", "identity theft" while one respondent correctly identified it as "phishing". Their responses, with grammatical errors, are in Table 9.

Table 9. Responses on why Absa Bank phishing email is not trusted

Reasons	n = 24
Its a scam	5
Prefer to go directly to the bank	5
These are hackers to commit fraud by stealing my bank details	4
Banks do not ask for personal details in emails	2
Its phishing	1
Not sure what to do if I don't get a refund	1
Its identity theft	1
Not comfortable that an amount will be deducted, they may want to steal all my money	1
Might be fraud	1
Don't feel comfortable sending my personal details on this channel	1
I don't use Absa and fake accounts can be created easily	1
Why don't they state the amount to be deducted? I would walk to them to find out the minimum amount	1

First National Bank Phishing Email. In the final phishing case, participants were presented with a phishing email purportedly from First National Bank (FNB) and which originated from the email address InContact@fnb.co.za. InContact is a familiar term to FNB clients as they receive transaction notifications with this description. Interestingly, the domain name is also legitimate. The email states that cardholders are at risk of having their account compromised and deactivated. As a result, they are required to open the attachment and follow instructions to activate their FNB card on the new security platform. The email further adds a warning that if they did not, it would lead to suspension of their ATM card. Participants were requested to select if they would comply with this request, and a majority (62%) indicated they would not. On further investigation into the reasons, 38.5% stated that they would query directly with the bank, 12.8% believed it to be a scam, 9% did not trust online banking, 7.7% stated that banks do not conduct their practices in this manner, and 6.4% noted dubious message elements such as missing logos, weak arguments, not addressing recipient by name, and no name for the admin, while the remainder supplied no reasons.

4.8   Responses to Browser Warning

An image of a Mozilla Firefox browser warning of blocking a malicious webpage was given. The warning has two buttons: one to allow the user to exit the webpage and the other allowing users to receive information as to why the page was blocked. There is also an embedded link in the warning which allows the user to ignore the warning. In the question it was stated that the warning was real and not fake. Participants had to choose from a list of actions they would take. Most (46.8%) chose to enquire why the page was blocked, 32.5% would obey the warning, while 18.3% would ignore the warning. The remainder chose the option: I know the webpage I want to go to is safe, I don't understand why this annoying message has come up. These findings suggest that users do not understand or trust warnings.

5   Discussion

Despite students coming from disadvantaged backgrounds, most students were actively involved in various SNSs and expressed their purpose for using it. Few participants gave adequate reasons to suggest that they understood that the Facebook links are malicious. Despite the images giving descriptions that were not directly related to the content displayed, most based their decisions on the appeal portrayed in the images. This may indicate that users apply a "heuristic mode" to processing information on SNSs thus supporting the study by Harrison et al. [28]. It further indicates that if the images presented were of more interest to the users, they might be more susceptible to clicking on them. Similarly, in the case of identifying safe webpages, the majority acknowledged that they were unable to determine if a webpage was safe while those who stated it was safe did not supply valid reasons. A small percentage were able to report on certain security indicators.

The phishing email purportedly originating from Facebook appealed to most users to open the attachment. This might be because most participants, as reported, use

Facebook and recognised the terminology given in the email. The phishing email purportedly originating from the University's Admin also appealed to most of the participants to comply with the request to click on the link. In a similar case, a legitimate email from the University's Human Resources Department, which appeared to possess all the common features of a phishing email, received similar results to the previous phishing example. This is an example of how challenging it is to educate users to identify phishing. This might be because the emails preyed on the social engineering principle of "authority" in order to persuade them to comply with the request [29]. However, in the cases of phishing emails purportedly originating from trusted South African banks, most of the participants chose not to click on the links. Most opted to ignore the emails while others stated that they did not trust those emails. Most respondents, for both banking cases, preferred to visit the bank directly to verify the request. This might indicate that either most participants were aware that scams typically impersonate banks or they were more vigilant when sending personal information such as banking details via email.

Regarding web browser warnings which aim to protect users, most participants appeared not to rely on the warning and chose to investigate further as to why their webpage was blocked. Again, this might have been due to a lack of knowledge of computer systems, as indicated in Table 1, or participants might have experienced fake warnings on sites that they had visited on their smartphones.

Referring to Table 1, participants who rated their abilities as *advanced* for both computer and Internet skills (n = 20), were further investigated to determine if they were better at detecting a safe website and phishing emails. Most (45%) stated they did not know if the webpage was safe, while 40% stated that it was a safe website. Majority (45%) would check attachment in the Facebook phishing email. For the University Admin phishing email, 50% would click the link. For the University Human Resources email, 45% would click on the link. Majority (50%) would ignore the Absa bank phishing email request while 25% stated they did not trust it. Finally, 60% would not view the attachment in the FNB phishing email while the remainder would comply with the request. This revealed that users who reported their skills as advanced, were not significantly better at detecting phishing than the rest of the sample population.

6 Conclusion

This paper revealed that average computer and Internet skill users might be increasingly aware of phishing emails impersonating financial institutions. This could be of concern for information security practitioners as most security education and training efforts in phishing continue to be focused mostly on protecting customers of financial institutions. The study also confirms that phishing is more effective especially if it has more contextual elements that are of interest or concern to the user. Phishing is also expanding into social media sites, enticing users into clicking on video and other malicious links directing to external websites. In South Africa, with the volume of controversial news events reported on social networking sites, phishers may catch their potential victims off-guard as they do not expect to be "phished" on such sites. In this regard, it is expected that phishing will continue to evolve on this platform adding more contextual elements, with the aid of Open Source Intelligence, to target particular types of users. Further research will focus more on statistical analysis exploring how the different responses correlate by gender and age.

References

1. Purkait, S.: Phishing counter measures and their effectiveness - literature review. Inf. Manag. Comput. Secur. **20**(5), 382–420 (2015)
2. Yates, D., Harris, A.L.: Phishing attacks over time: a longitudinal study. In: Twenty-First Americas Conference on Information Systems, Puerto Rico (2015)
3. Symantec, Internet Security Threat Report 2017, vol. 22, April 2017. https://www.symantec.com/content/dam/symantec/docs/reports/istr-22-2017-en.pdf. Accessed 9 Mar 2018
4. APWG, Phishing Activity Trends Report, 4th Quarter 2016. https://docs.apwg.org/reports/apwg_trends_report_q4_2016.pdf. Accessed 10 Mar 2018
5. APWG, Phishing Activity Trends Report, 3rd Quarter 2017. http://docs.apwg.org/reports/apwg_trends_report_q3_2017.pdf. Accessed 10 Mar 2018
6. ProofPoint, Quarterly Threat Summary–Q4 2016 & Year In Review, https://www.proofpoint.com/sites/default/files/proofpoint_q4_threat_report-final.pdf
7. Roberts, J.J.: Facebook and Google Were Victims of $100M Payment Scam, Fortune, 27 April 2017. http://fortune.com/2017/04/27/facebook-google-rimasauskas/
8. Abbasi, A., Lau, R.Y., Brown, D.E.: Predicting behavior. IEEE Intell. Syst. **30**(3), 35–43 (2015)
9. Metzger, M.J., Flanagin, A.J.: Credibility and trust of information in online environments: the use of cognitive heuristics. J. Pragmat. **59**, 210–220 (2013)
10. Mayhorn, C.B., Welka, A.K., Zielinska, O.A., Murphy-Hill, E.: Assessing individual differences in a phishing detection task. In: Proceedings 19th Triennial Congress of the IEA, Melbourne (2015)
11. Wombat Security Technologies, "State of the Phish 2018 Report". https://www.wombatsecurity.com/state-of-the-phish. Accessed 10 Apr 2018
12. Statista, Number of monthly active Facebook users worldwide as of 4th quarter 2017 (in millions). https://www.statista.com/statistics/264810/number-of-monthly-active-facebook-users-worldwide/. Accessed 22 Mar 2018
13. Patricios, O., Goldstuck, A.: SA Social Media Landscape 2018. World Wide Worx (2018). http://website.ornico.co.za/2017/09/sa-social-media-2018/. Accessed 12 Apr 2018
14. Dhamija, R., Tygar, J.D., Hearst, M.: Why phishing works. In: Proceedings of the SIGCHI Conference on Human Factors in Computing Systems, pp. 581–590. ACM, Montreal (2006)
15. Wu, M., Miller, R.C., Garfinkel, S.L.: Do security toolbars actually prevent phishing attacks? In: Proceedings of the SIGCHI Conference on Human Factors in Computing Systems, pp. 601–610. ACM, Montreal (2006)
16. Downs, J.S., Holbrook, M.B., Cranor, L.F.: Decision strategies and susceptibility to phishing. In: Proceedings of the 2nd Symposium on Usable Privacy and Security, pp. 79–90. ACM, Pittsburgh (2006)
17. Egelman, S., Cranor, L.F., Hong, J.: You've been warned: an empirical study of the effectiveness of web browser phishing warnings. In: Proceedings of the 26th Annual SIGCHI Conference on Human Factors in Computing Systems, pp. 1065–1074. ACM, Florence(2008)
18. Jagatic, T.N., Johnson, N.A., Jakobsson, M., Menczer, F.: Social phishing. Commun. ACM **50**(10), 94–100 (2007)

19. Silic, M., Back, A.: The dark side of social networking sites: understanding phishing risks. Comput. Hum. Behav. **60**, 35–43 (2016)
20. Hameed, K., Rehman, N.: Today's social network sites: an analysis of emerging security risks and their counter measures. In: International Conference on Communication Technologies (ComTech), pp. 143–148. IEEE, Pakistan (2017)
21. Halevi, T., Lewis, J., Memon, N.: A pilot study of cyber security and privacy related behavior and personality traits. In: Proceedings of the 22nd International Conference on World Wide Web Companion, pp. 737–744. ACM, Rio de Janeiro (2013)
22. Vishwanath, A.: Habitual Facebook use and its impact on getting deceived on social media. J. Comput. Mediat. Commun. **20**, 83–98 (2015)
23. Vishwanath, A.: Getting phished on social media. Decis. Support Syst. **103**, 70–81 (2017)
24. Mouton, F., Malan, M.M., Venter, H.S.: Social engineering from a normative ethics perspective. In: Information Security South Africa, Johannesburg, pp. 1–8 (2013)
25. Langheinrich, M., Karjoth, G.: Social networking and the risk to companies and institutions. Inf. Secur. Tech. Rep. **15**, 51–56 (2010)
26. ProofPoint, The Human Factor Report 2016. https://www.proofpoint.com/sites/default/files/human-factor-report-2016.pdf. Accessed 22 Mar 2018
27. Luo, X., Zhang, W., Burd, S., Seazzu, A.: Investigating phishing victimization with the Heuristic-Systematic model: a theoretical framework and an exploration. Comput. Secur. **38**, 28–38 (2013)
28. Harrison, B., Svetieva, E., Vishwanath, A.: Individual processing of phishing emails How attention and elaboration protect against phishing. Online Inf. Rev. **40**(2), 265–281 (2016)
29. Ferreira, A., Coventry, L., Lenzini, G.: Principles of persuasion in social engineering and their use in phishing. In: Tryfonas, T., Askoxylakis, I. (eds.) HAS 2015. LNCS, vol. 9190, pp. 36–47. Springer, Cham (2015). https://doi.org/10.1007/978-3-319-20376-8_4

Information Availability and Security
in Foreign Corrupt Practices Act Investigations

Tetyana Loskutova[✉] and Rivaj Parbhu

Control Risks, Culross Court, 16, Johannesburg 2191, South Africa
tetyana.loskutova@gmail.com,
rivaj.parbhu@controlrisks.com

Abstract. Foreign Corrupt Practices Act (FCPA) deals with businesses found guilty of bribing foreign officials. The increasing number of cases and high financial penalties present a growing concern for businesses operating or planning to start operating abroad. The ratings of Transparency International offer an indicator of corruption in countries; however, the analysis shows that this indicator is not correlated with the occurrence of FCPA cases in a particular country. This article proposes that the level of availability and security of information is more important in predicting and potentially preventing the need for FCPA investigations. Using the data of cases filed in 2016–2017, the article discusses how the factors of information availability and security influence the likelihood of FCPA investigation in a country. The article contributes to empirical studies on corruption by focusing on fact-based data on corruption as opposed to perception-based data and shows that these two sets of data do not correlate. The positive correlation between the availability of information and the number of FCPA cases especially in the countries with low GDP suggests that companies can leverage from the availability of information to take action against bribery before it is investigated.

Keywords: Bribery · Information · FCPA

1 Introduction

The Foreign Corrupt Practices Act (FCPA) was introduced in 1977 and applies to all U.S. persons, companies originating from the U.S., certain foreign issuers of securities, and foreign firms and persons who cause directly or through agents an act of furtherment of corrupt payments within the territory of the United States. FCPA regulations are often discussed in the law research [1, 2]; however, Koehler [3] defined the FCPA as a general business issue that needs to be on the radar of managers operating in the global marketplace. The recent McKinsey's and KPMG's corruption cases in South Africa confirm that FCPA investigations can cause considerable disruption to a business in, potentially, any country.

Bribery payments are covert acts that are not easy to detect [4]. Even if detected, FCPA cases are difficult to support with enough evidence. Based on that, it seems plausible that access-to-information laws have a direct impact on both the discovery and resolution of FCPA investigations. Access-to-information laws are balanced against the

H. Venter et al. (Eds.): ISSA 2018, CCIS 973, pp. 60–75, 2019.
https://doi.org/10.1007/978-3-030-11407-7_5

requirements for protection of private information, such as Protection of Private Information Act in South Africa and similar laws in other countries. Companies that operate in several jurisdictions find it increasingly difficult to navigate the landscape of often contradictory regulatory requirements. For example, a company is typically subject to U.S. trade sanctions that require information disclosure if its parent company is from the United States or if the company has U.S. Employees. At the same time, the company is also subject to local laws that may require information protection and non-disclosure of private information. While the explanation of the regulatory requirement fits firmly into the area of law, managers may benefit from better understanding of general trends of FCPA prosecutions, investigations, and factors contributing to them.

1.1   The Gap in Knowledge

Previous authors pointed to the lack of empirical as opposed to descriptive research on corruption [5]. Descriptive research usually deals with one country [6–8]. Multiple-country comparisons usually rely on perceptions of corruption [6, 9–11]. However, management could benefit from the knowledge of actual corruption prosecutions as opposed to perceptions and non-generalizable descriptions. This is especially useful for the management of international firms who deal with corruption as a cultural practice of a foreign country and who have a limited ability to get a deep understanding of this other culture. Most of the previous research on the FCPA is also descriptive and deals with the interpretation of particular cases [1, 2]. Despite providing useful insights, such research misses the more general trends that are particularly important for strategic management whose job is to leverage from broad recognizable patterns of corruption and suggest strategies for expansion/shrinkage of business in various countries.

FCPA investigations mostly point to the confirmed or alleged cases of bribery. Bribery is a part of the larger problem of corruption, which also includes embezzlement, financial fraud, self-dealing, extortion [1, 12]. Thus, the research on FCPA cases is an opportunity to add a quantitative measure to corruption as opposed to corruption perception [13].

Previous researchers of information influence on corruption reported incoherent results. The adoption of the Internet has been found to have a positive effect on the reduction of corruption, but this effect had yet to be fully realised [10]; this conclusion was based on significant but small correlations between the adoption of the Internet and corruption perceptions. In another research, using data from 128 countries between 1984 and 2004 authors found that the adoption of Freedom of Information (FOI) laws had no particular effect on corruption except in developing countries, where the adoption of FOI laws appeared to increase the perception of corruption [11]. Other authors confirmed the effectiveness of the Right to Information (RTI) laws for curbing corruption based on interviews with both bureaucrats and activists [7].

Many previous authors inquired which factors are important indicators of corruption and what is the role of information and communication technology (ICT) in exposing corruption. Previous authors [14] found that the Corruption Perception Index (CPI) by Transparency International (TI) depends mostly on historical colonialism, economic measures such as Gross Domestic Product (GDP), and the historical development of political institutions - factors that are hard to change. The debate has also remained unresolved about the accuracy of corruption measures. The questions were asked about how corruption measurements [15] and exposed corruption relate to the overall level of corruption in the country. For instance, perception-based indexes, such as CPI, rely on opinions (of local people, businesspeople, and experts), which depend on what people read in newspapers, what political rhetoric they are exposed to, and what they hear from others [15]. Other authors questioned the overall definition of corruption and the possibility of eliminating corruption as a cultural norm [4, 16]. Srivastava, Teo and Devaraj [5] suggested that only the integration of psychological and economic could reflect the full picture. This article does not intend to engage in this philosophical debate; instead, it aims to demonstrate quantifiable facts and statistical evidence to support further philosophical elaboration.

1.2 Research Purpose

The purpose of this article is both theoretical and practical. The theoretical goal is to get a better understanding of what combination of socio-economic and information sharing practices leads to the higher number of FCPA cases. The number of FCPA cases is taken both as an indicator of bribe-paying behaviour and pathways to the prosecution of such a behaviour. The practical contribution is expected to take the form of recommendations for businesses on how to anticipate and prevent bribery, which could lead to FCPA investigation, and mitigate the impact of FCPA investigations.

2   Literature Review

The general information about the prevalence of corruption is largely inaccessible because corruption deals are covert and often no evidence of them exists [17]. Information transparency is often considered to be the opposite of corruption [17]. Under conditions of secrecy, information disclosure, often associated with whistleblowers becomes dangerous for those who disclose the information. Rothschild and Miethe [18] found that whistleblowers suffered significant retaliation from management especially when the information revealed routinized corrupt behaviour essential to organisation's profit-making. In other words, conditions of information secrecy are associated with a significant barrier to breaking corrupt patterns of behaviour. However, another pattern of crime is based on the illegal use of information, such as identity theft, leakage of unverified government information, location of protected persons, corporate espionage, and so on. The existence of this type of crime explains the need for keeping some of the information secret, especially in environments where other forms of legal protection are unreliable, and the level of crime is high. Thus, information – used both to reveal and perpetuate corruption - is akin to currency in corruption deals.

Most of the previous research dealt with the perception-based indicators of corruption. Perceptions of corruption are also used by TI – the world's authority in providing corruption ratings. Despite being widely used, corruption perceptions are subject to criticism and disagreement in academia. Mashali [6] found that when citizens perceived high levels of corruption in the state departments, this perception drove the statesmen to become corrupt. This is aligned with the constructivist view of corruption as an informal institution that perpetuates itself [4, 16, 19]. Thus, sharing of information about corruption may be associated with corruption perpetuation. Vadlamannati and Cooray [11], on the other hand, claimed that the perception of corruption when combined with the existence of FOI laws tends to decrease corruption over time. Yet another opinion is that perception of corruption is driven by the accessibility to information such as discussion of corruption in the media, informal conversations within social groups, and so on [15]; it is plausible that through these pathways the perception of the level reinforces itself through creating a stable interpretation of the level of corruption, which may be isolated from the reality to some degree. In such a case, a more systematic means of disclosing information about corruption may be essential. Relly [19, 20] developed a model which confirmed that the legislation for media rights, the use of the Internet and cellphones, electoral pluralism, and other elements of political culture negatively relate to the level of perception of corruption. Overall, the problem with using the perception of corruption as a dependent variable of the level of information accessibility is in the theoretical probability that the perception of corruption is dependent on what information is shared and how it is presented [21]. Thus, instead of perception, more objectives measures of corruption (such as the number of cases) should be used to define the relationship between the availability of information and the level of corruption.

In line with these findings, Okello-Obura [12] claimed that the main difference between countries is the level of corruption and the systems that are in place to prevent and expose corruption. The previous discussion on the ease of perpetuation of corruption and the difficulty of breaking the pattern also confirms that it is better to prevent corruption than to cure the damages [8]. The FCPA regulations are one of the systems put in place to expose corruption; FOI, RTI laws, and accounting standards are the others [8]. Accounting is perhaps one of the oldest systematic controls that are in place and has been discussed in detail by many scholars of accounting. Zaman and Ionescu [8], for example, demonstrated how simultaneous undervaluing and overvaluing of assets whose market value is difficult to estimate, creates opportunities for companies to both lower their tax bills and increase their value in the eyes of potential investors. Higher transparency of corporate information together with open-to-public electronic systems for registering asset-exchange transactions may help the reduction and even elimination of corruption through double accounting.

Another systemic measure for fighting corruption is e-governance, which is defined as the use of ICT by governments to expedite and improve the provision of services to its citizens [5]. Srivastava, Teo, and Devaraj [5] found that e-governance is negatively associated with the level of corruption in national institutions: political, legal, and the media. Building upon Serra's [14] sensitivity analysis which established that the existence of long-established democratic institutions in a country is robustly associated with the reduction of corruption, it is possible to infer that e-governance could be the mechanism for the establishment of such democratic institutions.

The other opinion is that systems for protecting information rights are essential to human wellbeing [22]. Some authors argue that the confidentiality of information is necessary for businesses to maintain their competitive advantage [3]. While both the proponents of the freedom of information and confidentiality offer convincing arguments, the situation is not easily comparable in different countries where the needs for disclosure are different due to the established cultural practices of doing business. For example, several European countries do not have formal laws for information sharing [23]; however, these countries offer their citizens access to extensive datasets covering information on public governance and business information. Thus, practically these laws are not required. On the contrary, European countries are putting forward the new European Union Data Protection Regulation [24], which has entered into force in May 2018. This regulation focuses on the restriction and confidentiality of access to information. At the same time, the U.S. Office of Foreign Assets Control (ORAC) imposes requirements on businesses to identify their clients in order to prevent money laundering and terrorism financing. This law requires the disclosure of such information to the government agents when the need arises. The differences in the focus of information regulation between the European Union and the United States could be explained by many cultural and historical factors, which are not the focus of this article. What is important for the present discussion is that for the businesses operating in several jurisdictions, these laws create a substantial compliance obstacle as the requirements are often contradictory.

Given the importance of information in both perpetuation and curbing of corruption, it is surprising that so little conclusive research links corruption indicators to information availability and quality. Previous research has established the correlation of corruption levels with the wealth of the nation, the history of political institutions, and history of colonization [14] – all the factors that are very difficult or even impossible to change. It could also be argued that lower levels of corruption lead to higher wealth, better political institutions and political and social stability, thus giving no answer regarding what practical measures should be used to achieve these lower levels. At the same time, information sharing and protection, as shown by successes of e-governance [5] and the developments in the social media, are rather fluid and easily influenced. Theoretically, sharing of verified information may offer the ability to lower the levels of corruption by providing a climate where secrecy is increasingly problematic and corrupt behaviour is difficult to hide. However, this may only be useful where the risk of losing private information is not critical to survival (as it is crucial in war-zones, highly criminalized environments, or very poor countries). The analysis in the article aims to evaluate the potential of informational measures in global anti-bribery efforts.

3   Hypotheses Development

TI's corruption perceptions index is one of the most widely-used indicators of corruption. It is based on the views on the public-sector corruption that are collected from surveying the general public, analysts, and business people. As noted in the previous research [6], perceptions may also cause perpetuation of corruption. Do perceptions of corruption increase the probability of a business being involved in an FCPA investigation? It is plausible that businesspeople feel pressure to pay bribes in more corrupt environments [1] and therefore become subjects of an investigation. To test the relation between the CPI and the probability of FCPA investigation, the following hypothesis is suggested:

Hypothesis 1. There is a correlation between the CPI and the occurrence of FCPA cases.

It is likely that perceptions of corruption are not the only factor contributing to the occurrence of FCPA cases. The media has been suggested to be one of the foundational institutions for curbing corruption [5]. The power of the media is in its ability to reach and influence a wide audience. This often comes at the cost of filtering information and favouring particular interpretations [21]. The manipulative power of the media is particularly high in the environments where verification of data through public means is not possible and the accountability cannot be enforced [24]. Accountability may be one of the motivations for whistleblowers to disclose information, the lack of it on the societal level may also mean the lack of personal motivation to notify the authorities of the cases of bribery and corruption. The lack of information access would also prevent potential whistleblowers from stepping forward because their information may be hard to verify and thus may not be taken seriously. To test the relationship of the openness of information and the effectiveness of revealing corruption the following is proposed:

Hypothesis 2. There is a relationship between the public access to information and the number of FCPA cases revealed.

The damage of corruption for businesses is not only in the long-ingrained unfair competition practices and reputational damages but also in the short-term damages suffered from being investigated. These damages may be even more unpleasant as some of the investigations are triggered by other businesses who are interested mainly in causing disruption in the workflow of the competitor [3]. Such occurrences are more probable where the tip-offs are difficult to verify, in other words, in environments with the limited access to information. The difficulty of verification may be measured using corruption case duration, that is, the time interval between the opening of the case and its closure. Duration can also be seen as an indicator of the amount of work required for an investigation.

Hypothesis 3a. Duration of FCPA cases is associated with the measures for information availability.

The difficulty of investigation is likely dependent on the judicial and governance systems that are in place. As more developed countries possess more developed judicial and governance systems, which are important for fighting corruption [14], it is plausible that the level of development would affect both the level of information availability and the occurrence and duration of FCPA cases.

Hypothesis 3b. The measures of information availability and FCPA cases are correlated with the socio-economic level in the country.

Finally, the question may be posed about the relationship of information security to corruption prevention or revealing corruption. The lack of information security often manifests in breaches. Potentially, breaches of information may aid the discovery of corruption:

Hypothesis 4. The number of information breaches correlates with corruption indicators.

4   Method

To test the hypotheses suggested above, the article relied on the data from secondary sources. For the initial analysis that aimed to reveal the potential correlations and predictive ability of different indicators, the article relied on a cross-sectional selection of data for 2016–2017. The data on FCPA cases, their dates, and involved countries was taken from the FCPA biannual report of Shearman and Sterling, LLP covering 2016–2017 [25]. Unlike the summary statistics presented in the report, this article used individual cases unsealed in a year instead of FCPA groups[1]. The advantage of using such a dataset is in a slightly more granular understanding of the involved businesses and individuals, as cases create a major hassle for companies and individuals preventing them from normal business activities. All of the datasets were processed using Python 3.6 and Pandas 0.22. PyMuPDF 1.13 package was used to scrape data from PDF reports. The values of indicators were extracted into Pandas Dataframe format (columns representing indicators, rows representing countries). The source code for the data extraction and processing is available in GitHub [26]. The description of the datasets is provided in Table 1.

Table 1. Description of datasets

Indicator	Description	(1) Range (2) Mean (3) STD	Date	Source
Count of FCPA cases	The number of FCPA cases unsealed in a country	(1) 1–78 (2) 6.8 (3) 11.2	2016–2017	[25]
Aggregate duration of FCPA cases	The number of years between the date the case commenced and the date it was finalised aggregated for all case per country	(1) 2–401 (2) 37.8 (3) 60.4	2016–2017	[25]
Gini coefficient	Gini coefficient measures inequality as the distribution of family income in a country. The lower the coefficient the more equal are families in the country in terms of income. Gini coefficient of zero corresponds to complete equality; Gini coefficient of 100 corresponds to complete inequality	(1) 24.5–62.5 (2) 39.6 (3) 8.2	2016	[27]
Corruption perceptions index	CPI is a complex index based on a combination of perceptions of business people and expert opinion. CPI focuses particularly on the perceptions of corruption in the public sector. The index ranges from zero to one hundred, where zero indicates perception of high corruption and one hundred – the perception of no corruption	(1) 0–87 (2) 40.1 (3) 16.0	2017	[28]

(continued)

[1] FCPA group is one or more FCPA cases that share a common bribery scheme, location or time interval.

Table 1. (*continued*)

Indicator	Description	(1) Range (2) Mean (3) STD	Date	Source
Gross domestic product (GDP)	GDP is the total sum of gross value added by all residents of the country. GDP includes product taxes and excludes subsidies. Values used in this article were measured in billions USD. Both nominal GDP and Purchasing Power Parity (PPP) were used	(GDP): (1) 0–18624 (2) 755 (3) 2529.8 (GDP PPP): (1) 3–21409 (2) 1219.8 (3) 3392.2	2017	[29]
Extent of corporate transparency	The index measures the following dimensions of Corporate Transparency: disclosure of ownership stakes, compensation, audits and financial prospects	(1) 0–9 (2) 5.0 (3) 2.5	2017	[30]
Disclosure index	This index defines to what degree investors are protected through disclosure of ownership and financial information	(1) 0–10 (2) 6.2 (3) 2.5	2017	[30]
Breaches	This is the number of isolated incidents of data breaches per country	(1) 0–1766 (2) 25.6 (3) 203.9	2016	[31]
Right to information. Promotional measures	Promotional Measures include the requirement for establishment of a central body for promoting information access, compiling consolidated report regarding the implementation of information access regulations, the appointment of persons responsible for ensuring the compliance with the requirements of information disclosure, public awareness-raising campaigns, the existence of a system for ensuring the standards of records management, creation of public registries of records, training programmes, and reporting of public authorities on the actions taken to implement their disclosure obligations	(1) 0–16 (2) 6.1 (3) 5.3	2017	[32]

The report by Shearman and Sterling, LLP [25] was preprocessed to extract the number of cases per country and to calculate the duration of cases, as the number of years between the date the case commenced and the date it was finalised. The duration was further processed as the mean duration of cases per country and the sum of years that the cases stayed open per country. The complete Right to Information dataset [32] was used; however, none of the indicators except for Promotional measures proved useful.

Overall, 75 countries were common among the datasets and were used for the analysis. Countries that were missing in indicator datasets were omitted. The list of countries is available in GitHub. Though omitted countries could potentially carry important information, the lack of indicator values usually corresponds to the practical difficulty of gathering the relevant information; thus, only assumptions could be made about the influence of these countries. Relying on such assumptions was considered inconsistent with the approach taken in this study. As a cross-sectional data, this dataset could not capture the change over time, thus, giving only an indication about the state of the world in 2016–2017. However, the short time interval allowed removing the dependency introduced by the development of the DOJ and the Securities Exchange Commission (SEC) units designated for FCPA investigations. Thus, the biannual snapshot is expected to show the differences in the FCPA investigations that are characteristic of the countries as opposed to being characteristic of the developments in FCPA investigation and enforcement practices.

5   Findings

Table 2 below presents correlations of information measures with the number of FCPA cases. For brevity, indicators from the Right to Information dataset that showed no significant correlations are not presented.

Table 2. Correlation with the count of FCPA cases

Measure	Correlation with the count of FCPA cases (p-values are given in brackets)
GDP, billion USD	36% (0.0018)
Promotional measures	27% (0.0189)
Corporate transparency	25% (0.0312)
Disclosure index	26% (0.027)
GDP PPP, billion USD	59% (0.0000)

Table 3 below presents correlations of information measures with the aggregate duration of FCPA cases.

Table 3. Correlation with the aggregate duration of FCPA cases

Measure	Correlation with the aggregate duration of FCPA cases (p-values given in brackets)
GDP, billion USD	32% (0.0046)
Promotional measures	28% (0.0161)
Corporate transparency	28% (0.0153)
Disclosure index	27% (0.0178)
GDP PPP, billion USD	54% (0.0000)

5.1 Corruption Perceptions

H1 suggested that there is a correlation between CPI and the occurrence of FCPA cases. No significant correlation was found (correlation is −12% with p-value of 0.24). This result shows that perceptions of corruption do not give country managers sufficient information about the risks of being investigated for bribery in line with the FCPA. As suggested in the previous research, these risks may be driven by the actual opportunity for corruption as well as by bad-meaning competitors [3]. Further results suggest that this opportunity may be partially explained by the availability and access to information.

5.2 Access to Information

The results showed a positive correlation between the availability of information and the number of cases. This is measured by Corporate Transparency: 25% with p-value 0.03 and Disclosure Index: 26% with p-value 0.02. It is important to note that these measures are cross-correlated (39% p = 0.026). Corporate Transparency is also correlated with Gini index at −34% (p = 0.004). This means that higher inequality is associated with lower Corporate Transparency. Corporate Transparency is also correlated with CPI (40% p = 0.0009), which means that higher Corporate Transparency is associated with lower corruption. Based on the dependency between Corporate Transparency and several other measures, it could be suggested that Disclosure Index is a more suitable measure for prediction of FCPA cases. Its contribution also stays significant when the duration of cases is concerned. Further Granger-causality testing is required to prove these suggestions.

Promotional Measures are significantly (p = 0.02) and positively at 27% correlated with the number of FCPA cases. This result may indicate that the promotion of information disclosure creates an environment where whistleblowers are more encouraged to come forward with the information about corrupt actions. Though an FCPA investigation is not in the immediate interest of companies, the companies may use this finding to promote information transparency and disclosure within the company thus gaining the opportunity to resolve problems internally before the information becomes known to the DOJ or the SEC.

5.3 Duration of FCPA Investigations

H3a suggested testing the correlation between the duration of FCPA cases and measures of information availability. For the duration, the sum of years that the cases lasted and the mean duration of cases was calculated. The sum of years was found to significantly correlate with Promotional Measures (28%, $p = 0.0161$), Corporate Transparency (27%, $p = 0.0153$), and Disclosure Index (27%, $p = 0.178$). As the sum of years includes both the count and the duration of cases, measures contributing to it are important in anti-bribery efforts.

On the other hand, the mean duration was not found to be significantly correlated with any of the tested measures. It can be concluded that the mean duration of cases is poorly explained by the variables used in this study. This could be explained by the higher reliance of the duration of a single investigation on the investigation-level factors than on the country-level factors. The sum of duration is more suitable as an indication of the amount of time spent on investigations in the country in total.

H3b tested the relationship between the measures of information availability, duration, and number of FCPA cases and socio-economic situation in the country. Gini index was found to be significantly and negatively correlated with CPI (30%, $p = 0.0079$) and corporate transparency (39%, $p = 0.0005$). In other words, higher Corporate Transparency is associated with lower inequality (higher Gini). CPI is a reversed index, that is, the higher the index the lower is the perception of corruption. Thus, lower corruption is associated with lower inequality or, in other words, in countries with lower inequality, people perceive corruption levels to be lower as well.

The other socio-economic measure, GDP PPP, was found to be significantly correlated with the number of cases (58%, $p < 0.0000$), Corporate Transparency (26%, $p = 0.027$), and Disclosure Index (23%, $p = 0.0474$). This confirms the previous findings about the importance of the nation's wealth in anti-corruption work as GDP PPP is associated with higher number of FCPA cases as well as slightly higher Corporate Transparency and Disclosure Index.

5.4 Information Breaches

Finally, H4 suggested that the lack of information security, which manifests in breaches, may also affect FCPA cases discovery. The analysis was done in 2 stages: with and without the U.S. data (see Table 4). This was done because the number of recorded breaches in the United States was more than 1700 compared a maximum of 71 cases in the rest of the dataset. In the analysis with the U.S. data, breaches were found to be significantly correlated with CPI (-28%, $p = 0.0164$) and GDP (82%, $p < 0.0000$). This could lead to the conclusion that the higher number of breaches is associated with higher perceived corruption. But without the U.S. data, the breaches were found to be significantly correlated with CPI (34%, $p = 0.028$) and GDP (27%, $p = 0.0195$). In other words, breaches are associated with lower perception of corruption, which could

Table 4. Information breaches

Measure		Correlation with the number of breaches
With U.S. data	GDP	83% (<0.0000)
	CPI	−28% (0.0164)
Without U.S. data	GDP	27% (0.0195)
	CPI	34% (0.028)

be explained by the higher level of information available in electronic form in countries with higher GDP and lower corruption levels.

6   Discussion and Implications

Overall, the findings indicated that information availability is associated with the discovery of FCPA cases. The analysis also addressed the limitation of corruption perceptions, which previous authors suggested may result in the perpetuation of corruption. The findings in this article confirmed the previous results that FOI laws increase the perception of corruption [9]. More precisely, the more practically tangible measure of FCPA cases increases with the increase in the level of Promotional Measures. The increase in the cases may drive the awareness and thus increase the perception of corruption. Previously, Costa [9] found that the perceptions of corruption do not decrease in subsequent years. This may be explained by the fact that societal perceptions are generally difficult to change. Thus, FCPA cases seem to be a more useful measure for evaluation of the effects of the promotion of information disclosure. Further longitudinal research is required to confirm the proposition about the influence of FOI laws on the reduction of corruption. The openness and availability of information may reveal the disconnect between the stable perceptions in a society and the reality, thus increasing the likelihood of societal change.

Despite the benefits of the discovery of the cases being generally obvious for the society, negative consequences are also possible. Koehler [3] demonstrated how an FCPA investigation may create many negative consequences for business firms, including pre- and post-enforcement professional fees, problems with mergers and acquisitions, market capitalization, and time reallocation from other business activities and goals. This may also explain the offensive use of the FCPA by competitors for gaining the edge in business competition. Stevenson and Wagoner [2] mentioned other major social implications of company prosecutions, including job loss, disruption of service, and loss of business for the U.S. companies. This immediate damage may also translate in to even wider societal negative implications, such as the increase in unemployment, the drop in GDP, and so on. Thus, corruption mitigation initiatives may result in unexpected consequences.

The duration of cases was found to be positively correlated with the information availability. Thus, it may seem that information availability does not contribute to expediting the prosecution. This counterintuitive relation may be explained by the aggregation of time, that is, more cases of shorter duration can take more time overall compared to one long case. The finding that out of all indicators in the Right to

Information dataset, only Promotional Measures significantly contribute to the propensity of FCPA investigations can be explained by the difference in the rights prescribed by law and the actual implementation of laws. This was noted in the previous research that discussed how activist groups sometimes have to fight for the enforcement of rights to information laws [33]. A form of such activism may be hacktivism, which achieves the goals of transparency through data breaches. On the other hand, breaches seem to result in the increase of the perception of corruption, which may draw attention to corrupt activities and lead to further discovery of FCPA cases. The recommendation for businesses is then to ensure that damage from information breaches is minimised. For example, promotion of information sharing among employees was previously found to be an effective measure for mitigating the impact of breaches [34].

Information sharing manifested in the measure of Corporate Transparency was also found to be important in revealing fraud cases. The atmosphere of general transparency and the encouragement of information sharing may also help with the creation of the atmosphere of safety for whistleblowers who often suffer retaliation from the management [18]. These results suggest that companies may reduce the damage to themselves by promoting information disclosure (for example, though the creation of departments or child companies that focus on making the information public). This may also assist the DOJ and the SEC with providing guidance on clear and quantifiable benefits of self-reporting as suggested in the previous research [35].

The overall low correlations between the indicators used in this study and the occurrence of FCPA cases may be interpreted as the confirmation of the previous finding that the adoption of the Internet has a positive effect on reduction of corruption, but this effect is yet to be fully realised [10].

6.1   Limitations

Cross-national studies introduce concerns of cultural differences across countries. This is particularly relevant if corruption is seen as a cultural institution. From the research point of view, taking a macro perspective inevitably closes off the views from ethnic-cultural and micro-individual perspectives. This study is also different from the organisational perspective: despite the propensity of corporations to unify practices, there exist differences in how businesses operate, especially in different and volatile political environments. Other limitations of this study are the reliance on secondary sources whose data collection procedures could not be verified and the limited time scope of the data.

6.2   Future Work

In the previous discussion, Yockey [1] urged to shift some of the punishments from bribe-paying companies to bribe-seeking officials. Building upon the findings of the importance of information and the previous work on the potential of e-governance to improve the corruption levels in a country, this article supports this conclusion. However, e-governance alters the agent-principal relationship between the public sector and the public [36]. This is likely to be a cybernetic relationship that is difficult to understand from a cross-sectional analysis; instead, such understanding would likely benefit from case study approaches.

Overall, further work should focus on defining the shape of the dependency between information availability and FCPA investigations. For example, it would be useful to find out whether there is a distinct level of information disclosure and promotion thereof that is the most favourable for the discovery of bribery and the socioeconomic factors that may define this level. Information security should be further investigated as a mediating and moderating factor in the relationship between transparency, corruption, information privacy, and financial crime. The results of the correlation of information beaches with the revelation of FCPA cases indicate that further research is required on the effects on hacktivism on corruption outcomes.

Finally, the limited time-scope of the analysis in this article is useful for an exploratory analysis across multiple datasets; however, it does not take into consideration the changes in the effects of information availability laws over time. Thus, a longitudinal study would be useful in the future.

7 Conclusion

This analysis contributed empirically to the literature exploring the relationship between the availability of information and corruption. It confirmed the previous findings on the importance of information for fighting corruption [37]. Unlike the previous works, that found relationships between hard-to-change social factors like GDP and historical colonization [14], this analysis focused on factors that could be practically influenced by businesses operating in a country.

The answers about the need of information are useful but they also indicate that there's a complex non-linear relationship between the rights of access to information and reduction of bribery. As socio-economic factors make significant contribution to the discovery and investigation of FCPA cases, it is possible that the increase in information accessibility may result in the higher number of FCPA investigations, which could in its turn negatively affect economic factors, such as unemployment and GDP. The more positive outcome could be that the increase in transparency may prevent both the possibility of doing corruption and the reification of perceptions about corruption, which could drive the perpetuation of corrupt behaviour. These results should be used by managers of multi-national corporations in developing policies for information sharing, promoting access to information, and ensuring the protection of whistleblowers.

References

1. Yockey, J.: Solicitation, extortion, and the FCPA. Notre Dame L. Rev. **87**, 781–840 (2011)
2. Stevenson, D., Wagoner, N.: FCPA sanctions: too big to debar. Fordham Law Rev. **80**, 775–820 (2011)
3. Koehler, M.: Foreign corrupt practices act ripples. Am. Univ. Bus. Law Rev. **3**, 291–350 (2014)

4. Estrin, S., Prevezer, M.: The role of informal institutions in corporate governance: Brazil, Russia, India, and China compared. Asia Pac. J. Manag. **28**, 41–67 (2011)
5. Srivastava, S., Teo, T., Devaraj, S.: You can't bribe a computer: dealing with the societal challenge of corruption through ICT. MIS Q. **40**, 511–526 (2016)
6. Mashali, B.: Analyzing the relationship between perceived grand corruption and petty corruption in developing countries: case study of Iran. Int. Rev. Admin. Sci. **78**, 775–787 (2012)
7. Agrawal, C.: Right to information: a tool for combating corruption in India. J. Manag. Publ. Policy **3**, 26–38 (2012)
8. Zaman, G., Ionescu, L.: Fighting corruption generated by accounting. Case study Romania. Econ. Comput. Econ. Cybern. Stud. Res. **50**, 247–261 (2016)
9. Costa, S.: Do freedom of information laws decrease corruption? J. Law Econ. Organ. **29**, 1317–1343 (2012)
10. Lio, M.-C., Liu, M.-C., Ou, Y.-P.: Can the internet reduce corruption? A cross-country study based on dynamic panel data models. Gov. Inf. Q. **28**, 47–53 (2011)
11. Vadlamannati, K., Cooray, A.: Transparency pays? Evaluating the effects of the freedom of information laws on perceived government corruption. J. Dev. Stud. **53**, 116–137 (2017)
12. Okello-Obura, C.: Effective records and information management as a catalyst for fighting corruption. Inf. Dev. **29**, 114–122 (2013)
13. Escaleras, M., Lin, S., Register, C.: Freedom of information acts and public sector corruption. Publ. Choice **145**, 435–460 (2010)
14. Serra, D.: Empirical determinants of corruption: a sensitivity analysis. Publ. Choice **126**, 225–256 (2006)
15. Gonzalez, A., Lopez-Cordova, J., Valladares, E.: The incidence of graft on developing-country firms. World Bank (2007)
16. Lauth, H.-J.: Informal institutions and democracy. Democratization **7**, 21–50 (2000)
17. Matthiolius, E.: Measuring transparency. Towards a new model of corruption research. MaRBLe **4**, 143–160 (2014)
18. Rothschild, J., Miethe, T.: Whistle-blower disclosures and management retaliation: the battle to control information about organization corruption. Work Occup. **26**, 107–128 (1999)
19. Relly, J.: Corruption, secrecy, and access-to-information legislation in Africa: a cross-national study of political institutions. In: Maret, S. (ed.) Government Secrecy, pp. 325–352. Emerald Group Publishing Limited (2011)
20. Relly, J.: Examining a model of vertical accountability: a cross-national study of the influence of information access on the control of corruption. Gov. Inf. Quart. **29**, 335–345 (2012)
21. Rucht, D.: Movement allies, adversaries, and third parties. In: Snow, D.A., Soule, S.A., Kriesi, H. (eds.) The Blackwell Companion to Social Movements, pp. 116–152. Blackwell Publishing, Maiden, MA
22. Britz, J., Hoffmann, A., Ponelis, S., Zimmer, M., Lor, P.: On considering the application of Amartya Sen's capability approach to an information-based rights framework. Inf. Dev. **29**, 106–113 (2013)
23. Centre for Law and Democracy. Global right to information rating map. http://www.rti-rating.org/. Accessed 18 Mar 2018
24. Transparency International: G20 position paper: open data and corruption (2017). https://www.transparency.org/whatwedo/publication/g20_position_paper_open_data_and_corruption_2017
25. Shearman and Sterling, LLP: FCPA digest. Recent trends and patterns in the enforcement of Foreign Corrupt Practices Act. Central Intelligence Agency, Washington, DC (2018)
26. Loskutova, T.: CorruptionCasesStats. In: DAUtilities. https://github.com/tetyanaloskutova/DAUtilites/blob/master/CorruptionCasesStats.ipynb. Accessed 8 July 2018

27. Central Intelligence Agency: Country comparison: Distribution of family income - Gini index. https://www.cia.gov/library/publications/the-world-factbook/rankorder/2172rank.html. Accessed 18 Mar 2018

28. Transparency International: Corruption perceptions index 2017. https://www.transparency.org/news/feature/corruption_perceptions_index_2017. Accessed 18 Mar 2018

29. World Bank: GDP current (US$). https://data.worldbank.org/indicator/NY.GDP.MKTP.CD. Accessed 18 Mar 2018

30. World Bank: Doing business project. https://datamarket.com/data/set/5kcv/extent-of-corporate-transparency-index-0-9. Accessed 18 Mar 2018

31. Gemalto: 2016 Mining for database gold, Washington, DC (2017). https://www6.gemalto.com/breach-level-index-report-full-2016-press-release

32. Centre for Law and Democracy: Global right to information rating. http://www.rti-rating.org/historical/. Accessed 18 Mar 2018

33. Webb, M.: Disciplining the everyday state and society? Anti-corruption and right to information activism in Delhi. Contrib. Indian Sociol. **47**, 363–393 (2013)

34. Safa, N., Von Solms, R.: An information security knowledge sharing model in organizations. Comput. Hum. Behav. **57**, 442–451 (2016)

35. Reilly, P.: Incentivizing corporate America to eradicate transnational bribery worldwide: federal transparency and voluntary disclosure under the foreign corrupt practices act. Fla Law Rev. **67**, 1683–1733 (2015)

36. Mahmood, R.: Can information and communication technology help reduce corruption? How so and why not: two case studies from South Asia. Perspect. Glob. Dev. Technol. **3**, 347–373 (2004)

37. DiRienzo, C., Das, J., Cort, K., Burbridge, J.: Corruption and the role of information. J. Int. Bus. Stud. **38**, 320–332 (2007)

The Current State of Electronic Consent Systems in e-Health for Privacy Preservation

Lelethu Zazaza[1,2(✉)] ⓘ, H. S. Venter[1] ⓘ, and George Sibiya[2] ⓘ

[1] University of Pretoria, Pretoria, South Africa
u13028023@tuks.co.za, hventer@up.ac.za
[2] Council for Scientific and Industrial Research, Pretoria, South Africa
gsibiya@csir.co.za

Abstract. Consent management is a significant function in electronic health information systems as it allows patients to manage the privacy preferences regarding their health information. Placing patients in control of the privacy of their health information ensures that the risks for reputational and personal harm are reduced. Several approaches towards patient consent management solutions, ranging from software prototypes to conceptual models, have been adopted in response to the need for privacy preservation. The purpose of this paper is to review these approaches and to identify areas that still need to be addressed – particularly in terms of the automated enforcement of consent directives, interoperability, as well as standardised healthcare data exchange.

Keywords: E-consent · Privacy by design · Information security

1 Introduction

Health Information Systems (HISs) have enabled healthcare staff to have easier access to patient information, however, they have also introduced the risk that patient information may be accessed by unauthorised personnel and not for purposes originally intended by the patient [1]. For this reason, patients should be informed not only why their data is being collected, stored or processed, but also who is accessing their data [2]. Such a requirement needs to be enforced through consent policies and privacy-preserving laws such as the Protection of Personal Information (PoPI) Act that allow the patient to permit or deny the disclosure of particular medical information from particular personnel [1, 3, 4]. Patients can choose who may access their medical information such as their HIV/AIDS status, previous abortions, substance abuse, psychiatric illnesses and genetic predisposition to diseases [5–7]. Improper disclosure of such sensitive information can influence decisions about a patient's education, access to credit, or employment, and it may even expose the patient to reputational or personal harm [5, 8]. An HIS has the obligation to protect patient data in accordance with their individual consent boundaries [2] and when the effective enforcement of consent directives prevents undue disclosure of information, patients gain greater trust in electronic health record (EHR) systems [9]. In addition to ensuring the privacy of patient data, the procurement of informed consent reduces medical errors such as incorrect medical dosages and consequently reduces the number of medical malpractice claims [10].

© Springer Nature Switzerland AG 2019
H. Venter et al. (Eds.): ISSA 2018, CCIS 973, pp. 76–88, 2019.
https://doi.org/10.1007/978-3-030-11407-7_6

Besides permitting and prohibiting the collection, access, use and disclosure of private health information, three other forms of consent directives exist, namely medical treatment consent, research participation consent, and advance care consent. It is imperative that a patient's consent be unambiguous, informed and given freely [4, 11, 12] – furthermore, it must be as easy to revoke consent as it is to give it [11].

The introduction of a consent management platform affords a patient the opportunity to update his/her consent directives as necessary [3, 13]. The availability of such a mechanism also places patients in control of their information, as they can decide which information may be made available and to whom. Unauthorised access is thus prevented and accountable parties can easily be identified. The available literature suggests that the widespread use and acceptance of e-consent remains a challenge owing to the following reasons:

- There is still a lack of privacy and security measures [14] in HISs, specifically regarding the enforcement and safeguarding of patients' consent directives;
- E-consent systems hinder the ease with which health practitioners can perform their medical duties [2] as the system will prohibit unauthorized users from performing specific actions until they are given the appropriate access rights;
- The lack of an intuitive e-consent system makes it difficult for patients to manage their consent directives [1].

This paper provides a comprehensive review of the current state of e-consent systems in health information systems and identifies areas that still need to be addressed in the electronic patient consent management domain. In the following section, background concepts relevant to the literature referred to in this paper are provided. Section 3 details the research methodology that was followed to collect data for the study. Section 4 presents the findings of the survey. A discussion follows in Sect. 5 and the paper concludes in Sect. 6.

2 Background

This section provides some background on electronic consent, privacy and information security as these concepts facilitate privacy preservation in e-health systems.

2.1 Electronic Consent

It is important to discuss electronic consent, as it is the mechanism that allows patients to exercise the directives relating to their medical treatment and personal health information. Consent is considered informed when the patient is provided with sufficient information on the relevant processes, when adequate opportunity is given to the patient to consider alternative options, and when all the patient's questions are answered [15].

Consent may be given in three formats, namely written, verbal and implied [16]. The **written** consent format is where the patient signs a document to confirm that he/she has entered into an agreement for a high-risk treatment or procedure [16]. Written consent is further categorised into paper-based and electronic-based formats.

With the introduction of e-health, physical signatures are no longer compulsory, and electronic signatures or activities such as ticking a box are acceptable instead [17]. Electronic consent can also be realised through tele-consent where video media are used to facilitate the consent process. Even with the adoption of e-health, patients are still giving written consent primarily through signing physical documents [7, 10, 15]. However, the continued use of physical documents is not ideal as paper and printing costs are expensive [10]; physical documents make patient information difficult to store, search and retrieve [15]; and it is difficult to enforce access control for physical documents [7]. Furthermore, forms filled in by hand are often incomplete, inaccurate or illegible [18]. In contrast, an electronic consent management system is considered a more efficient and reliable approach [14].

Verbal consent occurs where oral confirmation is given for a low-risk treatment or procedure [16], whereas **implied** consent is given when the patient indicates agreement to a health practitioner's instructions (e.g. extending the arm to provide a routine blood sample for testing; taking or swallowing medication provided; attending an appointment for the purpose of receiving information or advice regarding management of the current condition) [16].

In e-health, consent implies that agreement is given for

- the collection, access, use or disclosure of information;
- medical treatment (agreement to undergo or reject specific medical treatments);
- participation in research; and
- advance care directives (e.g. Do Not Resuscitate orders).

Five directive options are available for e-consent: no consent; opt-in; opt-in with exceptions; opt-out; and opt-out with exceptions. An e-consent directive should also specify the subject of care, the grantee, the purpose and the time period covered by the consent [2]. Figure 1 illustrates the elements of an e-consent directive.

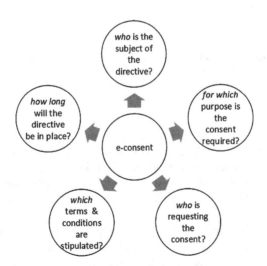

Fig. 1. e-Consent directive components [2]

The following section discusses the role of privacy and information security in e-consent.

2.2 Privacy and Information Security

Patients are the rightful owners of data that reside in HISs, and as such they may decline to disclose information that they feel may cause discrimination or stigma [19, 20]. In healthcare, the implications for practitioners who do not pay proper regard to the privacy of patients include sanctions from the Health Professions Council of South Africa, breach of privacy lawsuits, monetary penalty or even imprisonment [21]. The South African Protection of Personal Information (PoPI) Act recognises the right to privacy as stated in the Constitution and, as such, its purpose is to protect the processing of personal information by public and private bodies [21]. The PoPI Act is based on the best features of international privacy legislatures and it has given rise to eight information-processing principles. These PoPI principles [22] are summarised below:

1. Accountability: The responsible party must ensure that the eight information-processing principles are adhered to.
2. Processing limitation: Processing of information must be lawful and personal information may only be processed if it is adequate, relevant and not excessive for the purpose for which it is processed.
3. Purpose specification: Personal information must be collected for a specific, explicitly defined and lawful purpose related to a function or activity of the responsible party.
4. Further-processing limitation: Sometimes personal information is received from a third party and must be passed on to the responsible party for further processing. In these circumstances, the further processing must be compatible with the purpose for which it was initially collected.
5. Information quality: The responsible party must take reasonable and practical steps to ensure that the personal information is complete, accurate and not misleading. He/she must update the information where necessary, taking into account the purposes for which it was collected.
6. Openness: Personal information may only be processed by a responsible party that notified the Information Protection Regulator in advance. Furthermore, the responsible party must provide certain prescribed information to the data subject (the person/patient involved) by stating what information is collected, and whether or not the supply of the information by that data subject is voluntary or mandatory.
7. Security safeguards: The responsible party must secure the integrity of personal information in its possession or under its control by taking prescribed measures to prevent loss of, damage to, unauthorised destruction of, and unlawful access to or processing of personal data.
8. Data subject participation: A data subject has the right to request a responsible party to confirm, free of charge, whether the responsible party holds personal information about the data subject. The latter may also request from a responsible party the record or a description of the personal information held, including information

about the identity of all third parties (or categories of all third parties) who have (or have held) access to the information. In addition, a data subject may request a responsible party to

(a) correct or delete personal information about the data subject in its possession or under its control that is inaccurate, irrelevant, excessive, misleading or obtained unlawfully;

(b) destroy or delete a record of personal information about the data subject that the responsible party is no longer authorised to retain.

When patient data are protected, patients gain greater trust in e-health systems and healthcare professionals [23–25]. Giving individuals control of their health information increases the quality and reliability of health data, which in turn reduces the occurrence of malpractice. When the quality and reliability of health research data is improved, the quality of healthcare is ultimately also enhanced [26].

An e-consent system or management platform needs to function beyond its responsibility to manage consent directives. It also needs to be supported by security functions that prevent unauthorised access to patient information [1]. A security layer ensures data integrity, data confidentiality, as well as nonrepudiation [1, 13]. Security approaches such as password protection, encryption, access control and audit trails can be used to monitor fraud and abuse, and to prevent unauthorised use and disclosure of data [24–26]. These approaches are essential, as insufficient data protection may subject a patient to embarrassment, social stigma and discrimination [23].

In the next section, the research methodology applied in the study is described.

3 Research Methodology

To provide an overview of the current state of electronic patient consent management, a literature review was conducted in the background section in which the information that is currently available on electronic patient consent management was examined and summarised. The information sources that were eligible, were papers that dealt with electronic consent in the e-health context. The specific criteria that were used to find eligible sources are discussed in the subsequent sections.

3.1 Search Criteria

Electronic journal databases such ACM Digital Library, IEEE Xplore Digital Library, PubMed Central, ScienceDirect and Springer Link were accessed during the period December 2017 to March 2018. Search terms including "patient consent management", "e-consent", "electronic consent", "e-health", "privacy" and "security" were applied. Boolean connectors such as AND and OR were used on the selected keywords in order to obtain more comprehensive search results. Altogether 33 papers met the required criteria and were used as literature sources for this paper.

3.2   Evaluation Criteria

The sources were subsequently evaluated against the concepts below:

- *Architectures, frameworks and standards* – whether the literature considered standards such as HL7, Basic Patient Privacy Consents (BBPC) or Clinical Document Architecture (CDA), because they help facilitate interoperability in health information systems. There is currently a lack of standards or guidelines on how e-consent systems can be implemented best [17].
- *Information security measures* – whether the literature considered information security approaches that value and ensure the privacy of patients' health information and maintain the confidentiality, integrity and availability of patient health information.
- *Patient directive management* – how patients are given control over their directives through settings that facilitate revocation, creation and modification.
- *Patient understanding* – whether the literature explains how the e-consent process will ensure that the patient is provided with sufficient information to ensure that the consent given is informed.
- *Policies or regulations* – whether the literature mentions the use of regulations that will guide the design of e-consent systems, as consent directives should be in line with the health institution's policies as well as privacy laws.

The above evaluation criteria are essentially design focused, and therefore the discussion in the authors' analysis will be divided into patient-centered design and privacy by design. Patient-centered design is aimed at asserting whether the design of a presented system had a patient's needs in. Privacy by design focuses on the use of secure and confidentiality-driven approaches that are adopted when systems that contain or use personal user information are implemented. A complete analysis follows in Sects. 4 and 5.

4   Findings

This section presents a concept matrix as well as figures that illustrate observations made from the selected literature sources.

Table 1 presents a comparison of topics that constituted the focus of the selected literature in the health e-consent domain. These focus areas are the same as the evaluation criteria specified in the previous section. From the concept matrix in Table 1, it is evident that even though several journal papers covered some of the focus areas, there is a lack of research that covers all of the concepts specified in the evaluation criteria.

Only 7 papers discussed the use of any standards or frameworks that should be used during the design of e-consent systems. Around 60% of the papers highlighted the importance of using security approaches that value and ensure the privacy of patients' health information and maintain the confidentiality, integrity and availability of patient health information. Only 2 papers mentioned how directives should be accessible and

Table 1. Concept matrix for electronic patient consent management

Paper(s)	Standard/framework	Information security	Directive management	Patient under-standing	Policy/regulation
[26]		✓		✓	✓
[27]		✓			✓
[28]		✓		✓	
[1, 5, 7, 8, 30–32]		✓			
[2, 33]	✓	✓			
[4, 34]	✓				
[35]			✓	✓	
[36]		✓	✓		✓
[18, 37–40]					
[15, 25, 41, 42]				✓	✓
[10, 43, 44]	✓	✓		✓	
[45]					✓

manageable by patients within an e-consent system. The importance of patient understanding and policy regulation were discussed in 10 and 8 papers respectively.

A complete e-consent management system should implement all of these concepts as the application of information security techniques and regulations are essential for the pursuit of privacy preservation.

Figure 2 illustrates the components that encompass consent in healthcare. Four components of consent in healthcare were prominent, namely directive formats, types, attributes and options.

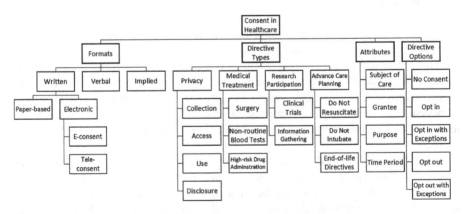

Fig. 2. Healthcare consent components

The directive options align with the need for patients to have the mechanism to manage their directives. The options should include no consent; opt-in; opt-in with exceptions; opt-out; and opt-out with exceptions.

The directive types that directly relate to information security are the privacy and research participation directives and it is also important for the appropriate privacy preserving policies and regulations to be applied.

A discussion of the foundational aspects of e-consent follows in Sect. 5.

5 Discussion

An e-consent system should have patient centricity as well as privacy centricity as its foundation; consequently, this section focuses on patient requirements and privacy by design in the e-health context.

5.1 Patient-Centred Design

The literature review found that comprehension, control and confidentiality are the main expectations that patients have when using e-consent systems.

Comprehension. Consent is informed when a patient had a conversation with a health practitioner during which the alternatives, advantages and disadvantages of a process were thoroughly discussed [17, 18] until the patient understood the situation and was able to assess the risks fully [45]. If a surgeon, for instance, does not obtain informed consent prior to a procedure, the patient may afterwards accuse him/her of battery or negligence. This is significant as most negligence claims are a result of patients not fully understanding the possible complications of a procedure [18].

One of the difficulties faced by patients during the consent process is the fact that they are unable to understand the policies or terms and conditions involved, often because of the lengthy and complex language used [17, 29, 46]. A study that explored user behaviours when providing electronic consent on health social networks showed that 73% of people did not carefully read the terms and conditions, and only 17% understood the contents [46]. Long and complex policies should be replaced with brief and lucid communications to help patients understand better. Additionally, multimedia can be employed to help enhance comprehension, particularly for children [29]. The use of multi-language support, additional educational resources, as well as quizzing mechanisms will increase the level of understanding and individuals will be in a better position to control their healthcare directives.

Control. Healthcare users have expressed the need for greater control over their consent directives [17]. This can be accomplished by adopting an individualised and transparent approach for each patient. Consent forms should be tailored for each patient [18] so that each component of the form is non-generic, relevant and complete. The patient should be able to express any of the consent directives, such as "no consent", "opt-in", "opt-in with exceptions", "opt-out" or "opt-out with exceptions" – as illustrated in Fig. 2. This freedom is similar to social media privacy control settings and, coupled with transparency and usability, autonomy is given to the patient.

Confidentiality. Concern about security and privacy issues in e-health has persisted ever since the first IoT botnet attack in 2013 [17]. A botnet attack can be used for denial-of-service attacks, for the collection of user information, or for stealthy user monitoring. Besides botnets, cookies are also a threat because even though they facilitate the functions of targeted advertising or keep login sessions alive, they were designed without proper consideration for information security [46]. Therefore, it is important to build systems that will take information security into account. For European citizens, the General Data Protection Regulation (GDPR), which comes into effect as from May 2018, will require from data controllers and processors to ensure security [17]. Non-adherence to the GDPR may lead to financial penalties [17]. In view of the GDPR, the Privacy-by-Design approach has been highlighted to facilitate security and privacy. The following section presents a discussion on Privacy by Design.

Table 2 illustrates the requirements as considered from the perspective of patients and healthcare practitioners.

Table 2. Technical and non-technical requirements for electronic consent management

Requirements		
Patient non-technical requirements	Health practitioner non-technical requirements	Technical requirements
Intuitive	Intuitive	Automated
Multi-lingual support	Workflow-friendly	Interoperable
Transparent		Secure
Informative		Auditable

5.2   Privacy by Design

Privacy by Design (PbD) is a concept developed to promote privacy and data protection in information technology and communication systems. Table 3 draws a comparison between the PbD principles and the PoPI principles. The principles for PbD [17, 47] are described as follows:

Table 3. Technical and non-technical requirements for electronic consent management

Privacy by design principle	PoPI principle and patient/system requirement
Proactive, not reactive	PoPI (7), automation, auditing
Privacy as default setting	PoPI (1)–(4)
Privacy embedded into design	PoPI (7)
Full functionality	Modifiable directive settings (control), notifications
End-to-end security	PoPI (7), confidentiality, auditing
Visibility and transparency	PoPI (1), (6), (8), clear intentions (comprehension)
Respect for user privacy	PoPI (5), (8), confidentiality

- *Proactive, not reactive*: PbD should anticipate privacy risks and prevent them from materialising.
- *Privacy as the default setting*: Personal data should automatically be protected by default with no added action required from the user.
- *Privacy embedded into design*: Privacy measures should be embedded into the architecture and design of information technology systems as the integral component.
- *Full functionality*: PbD should ensure that even though privacy is the core objective, it does not impair other functionalities of the system.
- *End-to-end security*: Privacy should be continuously enforced across the entire lifecycle of the data. Without strong security, privacy cannot be realised.
- *Visibility and transparency*: All stakeholders should operate according to the stated promises.
- *Respect for user privacy*: A user-centric approach should be undertaken so that users can control their data. This involves requesting consent from the user and ensuring that the users have access to activities surrounding their information.

6 Conclusion

Health information systems enable the collection and use of electronic health data, which in turn provides benefits to various stakeholders [23, 24, 26, 46]. In most cases, the electronic health data found in medical systems is patient data. With their data being exchanged electronically, patients still need a means to give consent about who should and who should not access their data. This requires an electronic consent management mechanism. With proper consent management in place, medical researchers can conduct their work more efficiently as there is increased access to accurate information:

- researchers can also use available data to investigate how high-quality and cost-effective healthcare may be provided;
- the quality of clinical care is improved as immediate access to information enables quick and informed decision making regarding diagnoses and treatments for healthcare service providers;
- patients can benefit by making informed decisions about service providers, medical treatments and health conditions in general.

The purpose of this paper was to provide a literature review on the current state of electronic consent management in healthcare. It showed that implementing an e-consent management system, even with the identified shortcomings, should be consideration for future research work. A survey should also be conducted to obtain the opinions of South African health practitioners and administrators on electronic consent management.

References

1. Coiera, E., Clarke, R.: e-Consent: the design and implementation of consumer consent mechanisms in an electronic environment. J. Am. Med. Inform. Assoc. **11**(2), 129–140 (2004)
2. Can, O.: A semantic model for personal consent management. In: Garoufallou, E., Greenberg, J. (eds.) MTSR 2013. CCIS, vol. 390, pp. 146–151. Springer, Cham (2013). https://doi.org/10.1007/978-3-319-03437-9_15
3. Bursa, O., Sezer, E., Can, O., Unalir, M.O.: Using FOAF for interoperable and privacy protected healthcare information systems. In: Closs, S., Studer, R., Garoufallou, E., Sicilia, M.-A. (eds.) MTSR 2014. CCIS, vol. 478, pp. 154–161. Springer, Cham (2014). https://doi.org/10.1007/978-3-319-13674-5_15
4. Heinze, O., Birkle, M., Köster, L., Bergh, B.: Architecture of a consent management suite and integration into IHE-based regional health information networks. BMC Med. Inform. Decis. Making **11**(1), 58 (2011)
5. Gaba, A., Havinga, Y., Meijer, H.J., Jan, E.: Privacy and security for analytics on healthcare data (2014)
6. Rindfleisch, T.C.: Privacy, information technology, and health care. Commun. ACM **40**(8), 92–100 (1997)
7. Eskeland, S., Oleshchuk, V.A.: EPR access authorization of medical teams based on patient consent. In: ECEH, pp. 11–22 (2007)
8. Russello, G., Dong, C., Dulay, N.: Consent-based workflows for healthcare management. In: IEEE Workshop on Policies for Distributed Systems and Networks, POLICY 2008, pp. 153–161. IEEE (2008)
9. Hu, L.L., Sparenborg, S., Tai, B.: Privacy protection for patients with substance use problems. Subst. Abuse Rehabil. **2**, 227 (2011)
10. Yu, B., Wijesekera, D., Costa, P.C.G.: Informed consent in electronic medical record systems. In: Healthcare Ethics and Training: Concepts, Methodologies, Tools, and Applications, pp. 1029–1049. IGI Global (2017)
11. Mense, E., Blobel, B., et al.: Hl7 standards and components to support implementation of the European General Data Protection Regulation (GDPR). Eur. J. Biomed. Inform. **13**(1), 27–33 (2017)
12. Abbas, R.M., Carroll, N., Richardson, I., Beecham, S.: The need for trustworthiness models in healthcare software solutions. In: HEALTHINF, pp. 451–456 (2017)
13. Moss, L., Shaw, M., Piper, I., Hawthorne, C., Kinsella, J.: Sharing of big data in healthcare: public opinion, trust, and privacy considerations for health informatics researchers. In: HEALTHINF, pp. 463–468 (2017)
14. Elkhodr, M., Shahrestani, S., Cheung, H.: Preserving the privacy of patient records in health monitoring systems. In: Theory and Practice of Cryptography Solutions for Secure Information Systems, pp. 499–529. IGI Global (2013)
15. Madathil, K.C., et al.: An investigation of the efficacy of electronic consenting interfaces of research permissions management system in a hospital setting. Int. J. Med. Inform. **82**(9), 854–863 (2013)
16. ACT Health: Informed consent. http://www.health.act.gov.au/publicinformation/consumers/informed-consent. Accessed 22 Mar 2018
17. O'Connor, Y., Rowan, W., Lynch, L., Heavin, C.: Privacy by design: Informed consent and internet of things for smart health. Procedia Comput. Sci. **113**, 653–658 (2017)

18. St John, E., Scott, A., Irvine, T., Pakzad, F., Leff, D., Layer, G.: Completion of hand-written surgical consent forms is frequently suboptimal and could be improved by using electronically generated, procedure-specific forms. Surgeon **15**(4), 190–195 (2017)

19. Ghazvini, A., Shukur, Z.: Security challenges and success factors of electronic healthcare system. Procedia Technol. **11**, 212–219 (2013)

20. Fernández-Alemán, J.L., Señor, I.C., Lozoya, P.Á.O., Toval, A.: Security and privacy in electronic health records: a systematic literature review. J. Biomed. Inform. **46**(3), 541–562 (2013)

21. Buys, M.: Protecting personal information: implications of the protection of personal information (PoPI) act for healthcare professionals. SAMJ: South Afr. Med. J. **107**(11), 954–956 (2017)

22. Ramdhin, A.: Protection of personal information bill: what should you be asking? https://www.werksmans.com/legal-briefs-view/protection-ofpersonal-information-bill-what-should-you-be-asking/. Accessed 01 Mar 2018

23. Gostin, L.O.: National health information privacy: regulations under the Health Insurance portability and accountability act. JAMA **285**(23), 3015–3021 (2001)

24. McGraw, D.: Privacy and health information technology: executive summary. J. Law Med. Ethics **37**(2 suppl), 121–149 (2009)

25. Wang, L.: The privacy rule: HIPAA standards for the privacy of individually identifiable health information. Empl. Benefits J. **27**(3), 59–63 (2002)

26. Hodge Jr., J.G., Gostin, L.O., Jacobson, P.D.: Legal issues concerning electronic health information: privacy, quality, and liability. JAMA **282**(15), 1466–1471 (1999)

27. Antal, H., Bunnell, H.T., McCahan, S.M., Pennington, C., Wysocki, T., Blake, K.V.: A cognitive approach for design of a multimedia informed consent video and website in pediatric research. J. Biomed. Inform. **66**, 248–258 (2017)

28. Asghar, M.R., Russello, G.: Actors: a goal-driven approach for capturing and managing consent in e-health systems. In: IEEE International Symposium on Policies for Distributed Systems and Networks (POLICY), pp. 61–69. IEEE (2012)

29. Blake, K., et al.: Use of mobile devices and the internet for multimedia informed consent delivery and data entry in a pediatric asthma trial: Study design and rationale. Contemp. Clin. Trials **42**, 105–118 (2015)

30. Chávez, E., Finnie, G.: Empowering data sources to manage clinical data. In: 2010 IEEE 23rd International Symposium on Computer-Based Medical Systems (CBMS), pp. 203–208. IEEE (2010)

31. Ge, Y., Ahn, D.K., Unde, B., Gage, H.D., Carr, J.J.: Patient-controlled sharing of medical imaging data across unaffiliated healthcare organizations. J. Am. Med. Inform. Assoc. **20**(1), 157–163 (2013)

32. Bergmann, J., Bott, O.J., Pretschner, D.P., Haux, R.: An e-consent-based shared EHR system architecture for integrated healthcare networks. Int. J. Med. Inform. **76**(2), 130–136 (2007)

33. Khan, A., McKillop, I.: Privacy-centric access control for distributed heterogeneous medical information systems. In: 2013 IEEE International Conference on Healthcare Informatics (ICHI), pp. 297–306. IEEE (2013)

34. Ko, Y.Y., Liou, D.M.: The study of managing the personal consent in the electronic healthcare environment. World Acad. Sci. Eng. Technol. **65**, 314 (2010)

35. Kondylakis, H., et al.: IEmS: a collaborative environment for patient empowerment. In: 2012 IEEE 12th International Conference on Bioinformatics and Bioengineering (BIBE), pp. 535–540. IEEE (2012)

36. Kondylakis, H., et al.: Donors support tool: Enabling informed secondary use of patients' biomaterial and personal data. Int. J. Med. Inform. **97**, 282–292 (2017)

37. Sonne, S.C., et al.: Development and pilot testing of a video-assisted informed consent process. Contemp. Clin. Trials **36**(1), 25–31 (2013)
38. Nwomeh, B.C., Hayes, J., Caniano, D.A., Upperman, J.S., Kelleher, K.J.: A parental educational intervention to facilitate informed consent for emergency operations in children. J. Surg. Res. **152**(2), 258–263 (2009)
39. Li, Y., Xie, M., Bian, J.: USign—a security enhanced electronic consent model. In: 2014 36th Annual International Conference of the IEEE Engineering in Medicine and Biology Society (EMBC), pp. 4487–4490. IEEE (2014)
40. Lentz, J., Kennett, M., Perlmutter, J., Forrest, A.: Paving the way to a more effective informed consent process: recommendations from the clinical trials transformation initiative. Contemp. Clin. Trials **49**, 65–69 (2016)
41. Warriner, A., et al.: A pragmatic randomized trial comparing tablet computer informed consent to traditional paper-based methods for an osteoporosis study. Contemp. Clin. Trials Commun. **3**, 32–38 (2016)
42. Whiddett, R., Hunter, I., Engelbrecht, J., Handy, J.: Patients attitudes towards sharing their health information. Int. J. Med. Inform. **75**(7), 530–541 (2006)
43. Yu, B., Wijesekera, D., Costa, P.C.: An ontology for medical treatment consent. In: STIDS, pp. 72–79 (2014)
44. Pruski, C.: e-CRL: a rule-based language for expressing patient electronic consent. In: Second International Conference on eHealth, Telemedicine, and Social Medicine, 2010, ETELEMED 2010, pp. 141–146. IEEE (2010)
45. Yu, B., Wijesekera, D., Costa, P.: Consent-based workflow control in EMRs. Procedia Technol. **16**, 1434–1445 (2014)
46. Rowan, W., O'Connor, Y., Lynch, L., Heavin, C.: Exploring user behaviours when providing electronic consent on health social networks: a just tick agree approach. Procedia Comput. Sci. **121**, 968–975 (2017)
47. Cavoukian, A.: Privacy by Design. Take the Challenge. Information and Privacy Commissioner of Ontario, Toronto (2009)

Detecting Manipulated Smartphone Data on Android and iOS Devices

Heloise Pieterse[1,2(✉)], Martin Olivier[2], and Renier van Heerden[3,4]

[1] Defence, Peace, Safety and Security, Council for Scientific and Industrial Research, Pretoria, South Africa
`hpieterse@csir.co.za`
[2] Department of Computer Science, University of Pretoria, Pretoria, South Africa
`molivier@cs.up.ac.za`
[3] National Integrated Cyber Infrastructure System, Council for Scientific and Industrial Research, Pretoria, South Africa
`rvheerden@csir.co.za`
[4] School of Information and Communication Technology, Nelson Mandela University, Port Elizabeth, South Africa

Abstract. Ever improving technology allows smartphones to become an integral part of people's lives. The reliance on and ubiquitous use of smartphones render these devices rich sources of data. This data becomes increasingly important when smartphones are linked to criminal or corporate investigations. To erase data and mislead digital forensic investigations, end-users can manipulate the data and change recorded events. This paper investigates the effects of manipulating smartphone data on both the Google Android and Apple iOS platforms. The deployed steps leads to the formulation of a generic process for smartphone data manipulation. To assist digital forensic professionals with the detection of such manipulated smartphone data, this paper introduces an evaluation framework for smartphone data. The framework uses key traces left behind as a result of the manipulation of smartphone data to construct techniques to detect the changed data. The outcome of this research study successfully demonstrates the manipulation of smartphone data and presents preliminary evidence that the suggested framework can assist with the detection of manipulated smartphone data.

Keywords: Digital forensics · Mobile forensics · Manipulation
Smartphone data · Smartphones · Android · iOS

1 Introduction

The 21st century is witnessing the rapid development of smartphone technology. The current technological advancements equip smartphones with improved capabilities and functionality that nowadays closely resemble a personal computer. Existing smartphone models support different connectivity options, various communication channels, the installation of third-party applications, as well as a

© Springer Nature Switzerland AG 2019
H. Venter et al. (Eds.): ISSA 2018, CCIS 973, pp. 89–103, 2019.
https://doi.org/10.1007/978-3-030-11407-7_7

complete operating system. The leading smartphone operating systems of 2018 are Google Android and Apple iOS. The prominence of both Android (69.87% market share) and iOS (28.82% market share) platforms directly relates to their provided capabilities and popularity among users [1]. Although other smartphone operating systems do exist, the combined market share of 98.69% guided this study to only focus on these platforms.

From a mobile forensics' perspective, which forms a sub-discipline of digital forensics, the data collected by smartphones, called smartphone data, can become important sources of digital evidence. Smartphone data includes any data of probative value that is generated by an application or transferred to the smartphone by the user [2]. The extensive market share of both Android and iOS smartphones ensures the diverse usage of the devices, which eventually leads to rich collections of smartphone data [3]. Smartphone data describe events (for example sending a text message or browsing a website) that occurred on the smartphone. Valuable smartphone data, such as contacts, text messages, call lists, browsing history and e-mails, provides a well-defined snapshot of user events and support the chronological ordering of these events [4]. The exact events recorded by a smartphone depend on several internal and external factors, such as smartphone settings, operation by the user and installed applications [5]. Regardless of the availability, the produced smartphone data can still offer insight during digital forensic investigations and provide important digital evidence.

The value of smartphone data as a form of digital evidence has, however, raised suspicion among users. Data retrieved from smartphones can offer contextual clues about the end-user, who the owner and user of the smartphone is, as well as activities performed involving the smartphone. Such clues can reveal who the user knows and communicated with, locations visisted, highlight personality traits and pinpoint close associates [6]. The presence of such information can be a cause for concern [7], which can drive end-users to apply manipulative techniques to the data and eliminate or remove any potential value. The motivation for manipulating smartphone data is two-fold. Firstly, benign end-users can deploy certain techniques to manipulate smartphone data deemed private or sensitive and minimise the exposure of such data. Secondly, end-users can use similar techniques to intentionally make changes to smartphone data to hide their involvement in criminal activities and erase incriminating events. These techniques and tools are commonly referred to as anti-forensics and are primarily used to "compromise the availability or usefulness of evidence to the forensic process" [8]. Several recent research studies [4,9–13] have investigated the effect and feasible use of anti-forensics in the smartphone environment. It is, therefore, possible for end-users to utilise anti-forensics to erase, manipulate or construct false data, ultimately misleading digital forensic investigations.

To counter and thwart the effects of anti-forensics, existing research presents several solutions. Verma et al. [14] preserve date and timestamps of Android smartphones by capturing system generated values and storing these values in a location beyond the smartphone. Govindaraj et al. [15] have designed a solution, called iSecureRing, which permits a jailbroken iPhone to be secure and ready for a digital forensic investigation by preserving timestamps in a secure location. Research conducted by Pieterse et al. [16] showcased the successful manipulation of timestamps stored in SQLite database on Android smartphones. The research also proposed the Authenticity Framework for Android Timestamps, which provides methods to identify manipulation timestamps. These solutions are, however, either platform-specific, require additional software to be installed on a smartphone prior to an investigation or only focus on a specific subset of smartphone data such as timestamps.

This paper attempts to eliminate the shortcomings of existing research by establishing an evaluation framework that assists with the identification of manipulated smartphone data on both Android and iOS platforms. To construct such a framework, it is necessary to determine what manipulative changes can be applied to smartphone data. This is possible by conducting exploratory experiments involving the manipulation of data on a Samsung Galaxy S5 Mini (Android version 6.0.1) and iPhone 7 (iOS version 10.0.1) smartphones. The steps followed to perform the manipulation form a generic process to generalise the manipulation techniques. Such manipulation of smartphone data is essentially an attack on the data's integrity and is best described using an attack tree. Using the attack tree, key traces left behind due to the manipulation of smartphone data leads to the formulation of the evaluation framework, which provides key indicators for digital forensics professionals to identify and pinpoint manipulated smartphone data. The immediate challenges to address in this paper are thus the following: (a) development of an effective and generic process to manipulate smartphone data on both Android and iOS platforms and (b) construct an evaluation framework capable of detecting manipulated smartphone data.

The remainder of this paper is structured as follows. Section 2 presents an overview of the Android and iOS platforms and discusses the structure of SQLite databases. The generic process for smartphone data manipulation, constructed using the results of the exploratory experiments, is discussed in Sect. 3. Section 4 presents an attack tree for smartphone data manipulation and Section introduces the evaluation framework to detect such manipulated data. Finally, Sect. 6 concludes the paper.

2   Background

With the continuous growth in functions and capabilities of smartphones supporting the Android and iOS platforms, valuable sources of smartphone data are collected on these devices. This section reviews the architecture and file system structure of the Android and iOS platforms. Attention is given to the storage location of the smartphone data on these platforms, as well as the accessibility of the data. Following the review of smartphone platforms is an overview of SQLite databases, which are a popular choice for persistent storage on smartphones.

2.1 Smartphone Platforms

Operating systems form the foundation of advanced capabilities and improved functionality showcased by smartphones today. They operate seamlessly and act as the intermediary layer between the user and the underlying hardware resources. High performance smartphone operating systems, which include Google Android and Apple iOS, are the current pace setters, as reflected by their combined market share of 99.9% in the 4th quarter of 2017.

The Google Android platform is an open source operating system provided by the Open Handset Alliance [17] and was officially announced in November 2007. The architecture of the platform is divided into six layers: system applications, Java API framework, native C/C++ libraries, Android runtime, hardware abstraction layer and Linux kernel [18]. This architecture ensures the effective operation of applications by allowing fluent communication between these applications and the lower layers. Until Android version 2.2 (Froyo), Android smartphones primarily used Yet Another Flash File System version 2 (YAFFS2) [19]. Android switched from YAFFS2 to Fourth Extended (EXT4) file system with the release of version 2.3 (Gingerbread) to more efficiently support multi-core chip sets [19]. The EXT4 file system also divides the disk space into logical storage units, which supports reduced management overhead and improves throughput [20]. With regards to digital forensic investigations, the logical storage units containing valuable smartphone data are the /data and /system partitions [21]. Access to these partitions is not permitted by default and is only accessible by rooting the Android smartphone. Rooting gives the user access to the root directory (/) and permits the execution of superuser privileges [17].

The Apple iOS platform is a proprietary and slimmed down version of the macOS [22] for Apple's mobile devices. The architecture of the iOS platform consists of five layers: applications, Cocoa touch, media, core services and core OS/kernel [23]. The iOS platform acts as an intermediary layer between the underlying hardware components and installed applications, causing the applications to interact with the hardware through a set of well-defined system interfaces [24]. A variation of the Hierarchical File System Plus (HFS+), called HFSX, was selected as the primary file system for iOS [25]. The single-threaded design and rigid data structures of HFSX struggled to keep pace with ever-improving technology. In 2016 Apple announced a new file system, called the Apple File System (APFS), for all Apple's mobile operating systems, including iOS [25]. Similar to the Android platform, iOS also divides the logical storage space into partitions. Traditionally, iOS smartphones are configured with two partitions: system and data [26]. Access to smartphone data stored on these partitions is not allowed by default and users must jailbreak the iOS smartphone. The term jailbreak originates from a Unix practice of placing services in a restricted set of directories called a "jail" and breaking free from these restrictions [27]. By jailbreaking an iOS smartphone removes restrictions put in place by Apple and elevates the privileges to root access [28].

2.2 SQLite Databases

SQLite is best described as an efficient software library that implements a lightweight Structured Query Language (SQL) database engine [29]. The main database file (.db, .db3 or .sqlitedb) contains a complete SQL structure that includes tables, indices, triggers and views [30]. The first page of the main database file is a 100-byte database header page. The remaining pages following the header page are structured as B-trees, where each page contains a B-tree index and B-tree table that holds the actual data [31].

During transactions, SQLite stores additional information in a secondary file called either a rollback journal or write-ahead log (WAL) file [32]. The purpose of this secondary file is to ensure the integrity of the data in the event of transaction failure. The WAL approach, which was introduced with version 3.7.0, preserves the original data in the main database file and appends changes to a separate WAL (.db-wal) file. The WAL file also contains a 32-byte file header and zero or more WAL frames. When a checkpoint occurs the updated or new records in the WAL file are written to the main database file. Once completed, the WAL file remains untouched and can be reused rather than deleted. Traditionally, SQLite performs an automatic checkpoint when the WAL file reaches a size of 1000 frames (approximately 4 MB in file size) [33]. The number of WAL frames are calculated using the WAL file size (minus the WAL header size) divided by the combined size of the header and frame.

3 Generic Process for Smartphone Data Manipulation

The manipulation of smartphone data occurs for different reasons by applying various techniques. The available techniques to manipulation smartphone data are modification, fabrication or deletion. Modification of the smartphone data refers to tampering or altering of existing smartphone data. With modification, the existing data is updated to reflect changed data. Fabrication describes the creation of new but false smartphone data. The fabricated or counterfeited data is inserted to represent actual data. Finally, deletion of smartphone data removes the data.

To establish a generic process for smartphone data manipulation, exploratory experiments involving both the Android and iOS default messaging applications are performed. The purpose of these experiments is to obtain access to the persistent data of the applications and attempt the manipulation, which is either the modification, fabrication or deletion, of the data. While performing the exploratory experiments, the steps followed to manipulate the smartphone data are carefully documented. From the observations, similarities are identified and collected into a generic process.

3.1 Manipulation of Android Smartphone Data

The first exploratory experiment focuses on the Android platform and uses a Samsung Galaxy S5 Mini, running Android version 6.0.1 (Marshmallow), as the test smartphone. To manipulate the smartphone data of Android's default messaging application, access to the file(s) responsible for storing the data is required. The Android platform stores all application-related smartphone data in the /data folder and access is only possible on a rooted smartphone, as mentioned in Sect. 2.1. Root access on the Samsung Galaxy S5 Mini is obtained using the CF Auto Root and Odin tools.

Android's default messaging application uses an SQLite database for data storage and is located in the /data/data/com.android.providers.telephony/database/ folder on the Android smartphone. At this point, manipulation in the form of deletion is possible by simply removing the SQLite database files (.db and .db-wal) and rebooting the smartphone. This deletes all of the smartphone data related to the application. Modification of existing data or adding newly fabricated data requires direct access to the SQLite database records. Applying changes directly to the data in the SQLite database files is not feasible due to the complex structure of the files and the possibility of applied changes being overwritten. It is, therefore, necessary to open and access the data in these file(s). Two approaches exist to access the SQLite database files: direct or off-device.

The direct approach involves the manipulation of the smartphone data by opening the SQLite database on the Android smartphone. This requires the use of an appropriate tool, such as the sqlite3 command-line program, to manually enter and execute SQL statements [34]. This program provides access to the SQLite database records (using the .open command) and allows for the manipulation of the smartphone data using the appropriate SQL statements (INSERT, UPDATE or DELETE). Android smartphones do not ship with a pre-installed sqlite3 command-line program. Absence of or failure to utilise the sqlite3 command-line program necessitates the use of the off-device approach.

The off-device approach requires an established communication channel between the smartphone and a connected computer. Establishing such a channel relies on the USB debugging functionality, which is not visible by default. Although not visible, going to Settings, About phone and tapping multiple times on the build number will enable Developer mode. Selecting Developer options and touching the check box next to "USB debugging" will enable this feature. Following the enabling of the "USB debugging" feature, it is possible to create a communication channel using the Android Debug Bridge (ADB). ADB is a versatile command-line utility that communicates with a connected Android smartphone [35]. The communication channel is established using adb shell, followed immediately by the su command. Using the established communication channel, the SQLite database files are first transferred to the /sdcard folder before downloading the files to the connected computer. The /sdcard folder is found across all Android smartphones, regardless of make or model, and allows end-users to store additional files and data. Using an SQLite editor to open the .db file causes an automatic checkpoint to occur, ensuring all the records in the .db-wal file are transferred and visible in the editor. It is now possible to manipulate the smartphone data using the available SQL statements (INSERT,

UPDATE or DELETE). After completing the manipulation of the smartphone data, the SQLite database is closed to ensure the changes are captured correctly.

To complete the manipulation of the smartphone data, the remaining .db file must be returned to the Android smartphone. Before this file can be returned to the /data/data/com.android.providers.telephony/databases/ folder, the original SQLite database (.db and .db-wal files) must be removed using the rm command. The removal of the original SQLite database files prevents the manipulated data from being overwritten. Thereafter, the .db file can be returned to the /data/data/com.android.providers.telephony/databases/ folder using the mv command. The only required file is the .db-wal file, which is generated following a smartphone reboot. The permission of the .db file must be changed using the chmod a=rw or chmod 666 command to create a new .db-wal file. The reboot also ensures the manipulated data is visible on the Android smartphone.

This concludes the exploratory experiment of manipulating Android smartphone data. The following section attempts the manipulation of smartphone data residing on an iPhone 7.

3.2 Manipulation of iOS Smartphone Data

The second exploratory experiment focuses on the iOS platform and uses an Apple iPhone 7, running iOS version 10.0.1, to perform the experiments. To manipulate the smartphone data that forms part of the default messaging application on the iPhone 7, access to the file(s) storing the data is required. The iOS platform stores application smartphone data in the /private/var/mobile/Library folder. Access to this folder is only permitted on a jailbroken smartphone, which is achieved by using the extra_recipe + yaluX jailbreak application and Impactor to transfer the application to the iPhone 7. Upon installing the application, the jailbreak executes and immediately reboots. The jailbreak status is confirmed by verifying the automatic installation of the Cydia application, a package manager for jailbroken iPhones.

iPhone's default messaging application uses a SQLite database for storing data. The SQLite database is found in the /private/var/mobile/Library/ SMS/ folder on the iPhone 7. At this point, manipulation in the form of deletion is possible by removing the SQLite database files (.db and .db-wal) and performing a smartphone reboot. Again, this removes all of the smartphone data related to the application. Modification of existing or the creation of counterfeited data necessitates access to the SQLite database records. Access to the records is possible via one of the following two approaches: direct or off-device.

The direct approach involves the manipulation of the smartphone data by opening the SQLite database on the iPhone 7. This approach relies on the presence and availability of the sqlite3 program on the iPhone 7. In contrast to Android, iOS comes pre-installed with the sqlite3 program. The program provides direct access to the SQLite database and permits the modification of existing data, fabrication of new data, as well as the removal of all or specific data. Should the sqlite3 program fail to effectively apply the changes to the smartphone data, it will be necessary to follow the off-device approach.

The off-device approach requires the transferral of the SQLite database (both the .db and .db-wal files) to a connected computer. A communication channel is established using the iFunbox and puTTy applications. Obtaining access to the iPhone 7 file system is possible using the standard iOS credentials, which is root (username) and alpine (password). Thereafter, the SQLite database files is first transferred to the /var/mobile/Media folder before downloading the files unto the connected computer. The /private/var/mobile/Media folder is similar to Android's /sdcard folder and allows users to store additional media and downloaded files. Using a SQLite editor, the .db file is opened and immediately causes an automatic checkpoint (see Sect. 2.2). It is now possible to manipulate the smartphone data using the available SQL statements (INSERT, UPDATE or DELETE). After completing the manipulation, the SQLite database is closed to ensure the changes are correctly captured.

For the manipulated data to reflect on the iPhone 7, it is necessary to return the .db file. Before returning the file to the /private/var/mobile/Library/ SMS folder, the existing SQLite database (.db and .db-wal files) must be removed using the rm command. These files, especially the .db-wal file, are removed to ensure the manipulated data is not overwritten. Thereafter, the .db file can be transferred to the /private/var/mobile/Library/SMS folder using the mv command. The only required file is the .db-wal file, which is created following a smartphone reboot. To generate the new and empty .db-wal file, the current permissions of the .db file must be changed using the chmod a=rw or chmod 666 command. This ensures the .db-wal file is created and the manipulated data is visible on the iPhone 7.

The successful manipulation of iOS smartphone data concludes the exploratory experiment. The following section consolidates the findings found across both exploratory experiments and formulates a generic process for smartphone data manipulation.

3.3   Generic Process

The exploratory experiments performed in the previous sections confirm that it is indeed possible to manipulate smartphone data on both the Android and iOS platforms. Although the focus was on the manipulation of text messages of the default messaging applications, the same steps can be followed to manipulate any other smartphone data. From these experiments, it is now possible to pinpoint various similarities among the steps followed to manipulate smartphone data. Using the collected similarities, a generic process is formulated that generalises the manipulation of smartphone data. The generic process consists of four distinct stages. Each individual stage describes the progression of the generic process to manipulate the smartphone data along with the requirements that must be met to successfully complete each stage, as well as the actual manipulation.

- **Phase 1:** ensures the selected smartphone is accessible by confirming the smartphone is either rooted (Android) or jailbroken (iOS).
- **Phase 2:** requires the selection of the application and identifying the location of the file(s), such as a SQLite database, storing the smartphone data. The data of the selected smartphone application must reside on the smartphone.
- **Phase 3:** identify the most appropriate approach to access the smartphone data: Direct or Off-device.
- **Phase 3.1:** the direct approach performs the manipulation of the smartphone data directly on the smartphone and relies on the presence of a program or utility to access the file(s).
- **Phase 3.2:** the off-device approach requires the transferral of the file(s) to the connected computer. Using the most appropriate program or utility, the contents of the file(s) is accessed and manipulated accordingly. Once completed, the file(s) is closed and returned to the smartphone to overwrite previous smartphone data. The returned file(s) is also assigned the necessary read/write permissions to ensure the smartphone application can interact with the manipulated smartphone data.
- **Phase 4:** requires a manual reboot of the smartphone.

This proposed generic process for smartphone data manipulation captures the steps to follow to modify, fabricate or delete smartphone data. The following section further investigates the manipulation of smartphone data by introducing an attack tree that encapsulates the various manipulation scenarios.

4   Attack Tree for Smartphone Data Manipulation

The established generic process for smartphone data manipulation provides the steps to affect changes to data. Such changes are essentially an attack on the integrity, availability and authenticity of smartphone data and is best described using an attack tree. An attack tree provides a formal and methodical way to describe various attacks against a system [36]. The attacks are represented using a conceptual tree structure with the main goal of these attacks listed as the root node. The nodes following the root describes the different avenues of achieving the goal, constructed using OR (choice between alternative steps) and AND (represents different steps to achieve the same goal) nodes.

The goal of this attack tree is the "manipulation of smartphone data" and is denoted by G. The intermediate goals are: deletion (I_1), modification (I_2) or fabrication (I_3). Following the intermediate goals are the sub-goals that describes the required steps to accomplish each intermediate goal and ultimately complete the set goal. There are two options for deletion: removal of the files holding the data which deletes all of the data (S_1) or removing specific data such as individual records (S_2). Removal of the file(s) requires physical access to the smartphone(S_5) by either rooting (Android) or jailbreaking (iOS) the smartphone. Once access is acquired, it is necessary to locate and remove the file(s) (S_6). This is followed by a reboot of the smartphone (S_7) and ensures the deletion

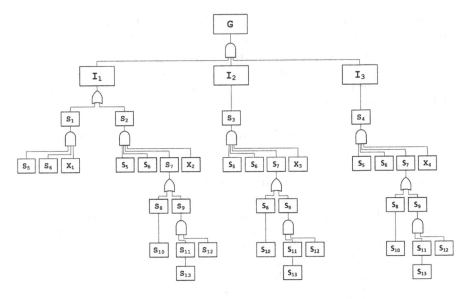

Fig. 1. Attack tree for smartphone data manipulation

of all the smartphone data related to the smartphone application. The removal of individual records also requires physical access to the smartphone and locating the file(s) holding the data. Since this attack focuses on the manipulation of specific data, it is necessary to access and open the file(s) containing the data (S_8). Options to open the file(s) are either directly on the smartphone (S_9) or off-device on a connected computer (S_{10}). To open and view the data requires the use of an appropriate utility or program to access the data (S_{11}). Should such utility or program be unavailable or the approach not be feasible, access to the file(s) holding the data must occur off-device on a computer connected to the smartphone. Off-device manipulation requires the transferral of the file(s) (S_{12}), which relies on an established connection between the smartphone and the connected computer (S_{14}). After performing the manipulating, the file(s) are returned to the smartphone via the established connection (S_{13}). This is again followed by a smartphone reboot (S_7) to ensure the removed data reflects on the smartphone.

The remaining manipulation techniques, modification (I_2) and fabrication (I_3), follows similar attack paths. To either change existing data (S_3) or insert fabricated data (S_4), it is necessary to open and access the data in the file(s). Therefore, these manipulation techniques follows a path identical to the removal of individual records. According to the descriptions above, the attack tree is constructed and presented in Fig. 1. This attack tree forms the basis for deriving attack scenarios to manipulate smartphone data.

The presented attack tree provides four distinct techniques to manipulate smartphone data. These four techniques (deletion of all data, deletion of specific data, modification of data or fabricating data) will have inherent side-effects that leaves various traces on smartphones. Traces specific to each sub-goal are listed in Table 1.

Table 1. Traces created due to the manipulation of smartphone data

Sub-goal	Trace created
S_1, S_2, S_3, S_4	The presence of a new and clean WAL file
S_5	Automatic installation of a root application
S_5	Unavailability of over-the-air (OTA) updates
S_7	Creation of a new entry in the reboot log
S_8	Discrepancy between WAL timestamp and application timestamp
S_9, S_{11}	Use of the `sqlite3` command-line program
S_{10}, S_{12}	Change in ownership of the `.db` file
S_{10}, S_{12}	Change in permissions for the `.db` file
S_{10}, S_{13}	The `.db` file size larger than `.db-wal` file
S_{14}	Enabled settings (USB debugging)

Collectively, the traces provides evidence that can assist with the identification of manipulated smartphone data. The following section further explores these traces by extracting key indicators and using the indicators to construct an evaluation framework for smartphone data.

5   Evaluation Framework for Smartphone Data

The collection of traces deduced from the various manipulation techniques encapsulated in the attack tree equips digital forensic professionals with the necessary information to evaluate smartphone data. There is, however, no structure or order to these traces, which can impact the effective use of the traces to detect manipulated smartphone data. To assist digital forensic professionals, key indicators are extracted from these traces and captured in an evaluation framework. Figure 2 presents the evaluation framework for smartphone data.

From the collected traces 10 distinct indicators are identified, which are listed in the above evaluation framework. Each indicator is a possible side-effect that occurs due to the manipulation of the smartphone data. Certain indicators, such as the root status and OTA updates, are not a direct indication of the intentional manipulation of smartphone data. However, the manipulation necessitates the need for rooting/jailbreaking the smartphone, which also impacts the availability of OTA updates. Therefore, a larger collection of present indicators is a better reflection of the manipulation of smartphone data.

To pinpoint these indicators, specific measurements are presented to assist digital forensic professional. Where necessary, explicit measures are specified for the different smartphone platforms. Each evaluated indicator produces a binary

No	Indicator	Measurements	Result
1	WAL File	➤ WAL file does not contain the latest stored records ➤ WAL file size < main database file size (if WAL frames < 1000)	[true/false]
2	Root Application	➤ *Android*: SuperSu or Superuser application installed ➤ *iOS*: Cydia application installed	[true/false]
3	OTA Updates	➤ Unavailable due to unauthorised changes (rooted/jailbroken)	[true/false]
4	Reboot	➤ Reboot entry logged present on the smartphone ➤ *Android*: reboots stored in /data/system/dropbox/ folder ➤ *iOS*: reboots stored in the /var/logs/lockdownd.log file ➤ A reboot entry immediately follows the WAL file timestamp	[true/false]
5	Application Usage	➤ WAL access timestamp proceed application last used timestamp ➤ *Android*: application logs in the /data/system/usagestats/ folder ➤ *iOS*: application logs in the /var/mobile/Library/Preferences/ folder	[true/false]
6	SQLite3 Usage	➤ *sqlite3* program used ➤ *sqlite3* program access timestamp proceed WAL timestamp	[true/false]
7	DB Ownership	➤ Changes to the SQLite database ownership ➤ *Android*: *UID* changed to *root* for both individual and group owners ➤ *iOS*: *UID* changed to *root* for individual owner	[true/false]
8	DB Permissions	➤ Changes to the SQLite database permissions ➤ *Android*: permissions change from -rw-rw---- to -rw-rw-rw for all files ➤ iOS: permissions change from -rw-rw---- to -rw-rw-rw for .db and .db-wal files	[true/false]
9	Main Database File	➤ WAL file size < main database file size (if WAL frames < 1000)	[true/false]
10	Additional Settings	➤ *Android*: USB debugging enabled	[true/false]

Fig. 2. Evaluation framework to identify manipulated smartphone data

result that reflects either a positive [**true**] or negative [**false**] result. A positive result indicates the evaluated measurement(s) are met while a negative result contradicts the indicator. All of the positive (pos_r) results of all the evaluated indicators (n) are accumulated and using Eq. (1), a manipulation score (M_s) is calculated.

$$M_s = \frac{pos_r}{n} \qquad (1)$$

Using the probability scale shown in Fig. 3, the calculated manipulation score can be plotted to reflect whether the evaluated smartphone data is either original or manipulation. Also, the probability scale allows the digital forensic professional to measure the certainty of the findings.

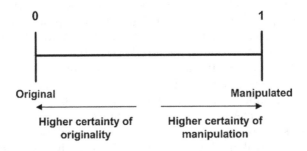

Fig. 3. Probability scale to measure manipulation

To confirm the effectiveness of the framework to identify manipulated smartphone data, the following manipulation technique is applied to smartphone data at a theoretical level: $I_1, S_2, S_5, S_6, S_8, S_9, S_{11}, S_7$. Application of this particular manipulation technique will cause the following indicators to present on a smartphone: WAL File, Root Application, OTA Updates, Application Usage, SQLite program and Reboot. All of these indicators meet the provided measurements and using Eq. (1), the calculated manipulation score is 0.6. Plotted on the probability scale shown in Fig. 3, the manipulation score confirms with a higher certainty the manipulation of the smartphone data. The result confirm that the evaluation framework for smartphone data can assist with the identification of manipulated data.

6 Conclusion

Smartphone data found on both Android and iOS devices can form an important component of digital forensic investigations. Available smartphone data provides a well-defined snapshot of user events. To protect their privacy or hide incriminating events, users can deploy anti-forensics to manipulate smartphone data. The challenges addressed in this paper were to show (a) that smartphone data can be manipulated and (b) construct an evaluation framework to detect such manipulated data. Challenge (a) was addressed by formulating the generic process to manipulate smartphone data on both the Android and iOS platforms. Challenge (b) was concluded by introducing the evaluation framework for smartphone data and confirming the framework can assist with the identification of manipulated data. Future work can build on this research by establishing other approaches to identify manipulated smartphone data.

References

1. NetMarketShare: Operating System Market Share. https://netmarketshare.com/operating-system-market-share.aspx. Accessed 04 June 2018
2. Pieterse, H., Olivier, M., van Heerden, R.: Evaluating the authenticity of smartphone evidence. Advances in Digital Forensics XIII. IAICT, vol. 511, pp. 41–61. Springer, Cham (2017). https://doi.org/10.1007/978-3-319-67208-3_3
3. Ayers, R., Brothers, S., Jansen, W.: Guidelines on mobile device forensics (draft). NIST Special Publication 800 (2013)
4. Albano, P., Castiglione, A., Cattaneo, G., De Maio, G., De Santis, A.: On the construction of a false alibi on the Android OS. In: Third International Conference on Intelligent Networking and Collaborative Systems (INCoS), pp. 685–690. IEEE (2011)
5. Pieterse, H., Olivier, M.: Smartphones as distributed witnesses for digital forensics. In: Peterson, G., Shenoi, S. (eds.) DigitalForensics 2014. IAICT, vol. 433, pp. 237–251. Springer, Heidelberg (2014). https://doi.org/10.1007/978-3-662-44952-3_16
6. Kala, M., Thilagaraj, R.: A framework for digital forensics in I-devices: jailed and jail broken devices. J. Adv. Libr. Inf. Sci. 2(2), 82–93 (2013)
7. Tsavli, M., Efraimidis, P.S., Katos, V.: Reengineering the user: privacy concerns about personal data on smartphones. Inf. Comput. Secur. 23(4), 394–405 (2015)
8. Harris, R.: Arriving at an anti-forensics consensus: examining how to define and control the anti-forensics problem. Digit. Invest. 3, 44–49 (2006)

9. Albano, P., Castiglione, A., Cattaneo, G., De Santis, A.: A novel anti-forensics technique for the Android OS. In: International Conference on Broadband and Wireless Computing, Communication and Applications (BWCCA), pp. 380–385. IEEE (2011)

10. Azedegan, S., Yu, W., Liu, H., Sistani, M., Acharya, S.: Novel anti-forensics approaches for smart phones. In: 45th Hawaii International Conference on System Sciences (HICSS), pp. 5424–5431. IEEE (2012)

11. D'Orazio, C., Ariffin, A., Choo, K.: iOS anti-forensics: how can we securely conceal, delete and insert data? In: 47th Hawaii International Conference o System Sciences (HICSS), pp. 4838–4847. IEEE (2014)

12. Karlsson, K., Glisson, W.: Android anti-forensics: modifying cyanogenMod. In: 47th Hawaii International Conference of System Sciences (HICSS), pp. 4828–4837. IEEE (2014)

13. Zheng, J., Tan, Y., Zhang, X., Liang, C., Zhang, C., Zheng, J.: An anti-forensics method against memory acquiring for Android devices. In: International Conference on Computational Science and Engineering (CSE) and Embedded and Ubiquitous Computing (EUC), pp. 214–218. IEEE (2017)

14. Verma, R., Govindaraj, J., Gupta, G.: Preserving dates and timestamps for incident handling in Android smartphones. In: Peterson, G., Shenoi, S. (eds.) Digital-Forensics 2014. IAICT, vol. 433, pp. 209–225. Springer, Heidelberg (2014). https://doi.org/10.1007/978-3-662-44952-3_14

15. Govindaraj, J., Verma, R., Mata, R., Gupta, G.: iSecureRing: forensic ready secure iOS apps for jailbroken iPhones. In: 35th IEEE Symposium on Security and Privacy (2014)

16. Pieterse, H., Olivier, M., van Heerden, R.: Playing hide-and-seek: detecting the manipulation of Android timestamps. In: Information Security for South Africa, pp. 1–8. IEEE (2015)

17. Lessard, J., Kessler, G.: Android forensics: Simplifying cell phone examinations. Small Scale Digit. Dev. Forensics J. **4**(1), 1–12 (2010)

18. Android: Platform architecture. http://developer.android.com/guide/platform/. Accessed 04 Oct 2017

19. Zimmermann, C., Spreitzenbarth, M., Schmitt, S., Freiling F.C.: Forensic analysis of YAFFS2. In: Sicherheit, pp. 59–69 (2012)

20. Kim, H.-J., Kim, J.-S.: Tuning the EXT4 filesystem performance for Android-based smartphones. In: Sambath, S., Zhu, E. (eds.) Frontiers in Computer Education, vol. 133, pp. 745–752. Springer, Heidelberg (2013). https://doi.org/10.1007/978-3-642-27552-4_98

21. Tamma, R., Tindall, D.: Learning Android Forensics. Packt Publishing Ltd., Birmingham/Mumbai (2015)

22. Tracy, K.: Mobile application development experiences on Apple's iOS and Android OS. IEEE Potentials **31**(4), 30–34 (2012)

23. Apple: iOS technology overview. http://developer.apple.com/library/content/documentation/Miscellaneous/Conceptual/iPhoneOSTechOverviewIntroduction/Introduction.html. Accessed 05 Oct 2017

24. Kanoi, M., Jdiet, Y.: Internal structure of iOS and building tools for iOS apps. Int. J. Comput. Sci. Appl. **6**(2), 220–225 (2013)

25. Tamura, E., Giampaolo, D.: Introducing Apple file system. Technical report. Apple, Inc. (2016)

26. Epifani, M., Stirparo, P.: Learning iOS Forensics. Packt Publishing Ltd., Birmingham/Mumbai (2016)

27. Zdziarski, J.: iPhone Forensics: Recovering Evidence, Personal Data and Corporate Assets, 1st edn. O'Reilly Media Inc., Sebastopol (2008)
28. Egele, M., Kruegel, C., Kirda, E., Vigna, G.: PiOS: detecting privacy leaks in iOS applications. In: NDSS, pp. 177–183 (2011)
29. Jeon, S., Bang, J., Byun, K., Lee, S.: A recovery method of deleted record for SQLite database. Pers. Ubiquit. Comput. **16**(6), 707–715 (2012)
30. SQLite: About SQLite. https://www.sqlite.org/about.html. Accessed 24 Apr 2018
31. Patodi, P.: Database recovery mechanism for Android devices. Ph.D. thesis. Indian Institute of Technology, Bombay (2012)
32. SQLite: Database file format. https://www.sqlite.org/fileformat.html. Accessed 24 Apr 2018
33. SQLite: Write-ahead logging. https://www.sqlite.org/wal.html. Accessed 24 Apr 2018
34. SQLite: Command line shell for SQLite. https://www.sqlite.org/cli.html. Accessed 25 Apr 2018
35. Android Studio: Android debug bridge (ADB). http://developer.android.com/studio/command-line/adb.html. Accessed 13 Jan 2018
36. Schneier, B.: Attack trees. Dr. Dobb's J. **24**(12), 21–29 (1999)

An Evaluation of the Password Practices on Leading e-Commerce Websites in South Africa

Silas Formunyuy Verkijika[(✉)]

Department of Computer Science and Informatics,
University of the Free State, Bloemfontein, South Africa
vekasif@gmail.com

Abstract. Despite the emergence of numerous authentication methods, passwords have remained the dominant authentication mechanism for e-commerce websites. However, password authentications if often widely criticized, especially due to the ease with which it can be compromised by end-users as they often have poor password security behaviors. Nevertheless, a plethora of evidence suggests that the blame should not only be placed on the users as many engage in poor password security practices because they lack sufficient guidance and support on how to maintain good password security behaviors. Indeed, many researchers over the years have shown that user password security behaviors can be significantly enhanced by provided guidance and support on how they can create and maintain strong passwords. Yet, it remains uncertain how well e-commerce website providers have learned these essential lessons. As such, this study is aimed at evaluating the password practices of e-commerce websites in South Africa (SA). After evaluating 37 leading e-commerce websites in the country, it was observed that the majority (92%) of the websites had poor password practices with over 81% offering no guidance for users to enhance their password behaviors. This problem is certainly worse than it should be in this day and age. Consequently, there is an urgent need for e-commerce service providers in SA to improve their password security practices as this is vital for enhancing the password behaviors of their website's users.

Keywords: Password restrictions · Password guidance · e-Commerce website
South Africa

1 Introduction

The proliferation of technology has provided numerous opportunities for people to change several aspects of their lives. One such change relates to the way people now conduct their shopping activities using the Internet. This phenomenon, generally termed as electronic commerce (e-commerce) has seen rapid development over the past decade [1, 2]. Many Global e-commerce giants like Amazon and eBay record billions of US dollars in revenue every year. In recent years, there have also been noticeable success stories among e-commerce businesses in South Africa (SA) such as Takealot and Spree [3, 4]. For example, Takealot recorded over 2.9 million transactions from a

© Springer Nature Switzerland AG 2019
H. Venter et al. (Eds.): ISSA 2018, CCIS 973, pp. 104–114, 2019.
https://doi.org/10.1007/978-3-030-11407-7_8

million customers in 2016, generating revenue of R2.3 million [3]. Similarly, Spree reported a 500% growth in 2014 [4]. Additionally, recent estimates suggest that e-commerce transactions in SA amounted to about R10 billion in 2017 [5]. Many factors account for the growth in e-commerce adoption around the world. However, a key factor that still continues to deter user adoption of e-commerce websites around the globe is the perceived security risk associated with e-commerce transactions [1, 6].

One of the most commonly used security measure in e-commerce websites is user authentication using passwords [7]. This is not surprising as passwords have remained the most dominant method of authentication amidst the growing alternatives [7, 8]. In fact, password mechanisms are widely preferred in online websites because of their ease of use, conceptual simplicity, and administrative inexpensiveness [9]. Password authentication as a concept is not a significant security problem in itself, but the greatest weakness of password authentication is the poor practices of the people who create and use these passwords [10]. As a result, passwords are more and more being subjected to a plethora of attacks by malicious individuals as they find it easy to exploit the human weaknesses associated with the creation and management of poor passwords [8]. Many studies over the years have shown that user online passwords are quite predictable and can easily be guessed [8]. This is a significant concern, especially for e-commerce users who store valuable information assets (e.g. credit card information, email addresses, bank account details) in their online e-commerce accounts. Moreover, users have been known to continuously misuse passwords and as such require support and guidance in creating and managing passwords [11, 12].

There is evidence suggesting that the password practices of online websites can be instrumental in improving the password security behaviors of its users [11]. In partic-ular, websites that provide guidance on the creation of strong passwords are likely to help their users to have better password behaviors [11]. Yet, despite the existing evi-dence, many websites still allow their users to figure things out for themselves, with even leading websites around the world still having poor password practices [12]. Since password use has remained widespread among e-commerce websites amidst the existing alternatives, it is imperative to ensure that best password practices are adopted by the website owners [10, 11]. In SA, little is known about the password practices on the country's leading e-commerce websites. Thus, the question this study seeks to answer is "what password security practices are implemented by SA e-commerce websites".

There is evidence suggesting that online consumers in the SA have poor password practices [13]. Moreover, a key concern observed among SA online consumers is that many tend to perceive themselves as proficient password users, yet their actual pass-word behaviors fall short of expectations [13]. This might suggest the lack of password support practices from the side of the country's online systems, as has been the case in some parts of the world [11, 12]. As such, if e-commerce websites in the country do not provide the needed guidance on good password practices, the users will continue to be at risk of potential exploitations due to their poor password practices. This is important because even if the website itself provides adequate security, but allows poor password practices, then its user's accounts can still be easily compromised as was the case with Apple iCloud [14]. Consequently, it is imperative to assess the current password practices on SA's e-commerce websites as this can provide valuable insights for the industry at large to refine their practices in a manner that will better support their users and improve their general password security behaviors. As such, the main objective of this is to evaluate the password practices of selected e-commerce websites in SA.

The rest of the paper is structured as follows. The next section presents the literature review which encompasses password restriction and guidance practices. Afterward, the methodology used for the selection and evaluation of the e-commerce websites is presented. Thereafter, the analyses and discussion of the findings are presented. Lastly, the conclusion of the study is presented.

2 Literature Review

There are two common categories of password practices that can be implemented on websites to enhance user password behaviors [10–12]. The first category deals with enforcing numerous restrictions that force the website users to create strong passwords, while the second category deals with the guidance provided by the website on how users can create strong passwords. Each of these categories is discussed below.

2.1 Password Restriction Practices

One of the most common approaches for enhancing the password security behaviors of website users is to enforce restrictions, as this ensures that all users of the website meet some minimum acceptable standards for creating passwords. Good password restriction practices are often common among enterprise information systems; however, these practices are often overlooked by public facing systems like e-commerce and e-government websites [12, 15]. Researchers over the years have emphasized the need for password restriction practices as effective implementation of these practices ultimately leads to the creation of better quality passwords by users [11]. Some of the common restrictions needed on e-commerce websites include enforcing minimum length of the password, preventing the user of the surname as password, preventing the use of the user ID as password, preventing the use of the word "password" or "123456" as a valid password, preventing the use of common dictionary words, and enforcing composition to create complex passwords.

General norms uphold that good passwords should have a minimum of 8 characters and also have a combination of different characters such as upper-case and lowercase letters, symbols and numerals [12, 16, 17]. These aspects help to enforce minimum length and composition thus making the passwords difficult to crack. Additionally, weak passwords are easily cracked with dictionary attacks and as such, it is increasingly advisable to restrict the use of common dictionary words as passwords [8, 16]. Some other essential restrictions include restricting the use of user ID and surnames as this infor-mation is often easily available to hackers and can serve as a starting point for cracking the user's password. Preventing the use of a user's surname as the password is particularly important when the website collects such information from the user [12]. Other password choices like "123456" and the word "password" have been widely revealed to be the most commonly used passwords for many years [18]. As such, malicious individuals are likely to use these passwords as a starting point when trying to crack a user's password.

Consequently, it is imperative for e-commerce websites to restrict the use of these common passwords to minimize their user's vulnerability to attacks.

2.2 Password Guidance Practices

In addition to providing restrictions, it is important for a website to provide guidance to users on the creation of quality passwords. This follows from the growing evidence suggesting that user password behavior can be significantly improved when guidance is provided [11, 19, 20]. Furnell [12] emphasised the need for password guidance on websites to be tangible enough to not only tell the user what needs to be done as is the case with restrictions but to further elucidate to the user why it is necessary to create a password in a certain manner. The provision of guidance does not necessarily mean that users will follow it; however, there is empirical evidence to suggest that guidance significantly improves user password behavior [11]. Some of the common guidance approaches used on websites include providing password meters and general tips on the creation of quality passwords [12]. Password meters enable the users to enhance their password behaviors by providing visual feedback on the strength of their passwords. Ur et al. [20] showed that pass-word meters helped users to create quality passwords. However, a key concern has been differences in the quality of password meters as some are poorly developed while others have good and stringent rules [11]. Password meters with stringent rules enable users to create better passwords [11, 20]. As such, it is imperative to ensure that available password meters on websites are well developed. In addition to password meters, web-sites can include advice to users on the creation of quality passwords. An example of password tips used by Amazon is presented below (Fig. 1).

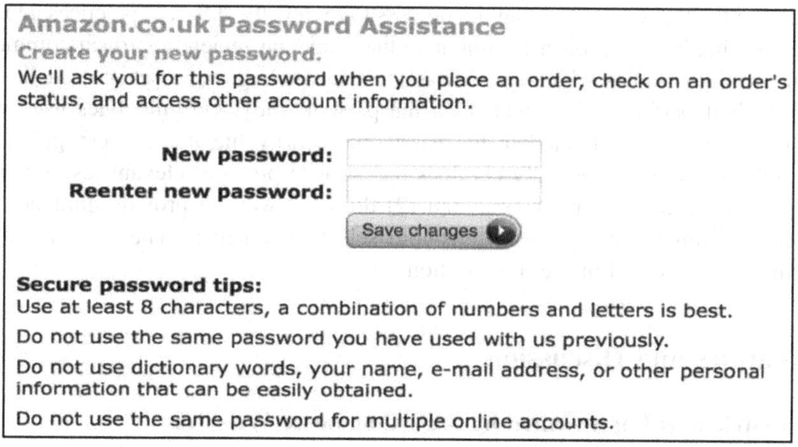

Amazon.co.uk Password Assistance
Create your new password.
We'll ask you for this password when you place an order, check on an order's status, and access other account information.

New password: [   ]
Reenter new password: [   ]

Save changes ▶

Secure password tips:
Use at least 8 characters, a combination of numbers and letters is best.
Do not use the same password you have used with us previously.
Do not use dictionary words, your name, e-mail address, or other personal information that can be easily obtained.
Do not use the same password for multiple online accounts.

Fig. 1. Password assistance by Amazon [12]

3   Methodology

3.1   Selection of e-Commerce Websites

The present study aimed at evaluating the password practices of SA e-commerce websites. Although there are many e-commerce websites in SA, there is no comprehensive database for these websites. However, there have been significant efforts by companies like uAfrica and Pricecheck to evaluate and recognize leading SA e-commerce websites through their e-commerce awards. In 2015, uAfrica (www.uafrica.com) released a list of 50 leading e-commerce websites in SA [21]. This study used this list as the primary database for recognized e-commerce websites in the country. Even though the 50 leading e-commerce websites do not represent all e-commerce websites in the country, focusing on leading websites have two major advantages. Firstly, the password practices of leading websites are likely to influence a wide pool of e-commerce end users as these websites attract the majority of e-commerce traffic in the country. Secondly, other providers often mimic the practices of leading websites and use them as standards for their own websites [12]. Thus, the password practices in leading websites could reflect that of the majority of SA e-commerce websites. Among the 50 leading e-commerce websites by uAfrica, 5 were eliminated from the present study because they were offline, while another 8 were eliminated because they did not have signup functionality. As such, a total of 37 e-commerce websites were evaluated in the present study (See Appendix).

3.2   Evaluation Approach

The password practices of the leading websites were evaluated by creating user accounts on the websites and using the process to review the different practices adopted by the website. This approach is similar to the guideline review approach commonly used in usability studies where an interface is evaluated against a set of guidelines to determine if it performs as expected. In the present study, the guidelines used were those that have been validated in the password security literature. These guidelines focused on two domains namely (1) does the website provide relevant restrictions to ensure users create good passwords and (2) does the website provide guidance and support that aims to enhance user password selection practices. The outcome of the assessment is presented in the next section.

4   Analyses and Discussion

4.1   Restrictions Implemented by SA e-Commerce Websites

One of the most common password restrictions implemented on most websites is the minimum length of the password. Table 1 presents the information on password restrictions among SA e-commerce websites.

It was observed that 14% of the websites had no password length restriction. It is quite uncommon, although not impossible to find leading websites that do not implement minimum password length [10, 12]. Short passwords are quite easy to crack,

Table 1. Minimum length restriction

Length Restriction	Frequency	%
None	5	14
4	2	5
5	9	24
6	17	46
7	1	3
8	2	5
12	1	3

so failing to provide password length restrictions is quite concerning. Also, it was seen that a total of 11 websites had their minimum length restrictions below 6. This is also a very weak practice as it is generally advisable to set minimum password length at 8, even though it is not uncommon to find that a majority of websites use 6 as the minimum password length. The majority of the websites (45%) set their minimum password length at 6 characters. This is not surprising as [12] found that 60% of the 10 world's leading websites he evaluated also set minimum password length at 6 characters. However, some of the websites like Google and Yahoo restrict their minimum passwords to 8 characters, which is in line with security recommendations. Among the SA e-commerce websites evaluated, only 2 (5%) used 8 characters as the minimum password length while one website required user passwords to have a minimum of 12 characters. While it is interesting to see a website that requires a minimum length of 12 characters, it is important to note that this is an acceptable practice used in many websites around the world [22]. In fact, some security experts even suggest that the minimum password length should be increased to 14 characters, especially because of the existence of rainbow tables where it is argued that the likelihood of finding a hash value for any password below 12–14 on an existing rainbow table is very high [23].

Table 2 presents the evaluation of other vital restrictions that websites can implement to improve password behavior.

Table 2. Other restrictions and enforcement of composition

Type of restriction	Websites enforcing the restriction	Websites not enforcing the restriction
Surname	1 (3%)	36 (97%)
"123456"	5 (13%)	32 (87%)
"password"	5 (13%)	32 (87%)
Dictionary words	4 (11%)	33 (89%)
Composition	4 (11%)	33 (89%)

It was observed that only 1 website (3%) restricted the use of the user's surname as a password. Also, five websites each had restrictions for use of common passwords like "123456" and "password". Additionally, four of the websites restricted the use of common dictionary words while four enforced the use of composition in creating passwords. Similar to [12], websites were considered to enforce composition when they required passwords to have characters in each of the following groups: upper case letter, lower case letter, numeric character, and special/punctuation characters. These findings are concerning as such poor password practices used by the majority of websites could ultimately result in users creating weak passwords that can be easily cracked.

Passwords with composition are usually considered to be highly secure as they are difficult to crack, especially when the composition includes upper and lower case letters, alphanumeric characters, and numbers [8, 20, 24]. As such the fact that up to 89% of the evaluated websites do not have password composition rules is a key concern as users of these websites are likely to have weak passwords that can be easily cracked. Nevertheless, some have argued that passwords with compositions even though more secure are difficult to memorize and use. Thus, website users do not prefer them [25, 26]. This could explain why the majority of the websites do not use password composition. However, as security concerns are vital for the adoption of e-commerce solutions [1, 6], it is imperative to ensure that users create strong passwords. It is quite possible for users to create complex passwords that they can easily remember [24]. One of the evaluated websites was highly security conscious by enforcing strong composition rules with users having to create a strong password with a minimum of 12 characters. The website even helped to auto-generate a complex password for users, which they can change when they log into the system. However, a key drawback to this approach is that system generated passwords are often more difficult to remember as they are random characters that offer little meaning compared to user-generated passwords. Nonetheless, the auto-generated passwords could serve as a guide for the users to understand how to effectively apply password composition rules.

4.2 Password Guidance Practices by SA e-Commerce Websites

In total, it was observed that 5 websites implemented password meters. Likewise, 5 websites also provided password tips for users as guidance for creating strong passwords. However, these websites were not necessarily distinct. In fact, 3 of the websites had both a password meter and provided tips for creating strong passwords, while 2 only implemented password meters and another 2 only provided password tips.

Password meters and tips have been shown to improve user password behavior in several studies [11, 19, 20]. Password meters and tips are important because they address some of the limitations of enforcing restrictions. For example, even though most of the websites set the password minimum length to 6 characters, they allowed common passwords like "123456" and "password" as well as common dictionary words as passwords. If such websites used a password meter or tips, their users will be able to know that such passwords are weak and still vulnerable to being cracked. The fact that only 3 websites (8%) use both a password meter while also providing password tips clearly indicates the lack of password guidance practices among these websites. This is a cause for concern as it indicates the existence of minimal efforts to improve the password security behaviors of their users. When password strength meters and password tips are implemented on a website, even novice users tend to effectively use the guidance to create strong passwords as they tend to feel in control of the situation.

5 Conclusion

Despite the criticisms of passwords, they have remained the primary authentication choice for most websites. Generally, end users are often criticised for misuse of passwords due to their poor password security behaviors. However, putting the blame on end-users is somewhat overstated, especially when service provides totally ignore the role they play in promoting poor password security practices. Indeed, many online service providers have highly overlooked essential lessons on how to improve the password security posture of their users. As highlighted above, the provision of password support and guidance mechanisms on websites can significantly improve the password security behaviors of users. Yet, many service providers continue to deploy e-commerce websites without providing any support/guidance or enforcing relevant restrictions that can enhance the security behaviors of end-users. As such, documenting the extent of this problem is the first step in creating awareness for service providers so that they can review and improve their current password practices. The present study is the first to document the extent of this problem among SA e-commerce websites.

The evaluation of SA e-commerce websites clearly showed the need for such studies as many of the websites are yet to adopt good password security practices. The implications of the findings are threefold. Firstly, evidence from SA shows that online consumers have poor password security behaviors. It is highly probable that their poor password behaviors could be a direct result of the lack of support and guidance in the password creation process as argued by many researchers. As such, e-commerce service providers need to play an active role in enhancing the security behaviors of their consumers by implementing good password security practices. Secondly, the extent of the problem suggests the need for training of website developers and designers in the country on the need for and implementation of good password security practices. Lastly, policymakers are also encouraged to consider enforcing legislation that mandates e-commerce websites to maintain a minimum set of password practices as this will be imperative in enhancing end-user security behaviors. Also, e-commerce websites owners should be encouraged to adopt multi-factor authentication as a means to limit the weaknesses of password mechanisms.

The study has two key limitations that also offer avenues for future studies. Firstly, the evaluation of password practices was limited to password practices during the initial registration with an e-commerce website. As such, other stages like password recovery and changing existing passwords were not covered. Future studies can also examine password practices at these other stages. Secondly, the study was limited to 37 e-commerce websites in South Africa. This only depicts a fraction of e-commerce websites in SA. As such, future studies can conduct an evaluation using a more comprehensive list of e-commerce websites in the country.

Appendix

Website Name	Website URL
Action Gear	https://www.actiongear.co.za/
Bidorbuy.co.za	https://www.bidorbuy.co.za/
Esque	https://www.esque.co.za/
Flook Sporting Deals	https://www.flook.co.za/
Futurama	https://www.futurama.co.za/
Gemboree	http://www.gemboreeshop.com/
Groupon South Africa	https://www.groupon.com/
HomeChoice	https://www.homechoice.co.za/home.aspx
iToys	https://www.itoys.co.za
Juniva.com	https://www.supps365.co.za/
Kapas Baby & Toddler	https://www.kapasbaby.com
Legwear Safari	http://www.legwearsafari.co.za
LekkeSlaap	https://www.lekkeslaap.co.za/
Loot.co.za	https://www.loot.co.za/welcome
Macaroon Collection	https://macarooncollection.co.za/
Mantality	http://www.mantality.co.za/
Norman Goodfellows	https://www.ngf.co.za/
Orms Direct	https://www.ormsdirect.co.za
Port2Port	https://www.port2port.wine/
Quicket	https://www.quicket.co.za/
Raru	https://raru.co.za/
Red Square	https://www.redsquare.co.za/
RunwaySale	https://www.runwaysale.co.za
SassyChic.co.za	https://www.sassychic.co.za
Seeds for Africa	https://www.seedsforafrica.co.za/
Simplicity	https://simplicity.co.za
Spree	https://www.spree.co.za/
Superbalist.com	https://superbalist.com/
Takealot.com	https://www.takealot.com/
TravelGround	https://www.travelground.com/
Travelstart	https://www.travelstart.co.za/
WebAntics Online	https://www.webantics.com/
Wellness Warehouse	https://www.wellnesswarehouse.com/
Wootware	https://www.wootware.co.za/
Yuppiechef.com	https://www.yuppiechef.com/
Zando	https://www.zando.co.za/
ZumbaWear South Africa	http://zumbawearsouthafrica.co.za

References

1. Kim, Y., Peterson, R.A.: A meta-analysis of online trust relationships in e-commerce. J. Interact. Mark. **38**, 44–54 (2017)
2. Verkijika, S.F.: Factors influencing the adoption of mobile commerce applications in Cameroon. Telematics Inform. **35**, 1665–1674 (2018). https://doi.org/10.1016/j.tele.2018.04.012
3. Mybroadband.co.za: Takealot's plan to grow its R2.3-billion annual revenue (2017). https://mybroadband.co.za/news/business/229775-takealots-plan-to-grow-its-r2-3-billion-annual-revenue.html. Accessed 26 Apr 2018
4. Fin24.Com: Spree records 500% growth (2014). https://www.fin24.com/Companies/Retail/Spree-records-500-growth-20140221. Accessed 26 Apr 2018
5. Smith, C.: How e-commerce is exploding in SA (2018). https://www.fin24.com/Economy/how-ecommerce-is-exploding-in-sa-20180316. Accessed 26 Apr 2018
6. Ndyali, L.: Adaptation and barriers of e-commerce in Tanzania small and medium enterprises. Dev. Country Stud. **3**(4), 100–105 (2013)
7. Herley, C., Van Oorschot, P.: A research agenda acknowledging the persistence of passwords. IEEE Secur. Priv. **10**, 28–36 (2012)
8. Shen, C., Yu, T., Xu, H., Yang, G., Guan, X.: User practice in password security: an empirical study of real-life passwords in the wild. Comput. Secur. **6**, 130–141 (2016)
9. Burr, W.E., Dodson, D.F., Newton, E.M., Perlner, R.A., Polk, W.T., Gupta, S., et al.: Sp 800-63-1: electronic authentication guideline. In: National Institute of Standards and Technology (2011)
10. Furnell, S.: An assessment of website password practices. Comput. Secur. **26**, 445–451 (2007)
11. Furnell, S., Khern-am-nuai, W., Esmael, R., Yang, W., Li, N.: Enhancing security behaviour by supporting the user. Comput. Secur. **75**, 1–9 (2018)
12. Furnell, S.: Password practices on leading websites–revisited. Comput. Fraud Secur. **12**, 5–11 (2014)
13. Butler, R., Butler, M.: The password practices applied by South African online consumers: perception versus reality. S. Afr. J. Inf. Manage. **17**(1), 1–11 (2015). Art. #638
14. Clover, J.: Celebrity iCloud accounts compromised by weak passwords, not iCloud breach (2014). www.macrumors.com/2014/09/02/apple-no-celebrityicloud-breach/. Accessed 28 Apr 2018
15. Verkijika, S.F.: Evaluating and improving the usability of e-government websites in Sub-Saharan Africa for enhancing citizen adoption and usage. Ph.D. thesis, University of the Free State, Bloemfontein, South Africa (2017)
16. Greene, S.S.: Security Program and Policies: Principles and Practices. Pearson, Indianapolis (2014)
17. Guo, Y., Zhang, Z.: LPSE: lightweight password-strength estimation for password meters. Comput. Secur. **73**, 507–518 (2018)
18. Splashdata: Worst passwords of 2017: Top 100 (2017). https://s13639.pcdn.co/wp-content/uploads/2017/12/Top-100-Worst-Passwords-of-2017a.pdf. Accessed 8 July 2018
19. Segreti, S.M., Melicher, W., Komanduri, S., Melicher, D., Shay, R., Ur, B., et al.: Diversify to survive: making passwords stronger with adaptive policies. In: Symposium on Usable Privacy and Security (SOUPS) (2017)
20. Ur, B., Alfieri, F., Aung, M., Bauer, L., Christin, N., Colnago, J., et al.: Design and evaluation of a data-driven password meter. In: Proceedings of the 2017 CHI Conference on Human Factors in Computing Systems, pp. 3775–3786. ACM (2017)

21. Stuart, T.: 50 of South Africa's top e-commerce sites (2015). http://ventureburn.com/2015/08/50-south-africas-top-ecommerce-sites/. Accessed 1 Apr 2018
22. Rankin, K.: Why final passwords are at least 12 characters (2016). https://getfinal.com/company-news/2016/03/08/why-final-passwords-are-at-least-12-characters/. Accessed 2 May 2018
23. Gamby, R.: Minimum password length best practices: are 14-character passwords necessary? (2012). https://searchsecurity.techtarget.com/answer/Minimum-password-length-best-practices-Are-14-character-passwords-necessary. Accessed 2 May 2018
24. Cross, M.: Social Media Security: Leveraging Social Networking While Mitigating Risk. Syngress, Waltham (2014)
25. Komanduri, S., Shay, R., Kelley, P.G., Mazurek, M.L., Bauer, L., Christin, N., et al.: Of passwords and people: measuring the effect of password-composition policies. In: Proceedings of the SIGCHI Conference on Human Factors in Computing Systems, pp. 2595–604 (2011)
26. Shay, R., Komanduri, S., Kelley, P.G., Leon, P.G., Mazurek, M.L., Bauer, L., et al.: Encountering stronger password requirements: user attitudes and behaviors. In: Proceedings of the Sixth Symposium on Usable Privacy and Security, pp. 1–20 (2010)

SA-EF Cube: An Evaluation Framework for Assessing Intelligent Context-Aware Critical Information Infrastructure Protection Solutions

Jan Hendrik van Niekerk[(⊠)] and Elizabeth Marie Ehlers

Academy of Computer Science and Software Engineering,
University of Johannesburg, Johannesburg, South Africa
janvanniekerk0@gmail.com, emehlers@uj.ac.za

Abstract. Advances in technologies such as cloud computing and Bring Your Own Technology (BYOT) environments have dramatically changed the way in which organisations do business. Critical Information Infrastructure (CII) is at the core of this revolution, yet it has become an almost impossible task to protect CII against all possible threats effectively. Multi Agent Systems (MASs) and have addressed Critical Information Infrastructure Protection (CIIP) from unique ways, yet these approaches often lack a sufficient contextualisation of the environment and its dynamism. Without a sufficient contextualisation of an environment and the dynamism that is associated with it, an automated CIIP mechanism will never be truly effective. To address this contextualisation problem that autonomous CIIP-mechanism face, the SA-EF Cube model is proposed. The model can be used as a "checklist" to assess if an autonomous CIIP solution covers the fundamental requirements to contextualise the problem domain of CIIP. The SA-EF Cube model is by no means exhaustive in nature, serves as solid foundation for an implementation checklist before any CIIP mechanism is contextualised and developed.

Keywords: Self-awareness · Ambient intelligence
Critical Information Infrastructure Protection · Multi Agent Systems
Evaluation framework · Artificial Immune Systems

1 Introduction

The 21st century has brought upon an influx of technological advances, which has drastically altered the way in which organisations drive business operations. Advances in cloud computing and BYOT environments (to name but a few) have had a positive impact from an employee productivity point of view for organisations, but the same beneficial technological advancements also bring additional risks to an organisation [1, 2]. Organisations have adopted CII as the core life-blood of the organisation [2], creating a dynamic environment where business is conducted in an electronic manner [3, 4]. Without the effective protection of CII being put in place, an organisation can be devastated from a reputational and financial point of view if any vulnerability is to be exploited [3, 4, 10].

© Springer Nature Switzerland AG 2019
H. Venter et al. (Eds.): ISSA 2018, CCIS 973, pp. 115–132, 2019.
https://doi.org/10.1007/978-3-030-11407-7_9

CIIP is the process whereby mechanisms, technologies and processes are put in place to protect CII from both internal as well as external threats [3, 5–8]. It is important to realise that CII can be physical or virtual by nature, creating complexities that should be considered during the holistic CIIP process. Figure 1 visualises the complexity of CII, and why protection thereof can be a difficult task [8, 10] – this is as a direct result of the distributed nature of CII. Furthermore, BYOT environments add additional complexity as on-demand networks will also form part of CII, and as such, requires the same level of "on demand" protection.

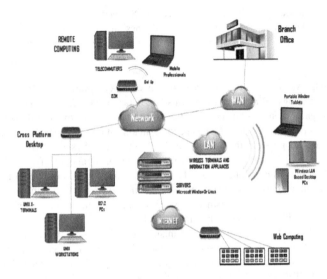

Fig. 1. Visualising the complexity of CII in the 21st century [9]

CIIP is made more complex in an organisation because of BYOT environment, internal and external information exchange, employee complacency and the globalised threat of cyber terrorism [11–15]. To visualise the inter-dependencies which arise within an organisation, Fig. 2 visualises a business model covering Information Security (IS) as part of planning for effective and efficient CIIP within an organisation. The dynamic relationship between the nodes and vertices indicate that changes to one node (component) can potentially impact another node, prompting careful consideration and due diligence to be executed during CIIP [2, 7, 17].

Conventionally CIIP is concerned with ensuring that the three CIA principles are met – these include confidentiality, integrity and availability of CII [2, 5, 7, 18]. Typical CIIP would be implemented within an organisation by one of three means:

- Protection by policy;
- Protection by hardware; and
- Protection by software.

The common issue that repeats throughout the approaches is the lack of robustness, flexibility and adaptability. Policies are often high-level directives which are defined by an organisation's appetite for risks in relation to certain CII aspects [19–21]. These policies are not regularly updated and suffer from a lack of employee awareness and application, creating soft vulnerabilities within an organisation's CII.

Protection by hardware enables an organisation to isolate CII from the external exploitation, but it does provide a single point of failure which is static by nature [8, 11, 12, 22, 23]. With the dynamism of CIIP and information exchange that occurs daily, the lack of robustness makes effective CIIP a difficult task.

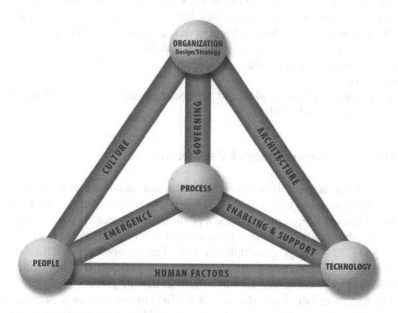

Fig. 2. Visualising inter-dependencies for an organisation's IS [16]

Protection by software can take on the form of something elementary such as anti-virus software, or something a bit more advanced such as an Intrusion Detection System (IDS). The caveat that occurs with this approach is that mechanisms are often expensive to implement and maintain, and there is a general lack of adaptability that is required for dynamic CIIP [24, 25]. One aspect is clear, conventional CIIP mechanisms, technologies and processes are indeed fallible.

2 Structure of Paper

This research paper starts off by providing a contextualised review of the problem domain – CIIP - and the considerations which would typically have to be made when implementing CIIP solutions. Included in this discussion is the typical approaches which are taken when providing CIIP, as well as the common caveats that these approaches would suffer.

This is then followed by a literature review in which non-conventional CIIP solutions are discussed. The non-conventional approach to CIIP specifically focuses on how MASs and their respective processes and components can be utilised to improve the overall effectiveness and efficiency of CIIP within an organisation.

Section 4 then elaborates on CIIP within an organisation, by specifically addressing contextualisation within the CIIP process. The importance of contextualisation of a dynamic environment is highlighted, as well as the general lack of contextualisation which occurs in non-conventional CIIP solutions.

Following on from the problem domain discussions and the general exclusion of contextualisation within dynamic problem domains such as CIIP, Sect. 5 focusses on proposing an evaluation framework (SA-EF Cube) for contextually aware CIIP solutions. The purpose of the evaluation framework is to serve as a checklist for new CIIP solutions during the various stages of research and development.

The research paper then concludes by performing a critical evaluation and discussing future work.

Next, section three looks at MAS and Artificial Immune Systems (AIS) approach-es which are geared towards CIIP.

3   CIIP: A Non-conventional Perspective

MASs have been at the forefront of concurrent and simultaneous problem-solving processes for quite some time [26, 27]. MASs can potentially be very useful for the problem domain of CIIP, as they provide a platform for automated distributed problem solving, whereby agents can achieve local utility as well as collaborate to reach global utility targets [28]. Deploying multiple agents into an environment enables the agents to solve problems concurrently, as each agent can perceive the environment and execute actions, post the deliberation and decision-making process [7, 28, 29].

MASs can potentially be useful within a CIIP environment as it provides some ideal characteristics which are suitable for the problem domain. These capabilities include self-deliberation processes, concurrent problem-solving capabilities and knowledge sharing between agents to improve collective utility [7, 28–31]. Some interesting applications of MAS to the problem domain of CIIP include:

- Utilising a fuzzy-logic driven, knowledge sharing and influencer approach where agents can learn and adapt [32];
- Establishing a platform whereby hardware and software agents collaborate to address the protection of CII that covers two of the three means addressed in Sect. 1 [33];
- The best characteristic selection approach whereby only the most suitable processes and components are incorporated into a MAS to provide the best possible utility [7, 34]; and
- Utilising evolutionary-inspired processes whereby agents can proliferate and co-exists in independent populations across CII [35].

Evolutionary-inspired CIIP refers to the use of AISs, their processes, components and dynamics. AISs is a research field wherein analogies are drawn between the Human Immune System (HIS) and computer-related applications thereof. At a very high level, the HIS provides the ideal analogy for effective and efficient CIIP [36, 37]. The HIS is self-sufficient, has self-regulation capabilities, can perform self-healing processes and can learn and adapt to new threats as and when they occur [37, 38].

There are quite a few HIS processes which provide promising analogies for CIIP. Processes such as Danger Theory[1] and Self/Non-self-discrimination[2] provide analogies for CIIP mechanisms to analyse, deliberate and discriminate/flag anomalous elements that can occur within CII [37, 39]. Some interesting applications of AISs to the problem domain of CIIP include:

- A Bee-colony inspired approach geared towards improving fault tolerance within CIIP [40];
- A sync-inspired Danger Theory approach whereby elements can sync with one another to calculate abnormalities between potentially harmful elements within an environment [41]; and
- A novel combination of Positive Selection and Negative Selection algorithms with a view to reduce several elements which are required to effectively govern the protection of an environment – which also improved the efficiency in which elements in an environment could be analysed [42].

The interesting applications of MASs and AISs which have been mentioned are by no means exhaustive, but provides some contextualisation to an underlying fundamental issue – contextualisation. Conventional and non-conventional CIIP mechanisms often suffer as a direct result of contextualisation being omitted.

It has been well established that CII operate in a dynamic environment where the only constant element is change [2, 3, 5]. Potential threats occur from both internal as well as external sources. It can be logically deduced then that any CIIP mechanism should be able to dynamically adapt and learn, taking into consideration the contextualisation of the environment, its state and the dynamism that is at play at any given instant [43, 44].

If any CIIP mechanisms are to be truly effective, it requires the ability to "understand" the environment, a term that is loosely used within any dynamic environment. "Understanding" an environment requires the ability to be instilled with knowledge, capacity to learn, capacity to proliferate and capacity to adapt to events as and when they occur.

Next, Sect. 4 discusses the contextualisation aspect of CII and CIIP mechanisms in more detail.

---

[1] A HIS process whereby elements are classified as harmful or not. This process enables non-self-elements to live within the environment as long as they are non-malicious in nature.

[2] A HIS process whereby discrimination occurs between elements which form part of the self and those which do not.

4 Self-awareness and Ambient Intelligence: A CIIP Perspective

Section one and section three hinted towards some form of contextualisation being present within MASs and AISs. MASs can be instilled with the ability to learn and deliberate, while an AIS can use the analogy of a memory cell to ensure an abstracted form of learning is realisable [7, 28, 37, 45]. Contextualisation or self-awareness is an important characteristic, which is highlighted in more detail later in this section.

Another key characteristic is Ambient Intelligence (AmI), which refers to the process whereby different research fields, components or technologies can be combined to explore a complex and dynamic problem from an innovative perspective [33, 46]. AmI is a key requirement if any CIIP mechanisms are to ensure effective security while still operating autonomously.

4.1 Self-awareness Within CIIP

At a very high-level, self-awareness refers to the abstracted cognitive ability that enables something or someone to create an understanding of an environment [47–49]. From a CIIP perspective, self-awareness can establish an intro- as well as extrospection capability that would enable a CIIP mechanism to adapt to an ever-changing environment and elements within the environment. This can be analogous to the process of mimicking reasoning.

Establishing an abstracted notion of reasoning within a CIIP mechanism or technology can potentially enable a CIIP mechanism to continually reach the maxi-mum possible utility regardless of the specific definition of utility [50, 51], effectively making the utility measurement process problem domain agnostic. Figure 3 provides a high-level overview of abstracted reasoning. As per Fig. 3, reasoning is a complex action which requires various capabilities which could overlap in certain regions.

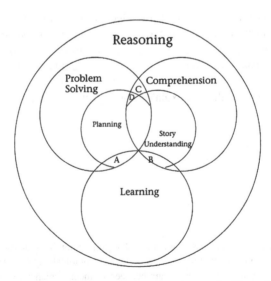

Fig. 3. The dimensions of abstracted reasoning applicable to CIIP [51]

For any automated CIIP mechanism to be truly effective and efficient in a dynamic environment, the mechanism requires the ability to deliberate (with reasoning) and adapt to elements in the environment as well as changes to the environment [7, 34, 46, 50]. MASs and AISs both provide some foundational characteristics with which self-awareness can be realised, but often self-awareness is not deliberately expressed as a characteristic of a solution that addresses CIIP [7, 34, 36].

4.2 Ambient Intelligence (AmI) Within CIIP

AmI was briefly introduced in Sect. 4 as the process whereby different research fields, processes and components are amalgamated in order to explore novel new approaches geared towards solving problems of a complex nature, one of which is CIIP. Within AmI, input and output are completely removed. Instead percepts and sensors play a key role.

The fundamental shift in using percepts and sensors promotes self-deliberation and reasoning capabilities in an abstracted manner. It also enables different approaches because of amalgamation, to facilitate communication and ensure complementary actions can follow [33, 43, 46, 52]. As was the case with self-awareness, AmI is often not deliberately expressed within CIIP mechanisms and technologies.

From a deductive reasoning approach, it would be beneficial to incorporate abstracted self-awareness and AmI into any CIIP mechanism, as it would enable such a mechanism to adapt to the dynamic nature of the problem domain, while exploring novel new approaches or solutions that can potentially improve the work that precedes it [44, 51, 52].

Section 4.3 will elaborate on why any CIIP mechanism should include self-awareness and AmI.

4.3 Dynamism of CIIP: Why You Would Need a Self-aware AmI Solution

Throughout Sects. 1 and 3, it has been well established that CIIP is a complex and dynamic problem domain. With a multitude of potential points of vulnerabilities introduced with aspects such as BYOT environments and geographically dispersed CII, ensuring effective and efficient CIIP is a difficult exercise [53, 54]. An organisation can also have CII outside the conventional CII (such as BYOT environments), making it difficult to govern security principles and protocols outside an organisation's physical and virtual environments.

Conventional CIIP mechanisms, technologies and policies would typically span a protection approach across two dimensions. Firstly, a preventative approach can be used to protect CII from known vulnerabilities and prevent those from being exploited [3, 55]. Secondly, a responsive approach can be taken post an exploitation of CII occurring [56].

The problem lies in ensuring end-to-end protection, as there are more than two dimensions that must be address. These two dimensions can potentially be addressed by implementing self-awareness and AmI within a CIIP mechanism. These requirements will be addressed in Sect. 5 as part of the evaluation model.

In order for an end-to-end CIIP solution to be realised, it will have to cover four dimensions of protection and not just the typical two mentioned previously.

These dimensions include:

- Proactive dimension – continuously search and explore CII for potential vulnerabilities and raise the required flags in order for overall CIIP to urgently address these;
- Preventative dimension – span the typical protection of CII in order ensure that the CIA principles mentioned in Sect. 1 are achieved;
- Reactive dimension – implementing capabilities into CIIP mechanisms that would enable them to instantaneously respond to stimuli from both internal and external elements, potentially preventing the exploitation of CII before it occurs; and
- Responsive dimension – Addressing CII after an exploitation has occurred to prevent the exploitation from reoccurring and to get the CIA principles associated with CII back up to speed.

Conventional CIIP mechanisms do not typically address the Proactive and Reactive dimensions, as these would require "contextualisation" of the environment, elements within and decision-making processes that occur [3, 56–58]. Recent MAS and AIS applications have addressed these problems, but only to a limited extent.

There is thus a clear requirement to incorporate abstracted self-awareness and AmI into any CIIP mechanism, to attempt to cover all four the dimensions of protection. With that in mind, Sect. 5 establishes an evaluation framework which can be used as a guideline to achieve this, which would be applicable to any conventional, or non-conventional CIIP mechanism.

5   An Evaluation Framework (EF) for Context-Aware CIIP Solutions

The purpose of an evaluation framework is to outline a set of guiding principles which can be followed when something is designed or implemented [58].

An EF effectively creates a "checklist" of aspects which should be addressed, creating a to-do list that can be referenced throughout the design life cycle of any new process, mechanism or technology [59, 60].

Although various EFs exist today, most of them are implementation specific, resulting in less than ideal "checklists" for a complex and dynamic problem domain such as CIIP [58–62]. There will never be a "one size fits all", but combining different aspects of EFs can yield interesting results [61].

Sections 1, 2, 3 and 4 discussed the importance of implementing self-awareness and AmI as part of any CIIP solution, as any CIIP solution would need to contextualise the environment in order to remain effective. The EF which is proposed in this section is by no means entirely exhaustive, but aims to establish a solid foundation for future EFs specific to the CIIP problem domain.

The purpose of the EF is to provide a checklist of considerations which assists in the design, development and implementation of new CIIP solutions in the future [59–61]. Before the EF is proposed, it would be beneficial to understand and revise a globally accepted EF – ISO27000 series.

These set of documents (in association with COBIT) sets a global standard for the implementation of Information Technology Governance (ITG) and Information Security Governance (ISG) [2, 5, 8, 63, 64]. These documents provide a high-level overview of considerations which must be made prior to the implementation of any ISG or ITG solution [63–65]. Figure 4 depicts the COBIT framework, providing a high-level overview. The COBIT document addresses a set of general ITG-related processes and elements which an organization should implement, discuss, assess and monitor.

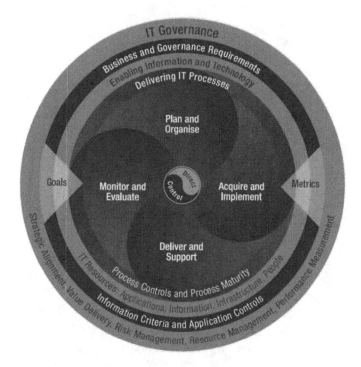

Fig. 4. Overview: COBIT 4.1 [65]

Although there is some overlap between what the documents aim to achieve, the most important take out from these EF documents is that they do not provide implementation specifics [64, 65]. Instead, they establish a checklist of minimum requirements that must be met. This is an important aspect which is utilised as part of the EF.

5.1 The SA-EF Cube – Self-aware Ambient Intelligent Evaluation Framework Cube

In accordance with what was mentioned in Sect. 4, the purpose of the SA-EF Cube is not to be entirely exhaustive when developing context-aware CIIP solutions, but to set the foundational framework which can be expanded upon in future research. The emphasis is placed on providing the outlying framework, dimensions and processes which form part of the SA-EF Cube.

At a very high level, the SA-EF Cube is effectively a checklist that describes aspects and dimensions which must be considered when any new CIIP solution is planned, designed and implemented. Emphasis is placed on having analogies of self-awareness and AmI embedded into any potential CIIP solution. Figure 5 depicts the SA-EF Cube.

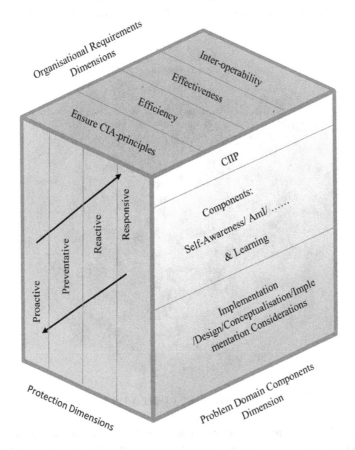

Fig. 5. The SA-EF Cube overview

The SA-EF Cube highlights three core dimensions, which can be used to address the fundamentals of CIIP. The three core dimensions are driven by:

- The components, processes and elements which can be used in the implementation of a CIIP solution;
- The dimensions of protection which need to be implemented to effectively protect CII; and
- The organisation's business requirements which act as a conduit for CIIP.

Each of the three core primary dimensions consists of a set of principles and directives. The role of the principles are to highlight areas which need to be addressed, while the directives provide high-level details on what is expected from that principle, specifically from a CIIP solution point of view. The rest of Sect. 5.1 addresses the three core dimensions in more detail, as well as provide the principles and directives which form part of the three dimensions.

It is important to note that the SA-EF Cube is intended to serve as a "checklist", and as such a scoring methodology relative to the CIIP mechanism would be beneficial. At a directive level, a person can score their planned approach with a score between 0 and 1 (in 0.25 intervals) based on their assessment as depicted in Table 1. These scores would then role up into overall principal score, before rolling up into an overall dimension-based score. Utilising this matrix style approach enables the developer of a contextually-aware CIIP solution to quickly gauge the areas where improvement is required. Table 1 depicts an example of what a rolled-up scoring matrix could look like:

Table 1. The SA-EF Cube assessment scoring example

Dimension	Principle	Directive	Finding	Score
Front	Pc 1	Dt 1	Not compliant	0
Front	Pc 1	Dt 2	Planned	0.25
Front	Pc 1	Dt 3	Somewhat adequate	0.5
Front	Pc 1	Dt 4	Almost sufficient	0.75
Front	Pc 1	Dt 5	Sufficient	1

For the remainder of this section, the SA-EF cube will be briefly discussed through the assessment of a top South African university's CIIP who is currently assessing implementing an additional layer of CIIP in the form of an AIS-inspired MAS. The conventional CIIP mechanisms would include a firewall, IDS, proxy and anti-virus software. For illustration purposes, an assessment is performed for all directives which form part of the Front-facing dimension.

5.2   The Front Facing Dimension

As per Fig. 5, the front facing dimension is focussed on creating an understanding of the problem domain, components which constitute the CIIP solution and how these components and processes fit together. The principle that governs this dimension is focusses on the contextualisation of the problem domain. For the rest of Sect. 5, principles will be denoted by Pc and directives by Dt.

Pc 1: Protection of Critical Information Infrastructure

- Dt 1 – Define what effective and efficient protection of CII constitutes within the applicable domain;
- Dt 2 – Outline the dynamisms and establish an understanding of the environment;
- Dt 3 – Identify CIIP-related policies and solutions which are currently operational within the target CII;

- Dt 4 – Attribute the role of each solution as per Dt 3 and establish a landscape overview of the CII-environment;
- Dt 5 – Establish potential approaches which describe how new CIIP solutions can fit into the target environment, in line with Dt 3 and Dt 4; and
- Dt 6 – Identify both the potential positive and negative impact that the envisioned solution can have on the current CIIP solutions (Table 2).

Table 2. The SA-EF Cube assessment scoring example of Pc 1

Directive	Score	Comment
Dt 1	1	Organisation has defined policies on what CIIP entails
Dt 2	.75	Not all dynamisms are well documented, especially BYOD environments
Dt 3	1	Well documented best practices
Dt 4	.75	Some CIIP solutions implemented hinder operations
Dt 5	.5	Current CIIP is very rigid, an application of MAS/AIS would not currently be possible
Dt 6	0	Current CIIP would not operate with additional non-conventional CIIP mechanisms

Pc 2: Components of the CIIP solution should be effective, efficient and intelligent by nature

- Dt 7 – Post assessment of Pc 1 and its directives, a clear understanding and acknowledgement is required that there is no all-encompassing solution;
- Dt 8 – Prior to the conceptualisation of any new CIIP solution, one or more research fields can be applied/amalgamated. Have the ideal characteristics of these research fields/components/processes been defined?;
- Dt 9 – The protection of CII is a problem of a dynamic nature. As such, and following on from Dt 8, has the areas of interest been well defined and established to address this dynamism?;
- Dt 10 – Has deliberation and decision-making processes been assessed in detail for any new solution?
- Dt 11 – An internalisation of a performance measurement is required to ensure proliferation of any CIIP solution. Does this measurement enable both local and global maximum utility to be achieved? Is all references to inputs and outputs replaced with percept, sensors and actuators?;
- Dt 12 – Does the proposed CIIP solution incorporate an abstraction of deductive reasoning?;
- Dt 13 – In accordance with Dt 11 and Dt 12, does the solution consist of components and processes which could be considered "intelligent"?;
- Dt 14 – Is cognition addressed in any form of analogy within the solution?;
- Dt 15 – An abstracted notion of self-awareness is required to contribute towards Dt 14; and
- Dt 16 – Does the proposed solution consider AmI in any form or factor, and contribute towards Dt 8, Dt 9 and Dt 14?

5.3   The Side Facing Dimension

As per Fig. 5, the side facing dimension is concerned with how the front facing dimension's Pcs and Dts address the protection of CII across the four dimensions of protection. As mentioned earlier in Sect. 4.3, typical CIIP solutions only address two of the four dimensions, often leaving potential vulnerabilities (Table 3).

Table 3. The SA-EF Cube assessment scoring example of Pc 2

Directive	Score	Comment
Dt 7	.5	Organisation will have to communicate to all stakeholders
Dt 8	1	Ideal characteristics well defined
Dt 9	1	Well documented in the form of a detailed report
Dt 10	.75	Yes, but the organisation is reliant on external professional support
Dt 11	1	The proposal to implement the MAS CIIP mechanisms does bare reference in all instances
Dt 12	.5	Given the detailed proposal, it would appear so, but an additional investigation is required
Dt 13	1	Intelligent and autonomous by nature
Dt 14	.5	Cognition is not as detailed as it should be
Dt 15	.75	Context-awareness is well documented
Dt 16	1	Yes, on all accounts

The side facing dimension is driven by the following Pc and Dts:

Pc 3: Ensure protection of CII in its dynamic environment occurs across all four dimensions of protection

- Dt 17 – The proposed CIIP solution should actively seek out changes in the environment that could lead to new vulnerabilities;
- Dt 18 – Does active protection against known internal and external threats form part of the underlying architecture of the CIIP solution?
- Dt 19 – Does the CIIP solution contain the ability to respond to the stimulation which is created by the presence of foreign elements? and
- Dt 20 – Does the CIIP solution consists of the ability to isolate exploitation events to limit the impact on CII and its operations?

5.4   The Organisational Requirements Dimension

As per Fig. 5, the top facing dimension places emphasis on the organisational requirements that drive CII and the protection thereof. It is important to realise that there is a direct relationship between the organisational requirements and the proposal of a new CIIP solution, specifically one that satisfies the list of Pcs and Dts.

The organisational requirements, the organisation's CII and the dynamism of the environment should factor into the design of any new CIIP solution. If a solution does not satisfy an organisation's requirements, the solution will fail inevitably.

The top facing dimension is driven by two Pcs:

- *Pc 4: Contextualisation of organisational requirements as input mechanisms for CIIP solution*
- Dt 21 – The CIA-principles are crucial in the CIIP process. Is this addressed in the proposed solution?
- Dt 22 – Efficiency is key and as such specific reference must made with regards to efficiency as a driver within the proposed solution;
- Dt 23 – Without effectiveness of CIIP solutions, CII will not be able to support and drive business processes. Is this taken into consideration in accordance with Dt 22;
- Dt 24 – When different elements are introduced into a dynamic environment, utility suppression and interference is bound to occur. Is this concern addressed within the context of the solution? and
- Dt 25 – There is no all-encompassing CIIP solution, but more effective solutions can be established by developing CIIP solutions that perform complementary functions. Is extensibility and integration taken into consideration?

Considering the scenario of a top South African university who is assessing implementing an AIS-inspired MAS, the team responsible for maintaining the CIIP within the organisation can utilise the scoring matrix to report back to stakeholders, as well as track their progress.

6 Critical Evaluation and Future Work

From a holistic perspective, the SA-EF Cube is effective in its endeavours to create a "checklist" scoring matrix which can be used when new CIIP solutions are designed, developed and implemented within the problem domain.

Although the purpose of the proposed EF is not to be entirely exhaustive by nature, and to act as a guideline for CIIP solutions, there are some areas of improvement which can be implemented. These also form part of the future work associated with the SA-EF Cube.

The SA-EF Cube establishes a basic guideline/checklist driven matrix which can be useful to new CIIP solutions, but industry standards and considerations will have to be considered. The reason that the ISO series documents are so widely received and recognised is as a direct result of the principles therein being completely aligned with organisational goals, objectives and key drivers. The SA-EF Cube model can benefit from consulting industry and organisational CIIP experts to incorporate their inputs into the model.

The SA-EF Cube provides a fundamental checklist approach, but given the 3-dimensional nature of the Cube, it would be beneficial to incorporate a more formal way of "scoring" a solution in accordance with the principled and directives which were listed in Sect. 5. The basic scoring matrix of the SA-EF Cube could also enable organisation to compare potential vendors and different solutions of CIIP, as well as benchmark their "overall health" against their industry standards once they exist.

7 Conclusion

Throughout this research paper, the emphasis for contextually aware CIIP solutions was made clear. For any automated CIIP solution to become truly effective and efficient, such a solution would require very specific aspects to be incorporated into the solution.

Self-awareness and AmI will play a pivotal role in such a solution, as without these characteristics a CIIP solution will not be able to proliferate and remain effective continually.

In order to assist in this process of incorporating contextualisation of an environment into any CIIP solution, the SA-EF Cube model was proposed which can be used a guideline document or checklist. The purpose of this EF was to ensure that all the high-level requirements are considered when a new CIIP solution is designed, developed, implemented and assessed.

The SA-EF Cube can benefit from some of the future work which was discussed in Sect. 6, but remains effective in its endeavors to provide a guideline document geared towards improving the future of CIIP solutions within an organisation.

References

1. Bruque, S., Moyano, J., Maqueira, J.M.: Use of cloud computing, web 2, 0 and operational performance: the role of supply chain integration. In: Academy of Management Proceedings, vol. 2014, no. 1, p. 10524. Academy of Management (2014)
2. von Solms, S.H., von Solms, R.: Information Security Governance. Springer, New York (2008). https://doi.org/10.1007/978-0-387-79984-1
3. Hadji-Janev, M.: Threats to the critical information infrastructure protection (CIIP) posed by modern terrorism. In: Critical Information Infrastructure Protection and Resilience in the ICT Sector, vol. 93 (2013)
4. Almklov, P.G., Antonsen, S.: Making work invisible: new public management and operational work in critical infrastructure sectors. Public Adm. **92**(2), 477–492 (2014)
5. Ellefsen, I., von Solms, S.: Implementing critical information infrastructure protection structures in developing countries. In: Butts, J., Shenoi, S. (eds.) ICCIP 2012. IAICT, vol. 390, pp. 17–29. Springer, Heidelberg (2012). https://doi.org/10.1007/978-3-642-35764-0_2
6. Theron, P.: Critical Information Infrastructure Protection and Resilience in the ICT Sector. IGI Global, Hershey (2013)
7. van Niekerk, J.H., Ehlers, E.M.: An immune-inspired multi-agent system for improved critical information infrastructure protection. Suid-Afrikaanse Tydskrif vir Natuurwetenskap en Tegnologie **34**(1) (2015)
8. Wilson, C.: Cyber threats to critical information infrastructure. In: Chen, T.M., Jarvis, L., Macdonald, S. (eds.) Cyberterrorism, pp. 123–136. Springer, New York (2014). https://doi.org/10.1007/978-1-4939-0962-9_7
9. Slideteam.net: Computer Networking, [image] (2015). http://www.slideteam.net/media/catalog/product/cache/1/image/9df78eab33525d08d6e5fb8d27136e95/0/9/0914_complex_networking_diagram_main_office_and_branch_office_wan_lan_and_cloud_ppt_slide_Slide01.jpg. Accessed 8 Mar 2016

10. Kuykendall, M., Wash, R.: Poor decision making can lead to cybersecurity breaches, Michigan State University (2015). http://msutoday.msu.edu/news/2015/poor-decision-making-can-lead-to-cybersecurity-breaches/. Accessed 8 Mar 2016
11. Gaines, J., Martin, E.: Bring Your Own Device: Implementation, Recommendations and Best Practices (2014)
12. Mishra, A., Jani, K.: Comparative study on bring your own technology [BYOT]: applications & security. In: 2015 International Conference on Electrical, Electronics, Signals, Communication and Optimization (EESCO), pp. 1–6. IEEE (2015)
13. Gharajedaghi, J.: Systems Thinking: Managing Chaos and Complexity: A Platform for Designing Business Architecture. Elsevier, San Diego (2011)
14. Skotnes, R.O.: Management commitment and awareness creation-ICT safety and security in electric power supply network companies. Inf. Comput. Secur. **23**, 302–316 (2015)
15. Naccache, D., Sauveron, D. (eds.): WISTP 2014. LNCS, vol. 8501. Springer, Heidelberg (2014). https://doi.org/10.1007/978-3-662-43826-8
16. ISACA: An Introduction to the Business Model for Information Security (2009). http://www.isaca.org/knowledge-center/bmis/documents/introtobmis.pdf. Accessed 9 Mar 2016
17. Kagan, A., Cant, A.: Information security: a socio-technical solution for homeland security threats within small to medium sized enterprises (SMEs). Homeland Secur. Rev. **8**, 147 (2014)
18. Sumra, I.A., Hasbullah, H.B., AbManan, J.-L.B.: Attacks on security goals (confidentiality, integrity, availability) in VANET: a survey. In: Laouiti, A., Qayyum, A., Mohamad Saad, M. N. (eds.) Vehicular Ad-hoc Networks for Smart Cities. AISC, vol. 306, pp. 51–61. Springer, Singapore (2015). https://doi.org/10.1007/978-981-287-158-9_5
19. Ellefsen, I.: The development of a cyber security policy in developing regions and the impact on stakeholders. In: IST-Africa Conference Proceedings 2014, p. 1–10. IEEE (2014)
20. Luiijf, E., Klaver, M., Nieuwenhuijs, A.: RECIPE–Good Practices for CIP Policy-Makers. The CIP report, vol. 9, pp. 13–14 (2011)
21. Robinson, N.: Information sharing for CIP: between policy, theory, and practice. In: Securing Critical Infrastructures and Critical Control Systems: Approaches for Threat Protection: Approaches for Threat Protection, vol. 324 (2012)
22. Ardagna, C.A., Asal, R., Damiani, E., Vu, Q.H.: From security to assurance in the cloud: a survey. ACM Comput. Surv. (CSUR) **48**(1), 2 (2015)
23. Bygstad, B.: Generative mechanisms for innovation in information infrastructures. Inf. Organ. **20**(3), 156–168 (2010)
24. Sophos: Security Threat Trends 2015 (2015). https://www.sophos.com/en-us/threat-center/medialibrary/PDFs/other/sophos-trends-and-predictions-2015.pdf. Accessed 6 Apr 2015
25. Bilge, L., Dumitras, T.: Before we knew it: an empirical study of zero-day attacks in the real world. In: Proceedings of the 2012 ACM Conference on Computer and Communications Security, pp. 833–844. ACM (2012)
26. Ferber, J.: Multi-agent Systems: An Introduction to Distributed Artificial Intelligence, vol. 1. Addison-Wesley, Reading (1999)
27. Jennings, N.R.: On agent-based software engineering. Artif. Intell. **117**(2), 277–296 (2000)
28. Wooldridge, M.: An Introduction to Multi Agent Systems. Wiley, West Sussex (2008)
29. Wooldridge, M., Jennigs, N.R.: Intelligent agents: theory and practice. Knowl. Eng. Rev. **10** (2), 115–152 (2009)
30. Daradoumis, T., Bassi, R., Xhafa, F., Caballé, S.: A review on massive e-learning (MOOC) design, delivery and assessment. In: 2013 Eighth International Conference on Parallel, Grid, Cloud and Internet Computing (3PGCIC), pp. 208–213. IEEE (2013)
31. Ouyang, M.: Review on modeling and simulation of interdependent critical infrastructure systems. Reliab. Eng. Syst. Saf. **121**, 43–60 (2014)

32. Shamshirband, S., Anuar, N.B., Kiah, M.L.M., Patel, A.: An appraisal and design of a multi-agent system based cooperative wireless intrusion detection computational intelligence technique. Eng. Appl. Artif. Intell. **26**(9), 2105–2127 (2013)
33. Tapia, D.I., Fraile, J.A., Rodríguez, S., Alonso, R.S., Corchado, J.M.: Integrating hardware agents into an enhanced multi-agent architecture for Ambient Intelligence systems. Inf. Sci. **222**, 47–65 (2013)
34. Heydenrych, M.: An adaptive multi-agent architecture for critical information infrastructure protection. Doctoral dissertation (2014). https://ujdigispace.uj.ac.za/bitstream/handle/10210/12370/Heydenrych,%20Mark.%20M.%20Sc.%202014.pdf?sequence=1. Accessed 10 Mar 2015
35. Byrski, A., Dreżewski, R., Siwik, L., Kisiel-Dorohinicki, M.: Evolutionary multi-agent systems. Knowl. Eng. Rev. **30**(2), 171–186 (2015)
36. Aickelin, U., Dasgupta, D., Gu, F.: Artificial immune systems. Search Methodologies, pp. 187–211. Springer, Boston (2014). https://doi.org/10.1007/978-1-4614-6940-7_7
37. Dasgupta, D., Nino, F.: Immunological Computation: Theory and Applications. Auerbach Publications, Boston (2008)
38. Ghosh, D., Sharman, R., Rao, H.R., Upadhyaya, S.: Self-healing systems - survey and synthesis. Decis. Support Syst. **42**(4), 2164–2185 (2007)
39. Phogat, S., Gupta, N.: Basics of artificial immune system and its applications. Int. J. Sci. Res. Educ. **3**(5) (2015)
40. Huang, S.J., Liu, X.Z.: Application of artificial bee colony-based optimization for fault section estimation in power systems. Int. J. Electr. Power Energy Syst. **44**(1), 210–218 (2013)
41. Shamshirband, S., et al.: Co-FAIS: cooperative fuzzy artificial immune system for detecting intrusion in wireless sensor networks. J. Netw. Comput. Appl. **42**, 102–117 (2014)
42. Van, T.N., Xuan, H.N., Chi, M.L.: A novel combination of negative and positive selection in artificial immune systems. VNU J. Sci. Comput. Sci. Commun. Eng. **31**(1), 22–31 (2015)
43. Acampora, G., Cook, D.J., Rashidi, P., Vasilakos, A.V.: A survey on ambient intelligence in healthcare. Proc. IEEE **101**(12), 2470–2494 (2013)
44. Mohamed, A., Novais, P., Pereira, A., Villarrubia González, G., Fernández-Caballero, A. (eds.): Ambient Intelligence - Software and Applications. AISC, vol. 376. Springer, Cham (2015). https://doi.org/10.1007/978-3-319-19695-4
45. Lewis, P.R., et al.: A survey of self-awareness and its application in computing systems. In: 2011 Fifth IEEE Conference on Self-Adaptive and Self-Organizing Systems Workshops (SASOW), pp. 102–107. IEEE (2011)
46. Bohn, J., Coroamă, V., Langheinrich, M., Mattern, F., Rohs, M.: Social, economic, and ethical implications of ambient intelligence and ubiquitous computing. In: Weber, W., Rabaey, J.M., Aarts, E. (eds.) Ambient Intelligence, pp. 5–29. Springer, Heidelberg (2005). https://doi.org/10.1007/3-540-27139-2_2
47. Duval, S., Wicklund, R.A.: Effects of objective self-awareness on attribution of causality. J. Exp. Soc. Psychol. **9**(1), 17–31 (1973)
48. Vago, D.R., David, S.A.: Self-awareness, self-regulation, and self-transcendence (S-ART): a framework for understanding the neurobiological mechanisms of mindfulness. Frontiers Hum. Neurosci. **6**, 296 (2012)
49. de Lemos, R., et al.: Software engineering for self-adaptive systems: a second research roadmap. In: de Lemos, R., Giese, H., Müller, H.A., Shaw, M. (eds.) Software Engineering for Self-Adaptive Systems II. LNCS, vol. 7475, pp. 1–32. Springer, Heidelberg (2013). https://doi.org/10.1007/978-3-642-35813-5_1
50. Yuan, E., Esfahani, N., Malek, S.: A systematic survey of self-protecting software systems. ACM Trans. Auton. Adapt. Syst. (TAAS) **8**(4), 17 (2014)

51. Cox, M.T.: Perpetual self-aware cognitive agents. AI Mag. **28**(1), 32 (2007)
52. Aarts, E., et al.: Ambient Intelligence: European Conference, vol. 8850. Springer, Cham (2015). https://doi.org/10.1007/978-3-319-14112-1
53. Laugé, A., Hernantes, J., Sarriegi, J.M.: Critical infrastructure dependencies: a holistic, dynamic and quantitative approach. Int. J. Crit. Infrastruct. Prot. **8**, 16–23 (2015)
54. Sansurooh, K., Williams, P.A.: BYOD in ehealth: herding cats and stable doors, or a catastrophe waiting to happen? Australian eHealth Informatics and Security Conference, Edith Cowan University (2014)
55. Bessani, A.N., Sousa, P., Correia, M., Neves, N.F., Verissimo, P.: The CRUTIAL way of critical infrastructure protection. Secur. Priv. **6**(6), 44–51 (2008)
56. Lopez, J., Setola, R., Wolthusen, S.D.: Overview of critical information infrastructure protection. In: Lopez, J., Setola, R., Wolthusen, S.D. (eds.) Critical Infrastructure Protection 2011. LNCS, vol. 7130, pp. 1–14. Springer, Heidelberg (2012). https://doi.org/10.1007/978-3-642-28920-0_1
57. Pastrana, S., Montero-Castillo, J., Orfila, A.: Evading IDSs and firewalls as fundamental sources of information in SIEMs. In: Advances in Security Information Management: Perceptions and Outcomes. Nova Science Publishers, Inc. (2013). http://www.seg.inf.uc3m.es/papers/2013nova-evasion.pdf. Accessed 12 Mar 2016
58. Sun, Y.L., Han, Z., Yu, W., Liu, K.R.: A trust evaluation framework in distributed networks: vulnerability analysis and defense against attacks. INFOCOM **6**, 1–13 (2006)
59. Kahan, B.: Review of evaluation frameworks, prepared for saskatchewan ministry of education (2008). http://www.idmbestpractices.ca/pdf/evaluation-frameworks-review.pdf. Accessed 13 Mar 2016
60. Kahan, B., Goodstadt, M.: The IDM manual - sections on: basics, suggested guidelines, evidence framework, research and evaluation, using the IDM framework, Centre for Health Promotion, University of Toronto (2005). http://idmbestpractices.ca/idm.php?content=resources-idm#manual. Accessed 13 Mar 2016
61. Patton, M.Q.: Developmental Evaluation: Applying Complexity Concepts to Enhance Innovation and Use. Guilford Press (2011)
62. Yusof, M.M., Kuljis, J., Papazafeiropoulou, A., Stergioulas, L.K.: An evaluation framework for health information systems: human, organization and technology-fit factors (HOT-fit). Int. J. Med. Inf. **77**(6), 386–398 (2008)
63. Disterer, G.: ISO/IEC 27000, 27001 and 27002 for information security management (2013). http://file.scirp.org/Html/4-7800154_30059.htm. Accessed 13 Mar 2016
64. Verry, J.: The relationship between the ISO 27001 and ISO 27002 standards (2013). http://www.pivotpointsecurity.com/blog/iso-27001-iso-27002-standards/. Accessed 13 Mar 2016
65. ISACA: COBIT 4.1: Framework for IT Governance and Control (2016). http://www.isaca.org/knowledge-center/cobit/pages/overview.aspx. Accessed 13 Mar 2016

Small and Medium-Sized Enterprises' Understanding of Security Evaluation of Cloud-Based Business Intelligence Systems and Its Challenges

Moses Moyo[✉] and Marianne Loock

University of South Africa (UNISA), Pretoria, South Africa
mosesm50@gmail.com, loockm@unisa.ac.za

Abstract. Although small and medium-sized enterprises (SMEs) are encouraged to seek new business opportunities by adopting and utilising cloud-based services, their understanding of threats, vulnerabilities and risk evaluation in the cloud environment, which is crucial in the success of cloud-based business intelligence (BI) adoption, is hardly known. The purpose of this study was to investigate SMEs' understanding of security evaluation of cloud-based BI and associated challenges. A cross-sectional survey was conducted among 109 SME owners/managers from selected South African provinces in which data was collected by means of an electronic and postal questionnaire. The study found that SME owners/managers were aware of conventional security challenges in the cloud-based services including BIs, had a basic understanding of security evaluation in general, understood the need to evaluate cloud-based BIs in terms of physically checking for vulnerabilities and data security and were not proficient in performing security evaluations of cloud-based BIs and relied on experts. SMEs face predicaments in evaluating cloud-based BI due to a lack of appropriate tools they can use. The study concluded that SME owners/managers have a basic understanding of security evaluation and challenges it poses.

Keywords: Cloud-based business intelligence · Security evaluation
Small and medium-sized enterprises

1 Introduction

The availability of many types of cloud-based services such as e-mails, online backup storage, online accounting, customer relations management and cloud-based business intelligence (BI) on the open web is a good development for small and medium-sized enterprises (SMEs) intending to adopt and use these technologies. Cloud-based BI is a concept that describes the components of a BI system delivered as services and data used by the BI system or stored in the cloud [1]. Cloud-based BI or BI in the cloud is the combination of two major cloud computing architectures as a flexible and cost-effective computing platform and BI technology as a support for swift organisational decision making [2]. A survey by Forest Technologies [3] found that the adoption of cloud-based services by South African SMEs was on the rise from 29% in 2014 to 39%

© Springer Nature Switzerland AG 2019
H. Venter et al. (Eds.): ISSA 2018, CCIS 973, pp. 133–148, 2019.
https://doi.org/10.1007/978-3-030-11407-7_10

in 2015 and to 50% in 2016. However, the cloud is an environment attractive for business opportunities to both unsuspecting SMEs and cyber criminals [4] and this requires SMEs to understand how to deal with cyber security challenges when migrating sensitive data, applications and transactions to the cloud [5]. According to Toesland [6], SMEs are a major target of cyber threats because their data are becoming increasingly valuable to cyber criminals and are also potentially easy routes to attacks on large enterprises which conduct transactions on the web. Literature also shows that a growing number of SMEs experience relentless cyber attacks by various threats that can breach data and application security by utilising vulnerabilities in cloud technologies used to offer services [6, 7]. Security breaches in cloud-based services compromise data confidentiality, integrity and availability [8] and this is likely to make SMEs reluctant to adopt and utilise cloud-based BIs.

SMEs are always encouraged to seek new business opportunities by adopting and utilising cloud-based services, despite the fact that their understanding of security evaluation of threats, vulnerabilities and risks in the cloud environment is hardly known. Chances are high that SMEs could end up selecting wrong cloud-based BIs, leading to business failure. According to Moore [9], the prospects of SME owners/managers selecting wrong BIs is usually increased by the presence of many cloud-based technologies as well as the lack of understanding of the technology to be adopted. Empirical studies on the adoption of cloud-based BI by South African SMEs explore the affordability of the technology, awareness and how it has been received among different types of SMEs [10, 11]. SME owners/managers' understanding of security evaluation of cloud-based services is very important for the adoption of cloud-based BIs by South African SMEs. SMEs need to work independently, without the influence of cloud technology vendors or cloud service providers (CSPs) when deciding on the cloud-based BIs and service providers most suitable for their business needs. Therefore, the purpose of this study was to evaluate SME owners/managers' understanding of security evaluation in cloud-based services, particularly BIs, they intended to adopt or had already adopted and challenges associated with the evaluation processes.

The study was guided by the following research questions (RQs):

RQ1: What is the state of adoption of cloud-based services by SMEs in South Africa?

RQ2: What is the level of awareness of security challenges associated with cloud-based services among South African SMEs?

RQ3: How do SMEs evaluate security in cloud-based services prior to adoption?

RQ4: How do SMEs understand security evaluation in cloud-based services?

RQ5: What challenges do SMEs face in evaluating cloud-based services, particularly BI?

The article is organised as follows: introduction, literature review, research methodology, results and analysis, findings and discussion, conclusions and limitations.

2   Literature Review

2.1   SMEs' Awareness of Security Challenges Associated with Cloud-Based Services

Of the three major cloud service models available, i.e. Infrastructure-as-a-Service (IaaS), Platform-as-a-Service (PaaS) and Software-as-a-Service (SaaS), in community or public clouds, SaaS is highly recommended for adoption and utilisation by SMEs that have constrained human and financial capacity to purchase and maintain substantial information technology (IT) resources [12]. Unlike in private clouds, low-cost or free-of-charge public clouds present serious security challenges for hosting BIs and sensitive data. Narayanan [13] argues that SMEs using SaaS face security threats related to scam e-mails, online malware, identity scams, misuse of company files on employees' own devices as well as insecure wireless networks. By hosting BIs in SaaS, SMEs lose control over their data and applications to CSPs and this makes it difficult for SMEs to ensure that correct security mechanisms are in place [14] and to ensure application availability when needed [15]. SaaS as a multi-tenant service allows different clients to store their sensitive data in the same location, although it is not intelligent enough to separate that data [16]. By exploiting security vulnerabilities in SaaS, hackers use less sophisticated means to bypass security controls and breach data security for many clients. The implication is that SMEs storing customer data in SaaS could eventually suffer financial loss and face legal liabilities related to data security breaches [17].

In SMEs the importance of security can be undermined by users who are ignorant of security threats and always judge security based mainly on their uninterrupted availability of the respective cloud service [18]. A study by Lacey and James [19] on SMEs as IT service users concludes that SMEs tend to view security as not their problem and therefore always seek to minimise their commitment and involvement in securing their information systems. Separate studies by Moyo and Loock [5] and Toesland [6] conclude that South African SME owners/managers are aware of security challenges associated with the adoption and utilisation of cloud-based BIs and this influences their disposition to adopt the technology. However, it is still not clear how SME owners/managers understand security evaluation in cloud-based BI and how they conduct the evaluations.

2.2   Techniques Used by SMEs to Evaluate Security in Cloud-Based BIs Prior to Adoption

Information system evaluation refers to a systematic process which involves data collection and analysis, making judgements and finally providing useful feedback about the worth or merit of the product or service being evaluated [20]. With regard to SMEs, evaluating cloud-based BIs can provide information on security needed to assist decision making on the most appropriate cloud-based BI for a particular enterprise [21]. The two types of evaluation employed in IT are prior-operational use evaluation (POUE), known as strategic, pre-implementation or formative evaluation, and operational use evaluation (OUE), referred to as post-implementation or summative evaluation [22]. POUE serves to support IT investment justification by predicting estimated costs and benefits, return on investment and management [22]. On the other hand, OUE is used to establish the impact of the system, providing a better understanding of system performance, and what it has accomplished in terms of its stated objectives [23]. SMEs should conduct POUE on cloud-based BIs in order to establish the security threats, vulnerabilities and risks associated with the adoption of the technology. Using POUE enables SMEs to gather required data to determine whether the cloud-based BIs they intend to adopt meet their needs and expectations in terms of data and application security. Heller [24] encourages SMEs to conduct their own evaluations when selecting cloud-based BIs to check whether most of the features the vendors claim to have are of real benefit to the enterprise.

Currently, there is no literature specific to cloud-based BI evaluation techniques for SMEs besides traditional technical evaluation techniques such as vulnerability scanning and testing, which are suitable for large business organisations with sound finance and IT security personnel [25]. Although the Cloud Security White Paper [26] outlines areas that potential cloud users need to evaluate in order to successfully adopt and use cloud-based services, it does not specify how this evaluation should be done. The White Paper also overlooks the fact that most potential adopters of cloud-based services may not be able to access CSPs due to different geographical locations and legislation. Heiser [27] argues that effective cloud-based services security evaluation processes need pragmatic and flexible use of multiple forms of CSP security posture information. In this regard, SMEs face increasing challenges to obtain that information.

2.3   Challenges SMEs Face in Evaluating Cloud-Based BIs

The existence of different cloud-based BI products in the market presents SMEs with selection challenges because they raise different security issues to be dealt with [28]. Unlike on-premises BIs where enterprises have to evaluate only technical and procedural aspects, evaluating cloud-based BIs requires enterprises to evaluate more areas of the clouds [29]. According to Willcocks [30], evaluation raises the issues of costs, benefits, risk and value of an IT system to an organisation and these could be assessed through an informal or formal evaluation process. CSPs are responsible for technical information infrastructure security whereas client enterprises are responsible for configuration and procedural security. This implies that SME owners/managers should be able to check whether CSP infrastructure is based on commonly used manufacturers that produce patches to deal with identified security vulnerabilities, and documentations of the vulnerabilities and patches are always available [31]. According to Moghe [32], lack of standardisation in cloud-based BIs presents a challenge to SMEs because they would have to devise a variety of strategies in evaluating cloud-based BIs.

3   Research Methodology

The study utilised a descriptive cross-sectional survey design because it enabled easy collection of data from a large sample over a large geographical area at low cost and without the influence of the researcher on respondents. The target population was all SMEs utilising the Internet/web-based systems for business transactions across the

Western Cape, Limpopo, Gauteng, Mpumalanga and Eastern Cape. The network sampling technique was used to select a sample of decision makers/owners/managers in SMEs already using or considering adopting cloud-based services. The information about suitable SMEs was obtained through owners/managers who had knowledge about other SMEs' utilisation of ITs in various provinces/districts. E-mails and phone calls were used to access all potential SME owners/managers, after which the questionnaires were sent either electronically or by post.

To account for questionnaire validity and reliability at the design stage Segars and Gover [33] and Chang et al. [34] encourage researchers to avoid or reduce any potential common method variance (CMV), a common source of bias. CMV bias was reduced by adopting constructs from different sources and mixing the ordering structure of the questions in order to reduce the likelihood of bias towards the theory-in-use. Respondents were assured of the anonymity and confidentiality of the study, and were informed that there were no right or wrong answers but were encouraged to answer questions as honestly as possible [34]. The questionnaire was tested and piloted to eliminate ambiguity of questions among local SME owners who volunteered to test the questionnaire. The reliability of the questionnaire was measured using SPSS and Cronbach's alpha was found to be 0.929. A copy of the survey questionnaire was distributed to a network sample of 380 respondents, in the form of 150 online Google forms and 230 copies posted. The questionnaire response rate was very low with only 113 (29.7%) returned; 109 (28.7%) of the respondents' questionnaires were analysed. Data were then processed using SPSS to generate frequency tables, graphs and descriptive statistics.

4   Results and Analysis

This section presents an analysis of the results of the study. Table 1 shows the distribution of respondents by type of enterprise.

Table 1. Distribution of respondents by enterprise

No. of employees	Frequency f (%)	Combined f (%)	Type of enterprise
10 to 20	21 (19.3)	67 (61.5)	Small enterprise (SE)
21 to 50	46 (42.2)		
51 to 100	25 (22.9)	42 (38.5)	Medium enterprise (ME)
101 to 150	11 (10.1)		
151 to 200	6 (5.5)		
Total	**109 (100)**	**109 (100)**	

The majority of the respondents in this survey, 67 (61.5%), were from small enterprises (SEs), 21 (19.3%) of which employed 10 to 20 workers and 46 (42.2%) employed 21 to 50 workers. The minority of the respondents, 42 (38.5%), were from medium enterprises (MEs), 25 (22.9%) of which employed 51 to 100 employees,

11 (10.1%) employed 101 to 150 employees and 6 (5.5%) employed 151 to 200 employees. In SMEs, the owners/managers are usually responsible for the day-to-day operations of the enterprise and make all the decisions in the adoption and use of cloud-based services in the organisation and may be the ones who use it most.

The results in Table 2 show the distribution of decision makers from which data were collected. 61 (56.0%) respondents were owners responsible for decision making in 16 (14.7%) MEs and 45 (41.3%) SEs; 48 (44.0%) respondents were hired managers who made decisions in 26 (23.9%) MEs and 22 (20.2%) SEs.

Table 2. Distribution of decision makers of cloud-based service adoption in SMEs

	Person in charge of decision making to adopt cloud-based services (n = 109)		
Type of SME	Owner f (%)	Hired manager f (%)	Total f (%)
ME	16 (14.7)	26 (23.9)	42 (38.5)
SE	45 (41.3)	22 (20.2)	67 (61.5)
Total	61 (56.0)	48 (44.0)	109 (100)

In this study, there were more owners than hired managers who were involved in decision making regarding the adoption and use of cloud-based services and other ITs.

4.1   RQ1: What Is the State of Adoption of Cloud-Based Services by SMEs in South Africa?

Responses regarding the state of adoption and use of cloud-based services, including cloud-based BIs, are shown in Fig. 1.

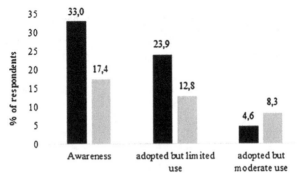

Fig. 1. State of adoption and use of cloud-based services

The results show that 36 (33.0%) of the respondents from SEs and 19 (17.4%) from MEs, overall 55 (50.5%) of the respondents, indicated that their enterprises were at the awareness stage of adopting cloud-based services. 40 (37%) respondents, consisting of 26 (23.8%) from SEs and 14 (12.8%) from MEs, indicated that their enterprises had adopted cloud-based technologies but put them to limited use. A minority, 14 (13.0%) respondents, 5 (4.6%) from SEs and 9 (8.3%) from MEs, had adopted cloud-based services and used them moderately.

4.2   RQ2: What Is the Level of Awareness of Security Challenges Associated with Cloud-Based Services Among South African SMEs?

Table 3 shows respondents' rating of their awareness of security challenges that affect the adoption of cloud-based services, particularly cloud BIs. A 4-point Likert-type rating scale from very much aware (4) to not aware (1) was used.

Table 3. Ratings of awareness in security challenges in cloud-based services

Security challenges	Ratings of selected security challenges in cloud services n = 109					
	Very much aware n (%)	Moderately aware n (%)	Little aware-ness n (%)	Not aware n (%)	Mean	Std. Dev
Hacking activities on web	62 (56.9)	36 (33.0)	7 (6.4)	4 (3.7)	3.4	0.9
Data theft	46 (42.2)	45 (41.3)	7 (6.4)	11 (10.1)	3.2	0.9
Data unavailability	48 (44.0)	34 (31.3)	7 (6.4)	20 (18.3)	3.0	1.1
Competitors sharing same data storage	46 (42.2)	25 (22.9)	18 (16.5)	20 (18.3)	2.9	1.1
Privacy breaches	36 (33.0)	35 (32.1)	27 (24.8)	11 (10.1)	2.9	1.0
Data confidentiality breaches	46 (42.2)	43 (39.4)	9 (8.3)	11 (10.1)	2.8	1.1
Information leakage in cloud	35 (32.1)	38 (34.9)	22 (20.2)	14 (12.8)	2.8	1.1
Loss of control of data to CSP	30 (27.5)	39 (35.8)	31 (28.4)	9 (8.3)	2.8	0.9
Difficulties in data migration to other providers	32 (29.4)	25 (22.9)	41 (37.6)	11 (10.1)	2.7	1.0
Ransomware effects	20 (18.3)	14 (12.8)	46 (42.2)	29 (26.6)	2.5	1.2
CSP closing down without notice	21 (19.3)	25 (22.9)	34 (31.2)	29 (26.6)	2.3	1.1

The results reveal that respondents' awareness of all key security challenges was rated as moderate (mean of 3.4), with hacking activities on the web topping the list, down to 2.7 for difficulties in data migration to other providers. The two least rated security challenges were awareness of the possibility of CSP closing down without notice (mean of 2.5) and ignorance of ransomware effects (mean of 2.3), which indicated respondents having very little awareness. An overall average mean score of 2.8 indicates that the majority of the respondents had nearly moderate awareness of most challenges being investigated.

4.3 RQ3: How Do SMEs Evaluate Security in Cloud-Based BIs Prior to Adoption?

To answer this question, respondents were asked how they selected cloud-based services they were currently using or intended to use, as seen in Fig. 2. The results show that 28 (25.7%) of the respondents from SEs and 6 (5.5%) respondents from MEs, with an overall minority of 34 (31.2%), searched for cloud-based services possibly for adoption from the web on their own. On the other hand, 39 (35.8%) of the respondents from SEs and 36 (33.0%) from MEs, i.e. the majority of 75 (68.8%) of the respondents, indicated that the cloud-based services they adopted or intended to adopt were recommended to them by experts in cloud technology. These results show that SMEs were also able to use the web to search for cloud-based services that met their needs.

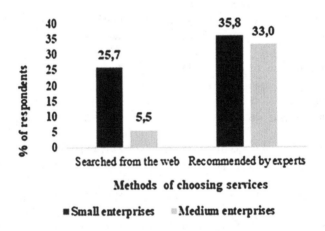

Fig. 2. Methods used to select cloud-based services by SMEs

Respondents were asked to rate the importance of evaluating a number of key aspects of security in the cloud. The results are shown in Table 4.

Based on the Likert scale of 4 (very important) to 1 (not important), the majority of the respondents, 102 (93.6%), rated password protection as the most important security aspect that must be evaluated, and 7 (6.4%) rated it as important, with a mean score of 3.9. Application programming interfaces were rated the second most important, with a mean of 2.6, with 32 (29.4%) respondents rating it very important, 70 (64.2%) as important and 7 (6.4%) as less important. The average mean of 3.1 shows that respondents regarded all the aspects as important to consider when evaluating cloud-based services.

Table 4. Ratings of the importance of evaluating selected security aspects

Security aspect evaluated	Ratings of importance of evaluation of security aspects n = 109					
	Very important f (%)	Important f (%)	Less important f (%)	Not important f (%)	Mean	Std. Dev
Password protection	102 (93.6)	7 (6.4)	0 (0)	0 (0)	3.9	0.5
Security management services	91 (83.5)	11 (10.1)	7 (6.4)	0 (0)	3.7	0.7
Firewall configurations	82 (75.2)	27 (24.8)	0 (0)	0 (0)	3.5	0.9
Software security	75 (68.8)	34 (31.2)	0 (0)	0 (0)	3.4	0.9
Up-to-date security patches	73 (67.0)	36 (33.0)	0 (0)	0 (0)	3.3	0.9
Contingencies and backups	73 (67.0)	29 (26.6)	7 (6.4)	0 (0)	3.3	0.9
Vendor or provider reliability	68 (62.4)	41 (37.6)	0 (0)	0 (0)	3.2	1.0
Organisational security and risk management	62 (56.9)	31 (28.4)	16 (14.7)	0 (0)	3.1	1.0
Human resources security	41 (37.6)	39 (35.8)	29 (26.6)	0 (0)	2.8	1.0
Physical security of provider	41 (37.6)	41 (37.6)	27 (24.8)	0 (0)	2.8	1.0
Security guideline by provider	48 (44.0)	41 (37.6)	11 (10.1)	9 (8.3)	2.8	1.1
Interoperability and portability	39 (35.8)	34 (31.2)	36 (33)	0 (0)	2.7	1.0
Application programming interfaces security	32 (29.4)	70 (64.2)	7 (6.4)	0 (0)	2.6	0.9

4.4 RQ4: How Do SMEs Understand Security Evaluation in Cloud-Based Services?

To determine the respondents' understanding of security evaluation in cloud-based BIs and related services, respondents were asked to rate a given number of statements on a Likert scale of 5 (strongly agree) to 1 (strongly disagree) (Table 5). The mean scores ranged between 4.6 and 3.8, close to strongly agree and agree, and the average overall mean was 4.2 for all items. This shows that respondents understood security evaluation in cloud-based services in terms of a variety of aspects indicated. The overall average mean rating score of 4.2 shows that respondents had a generic understanding of what each aspect meant with regard to cloud-based BIs.

As a follow-up, respondents were asked to indicate how they understood evaluation of cloud-based BI and other services, as seen in Table 6 below.

The majority of the respondents understood security evaluation of cloud-based services as assessing the effectiveness of the following security controls: data security - 91 (83.5%) strongly agreed and 18 (16.5%) agreed, with a mean of 4.8; application

Table 5. Understanding of security evaluation in cloud services

Aspect	Ratings of security evaluation understanding n = 109					
	Strongly agree f (%)	Agree f (%)	Not sure f (%)	Disagree f (%)	Mean	Std. Dev
Checking information asset accessibility publicly by unauthorised cloud users	64 (58.7)	45 (41.3)	0 (0)	0 (0)	4.6	0.5
Checking the chances of being tricked into signing a contract by a poor-performing CSPs	64 (58.7)	36 (33)	0	6 (5.5)	4.4	0.9
Checking that expected results match CSPs' claims	55 (50.5)	45 (41.3)	6 (5.5)	3 (2.8)	4.4	0.6
Checking whether CSP employees can access and manipulate enterprise data without permission	47 (43.1)	46 (42.2)	16 (14.7)	0 (0)	4.3	0.7
Checking the level of control of data in the cloud I will have	48 (44)	47 (43.1)	13 (11.9)	3 (2.8)	4.3	0.7
Identifying and understanding exposure to risk and capability of managing it	35 (32.1)	65 (59.6)	6 (5.5)	3 (2.8)	4.2	0.6
Checking reported cases on whether unexpected changes to data/information in a particular cloud once occurred	46 (42.2)	36 (33)	18 (16.5)	9 (8.3)	4.1	1.0
Checking whether processes or functions on clouds can be manipulated by outsiders	28 (25.7)	56 (51.4)	18 (16.5)	7 (6.4)	4.0	0.7
Identifying the possible sources of conflict with the cloud provider in terms of SLAs	26 (23.9)	51 (46.8)	22 (20.2)	10 (9.2)	3.9	0.7
Checking reports on periods of time when the cloud was unavailable to the users	26 (23.9)	42 (38.5)	32 (29.4)	9 (8.3)	3.8	0.9

security - 84 (77.1%) strongly agreed and 25 (22.9%) agreed, with a mean of 4.8; system security - 73 (67.0%) strongly agreed and 36 (33.0%) agreed, with a mean of 4.7; network security - 84 (77.1%) strongly agreed, 18 (16.5%) agreed and 7 (6.4%) were not sure, with a mean of 4.7, and physical security of data centres from cloud providers - 36 (33.0%) strongly agreed, 53 (48.6%) agreed, 11 (10.1%) were not sure and 9 (8.3%) disagreed. From these results, it could be deduced that SME owners/managers had a clear understanding of what security evaluation entailed and the critical areas of the cloud to be evaluated.

Table 6. Meaning of evaluation of cloud-based services and BIs

Aspect	Ratings of what security evaluation means for each control n = 109					
	Strongly agree f (%)	Agree f (%)	Not sure f (%)	Disagree f (%)	Mean	Std. Dev
Data security	91 (83.5)	18 (16.5)	0	0 (0)	4.8	0.4
Application security	84 (77.1)	25 (22.9)	0	0 (0)	4.8	0.4
System security	73 (67.0)	36 (33.0)	0	0 (0)	4.7	0.5
Network security	84 (77.1)	18 (16.5)	7 (6.4)	0 (0)	4.7	0.6
Physical security of data centres for cloud providers	36 (33.0)	53 (48.6)	11 (10.1)	9 (8.3)	4.1	0.9

4.5   RQ5: What Challenges Do SMEs Face in Evaluating Cloud-Based Services, Particularly BIs?

Respondents indicated the extent to which common security challenges were likely to affect their effort in evaluating cloud-based services they intended to adopt and use, as seen in Table 7. The results are arranged with regard to their mean score of the Likert rating scale from very serious (4) to not serious (1).

Table 7. Ratings of the common security challenges in evaluating cloud-based services

Security aspect	Ratings of security evaluation challenges n = 109					
	Very serious f (%)	Serious f (%)	Less serious f (%)	Not serious f (%)	Mean	Std. Dev
Evaluating vulnerabilities in interface of applications	82 (75.2)	27 (24.8)	0	0	3.8	0.4
Security that cloud providers claim they give	68 (62.4)	32 (29.4)	9 (8.3)	0	3.5	0.6
Getting information from cloud providers	71 (65.1)	18 (16.5)	20 (18.3)	0	3.5	0.8
Ability of provider to meet requirements	48 (44)	52 (47.7)	9 (8.3)	0	3.4	0.6
Authentication of users/applications/processes	58 (53.2)	40 (36.7)	11 (10.1)	0	3.4	0.7
Robustness of separation between data belonging to different customers	64 (58.7)	25 (22.9)	20 (18.3)	0	3.4	0.8
Lack of tools to evaluate cloud-based BIs	46 (42.2)	54 (49.5)	9 (8.3)	0	3.3	0.6
History of data breaches in a particular cloud	48 (44.0)	43 (39.4)	18 (16.5)	0	3.3	0.7

(*continued*)

Table 7. (*continued*)

Security aspect	Ratings of security evaluation challenges n = 109					
	Very serious f (%)	Serious f (%)	Less serious f (%)	Not serious f (%)	Mean	Std. Dev
Certainty about survival of cloud provider	61 (56.0)	30 (27.5)	9 (8.3)	9 (8.3)	3.3	0.9
Establishing the physical location of the cloud provider	47 (43.1)	46 (42.2)	7 (6.4)	9 (8.3)	3.2	0.9
Physical security evaluation of provider	46 (42.2)	34 (31.2)	18 (16.5)	9 (8.3)	3.1	1.0
Trust of provider and employees	55 (50.5)	18 (16.5)	27 (24.8)	9 (8.3)	3.1	1.0
Enterprises with which the cloud was shared	48 (44.0)	41 (37.6)	20 (18.3)	0	3.1	1.1

The results show that respondents rated all items as challenges to the evaluation of security in cloud-based services as serious to nearly very serious, with mean scores ranging from 3.1 to 3.8. Evaluating vulnerabilities in the cloud-based application interfaces posed the most serious challenges as indicated by the majority of the respondents: 82 (75.2%) rated this very serious and 27 (24.8%) rated it serious, with a mean score of 3.8. The security challenge rated the least serious was evaluating the enterprises with which the cloud-based services were shared: 48 (44%) respondents rated it as very serious, 41 (37.6%) rated it as serious and 20 (18.3%) as less serious, with a mean of 3.1. With the majority of the respondents regarding these challenges as serious, this affects the manner in which SMEs evaluate cloud-based services and eventually adopt and use the services. The overall mean score of 3.4 indicates that respondents considered the majority of the security aspects as serious.

5   Findings and Discussions

This subsection presents the findings of the study based on the research questions.

5.1   State of Adoption of Cloud-Based BI by SMEs in South Africa

The state of adoption of cloud-based services such as BI by SMEs has been found to be in three stages: awareness (50.4%), adoption with limited use (36.2%) and adopted with extensive use (12.9%). These findings are consistent with the projections made independently by Forest Technologies [3]. As a new technology for SMEs, the level of awareness of its existence is generally high among SME owners/managers.

5.2   Level of Awareness of Security Challenges Associated with Cloud-Based Services Among South African SMEs

Hacking activities on the web, data confidentiality breaches in the cloud, data availability issues, various forms of data theft, sharing of the same data storage with competitors and data privacy breaches were commonly known by the majority of respondents, whereas challenges related to ransomware and possibility of the provider closing down without notice were least known by most of the respondents. Technical paper by Muntean [1] and Boonsiritomachai et al. [11] allude to a number of security challenges that SMEs face in their quest to adopt cloud-based services. A study by Moyo and Loock [5] also attributes the poor adoption and use of cloud-based services, particularly BIs, to several security challenges that SMEs have to overcome if they are to successfully adopt and utilise these services. SMEs are aware of the devastating effects of various threats in cyber space on their business profitability if they risk adopting cloud-based BI without due evaluation [26].

5.3   SMEs' Evaluation of Security in Cloud-Based BIs Prior to Adoption

The majority (68.8%) of the SME owners/managers relied on experts' opinions regarding which service to adopt and were not able to perform security evaluations themselves. However, 31.2% of the owners/managers were able to perform searches for cloud-based services on the web and evaluate the services before adoption and use. The majority of respondents were aware of the importance of evaluating cloud services before adopting them. The majority (75% to 94%) of the owners/managers thought that password protection, security management services and firewall configurations were very important areas to be evaluated in cloud-based BIs. Although a number of studies encourage SMEs to evaluate the cloud before adoption, they provide piece-meal suggestions on what and how to evaluate envisaged security challenges [26].

5.4   SMEs' Understanding of Security Evaluations in Cloud-Based BIs

SME owners/managers understood security evaluation in cloud-based services from a practical perspective in which they preferred checking information assets for vulnerabilities that could possibly be accessed publicly by unauthorised cloud users, guarding against being tricked into signing a contract by a poor-performing cloud provider and verifying that the process or function provided the expected results as claimed by the cloud provider. Literature emphasises that cloud clients such as SMEs have an obligation to understand technical infrastructure security, data security, standards and procedures pertaining to the cloud-based service they want to adopt [31]. Similarly, Antoo et al. [4] point out that SMEs should understand the evaluation of cloud-based services in terms of security vulnerabilities, threats and risks in internal network controls, data storage and service level agreements (SLAs) of their CSPs with regard to their requirements and security policies. The Cloud Security White Paper [26] emphasises the importance of having a clear understanding of how to evaluate the physical infrastructure in the data centre, applications hosted by CSPs that manage clients' data, and the policies and procedures used to continuously maintain security in the cloud environment. The findings of this study suggest that SME owners/managers should be actively involved in the process of evaluating cloud-based BIs to make correct decisions about services to be adopted.

5.5 Challenges that SMEs Face in Evaluating Cloud-Based Services, Particularly BIs

While SME owners/managers may have some understanding of security evaluation in cloud-based services, they also face serious challenges in evaluating the identified areas due to complications that range from accessibility to legal issues [5]. The major obstacle is a lack of proper tools to evaluate cloud-based services to determine how secure the services and CSP are [26]. SME owners/managers lack technical skills in evaluating IT systems and they tend to rely on expertise from outside the organisation, which is also too expensive for them [29]. It is difficult for SME owners/managers to force CSPs to divulge every detail about the service they provide, although legally they should do so. Not all CSPs can provide a totally secure service as they are unable to vet their clients who use a virtual space. Due to different geographical locations, SME owners/managers are unable to evaluate the physical security of data centres and also to monitor unauthorised access to their data by the provider's employees [9]. Generally, studies which encourage the adoption of cloud-based services by SMEs do so on the strength of benefits that adopters may derive from the technology while overlooking or downplaying the security challenges that come with the cloud [15]. On the other hand, SME owners/managers are not prepared to risk their businesses by adopting services they are not certain about.

6 Conclusions

The majority of the SME owners/managers surveyed understood security evaluations in terms of physically checking for vulnerabilities in cloud-based BIs and the security of data that were likely to be accessed publicly by unauthorised cloud users, guarding against being tricked into signing contracts by a poor-performing and unreliable cloud provider and verifying whether the process or function was capable of providing the expected results as claimed by the CSP. Although the majority of SME owners/managers were not able to perform security evaluations, their level of understanding of the need for these evaluations was fair. SME owners were also aware of the areas of cloud-based BIs that needed to be evaluated. A number of SME owners/managers conducted their own search of cloud-based services on the web, deviating from the traditional practice of depending on expertise from outside their businesses. The ability of SME owners/managers to evaluate cloud-based services was affected by a number of factors beyond the control and comprehension of the adopters.

7 Limitations and Further Research

The findings of this study cannot be generalised to all SMEs in South Africa due to the fact that it was a cross-sectional study whose results may change within the foreseeable future as more easy-to-use technology emerges and the adopters improve their understanding of security issues. Secondly, the use of postal/online questionnaires have their own strengths and shortfalls, resulting in a very low response rate which constrains generalisation. Further studies are in progress in using the findings of longitudinal research in developing a security framework to evaluate cloud-based BIs by SMEs in South Africa.

References

1. Muntean, M.: Considerations regarding business intelligence in cloud context. Informatica Economica **19**(4), 55–67 (2015)
2. Tamer, C., Kiley, N., Ashrafi, N., Kuilboer, J.: Risks and benefits of business intelligence in the cloud. In: Proceedings of the Northeast Decision Sciences Institute Annual Meeting, p. 86 (2013)
3. Forest Technologies: SME Survey 2015: The Greening of the SME Sector (2015). http://www.smesurvey.co.za/press.html
4. Antoo, M., Cadersaib, Z., Gobin, B.: PEST framework for analysing cloud computing adoption by Mauritian SMEs. Lect. Notes Softw. Eng. **3**(2), 107–112 (2015)
5. Moyo, M., Loock, M.: South African small and medium-sized enterprises' reluctance to adopt and use cloud-based business intelligence systems: a literature review. In: The 11th International Conference for Internet Technology and Secured Transactions (ICITST-2016), pp. 250–254 (2016)
6. Toesland, F.: Why SMEs are big targets for cybercrime (2016). https://www.raconteur.net/technology/why-smes-are-big-targets-for-cyber-crime
7. Madzima, K., Moyo, M., Dzawo, G., Mbodila, M.: Mobile security threats: a survey of how mobile device users are protecting themselves from new forms of cybercrimes. In: Proceedings of the 10th International Conference on Cyber Warfare and Security, ICCWS 2015, pp. 123–133 (2015)
8. Akinola, K.E., Odumosu, A.A.: Threat handling and security issue in cloud computing. Int. J. Sci. Eng. Res. **6**(11), 1371–1385 (2015)
9. Moore, J.: Business Intelligence Takes to Cloud for Small Businesses (2014). https://www.cio.com/article/3237786/business-intelligence/9-ways-youre-failing-at-business-intelligence.html#tk.drr_mlt
10. Mohlameane, M.J., Ruxwana, N.L.: The potential of cloud computing as an alternative technology for SMEs in South Africa. J. Econ. Bus. Manage. **1**(4), 396–400 (2014)
11. Boonsiritomachai, W., McGrath, M., Burgess, S.: A research framework for the adoption of business intelligence by small and medium-sized enterprises. In: 27th Annual SEAANZ Proceedings for Small Enterprise Association of Australia and New Zealand Conference, 16–18 July 2014, pp. 16–28 (2014)
12. Chang, V., Kuob, Y., Ramachandrana, M.: Cloud computing adoption framework: a security framework for business clouds. Future Gener. **57**(2015), 24–41 (2015)
13. Narayanan, S.: Tackling the cyber security challenges faced by SMEs (2013). http://www.cisoplatform.com/profiles/blogs/tackling-the-cyber-security-challenges-by-smes

14. European Union Agency for Network and Information Security. Security framework for governmental clouds (2015). http://www.enisa.europa.eu/activities/Resilience-and-CIIP/cloud-computing/governmental-cloud-security/security-framework-for-govenmental-clouds

15. Chou, T.: Security threats on cloud computing vulnerabilities. Int. J. Comput. Sci. Inf. Technol. (IJCSIT) 5(3), 79–88 (2013)

16. Fernandes, D.A.B., Soares, L.F.B., Gomes, J.V.M., Freire, M., Inacio, P.R.M.: Security issues in cloud environments: a survey. Int. J. Inf. Secur. (IJIS) 2013(1), 1–62 (2013)

17. Subashini, S., Kavitha, V.: A survey on security issues in service delivery models of cloud computing. J. Netw. Comput. Appl. 34(1), 1–11 (2011)

18. Oza, N., Karppinen, K., Savola, R.: User experience and security in the cloud – an empirical study in the Finnish Cloud Consortium. In: The 2nd IEEE International Conference on Cloud Computing Technology and Science, pp. 621–628 (2010)

19. Lacey, D., James, B.E.: Review of Availability of Advice on Security for Small/Medium Sized Organisations (2010). https://ico.org.uk/media/about-the-ico/documents/1042344/review-availbllity-of-security-advice-for-sme.pdf

20. Mussa, M., Kipanyula, M.J., Angello, C., Sanga, C.A.: Evaluation of Livestock Information Network Knowledge System (LINKS) based on user satisfaction definition of information system evaluation. Int. J. Inf. Commun. Technol. Res. 6(8), 115–130 (2016)

21. Wise, L.: Evaluating business intelligence in the cloud (2016). http://www.cio.com/article/3041639/business-intelligence/evaluating-business-intelligence-in-the-cloud.html

22. Al-yaseen, H.M.: Challenges of implementing healthcare information systems in developing countries: using a mixed method research. J. Emerg. Trends Comput. Inf. Sci. 3(11), 1521–1529 (2012)

23. Al-Yaseen, H., Al-Jaghoub, S., Al-Shorbaji, M., Salim, M.: Post-implementation evaluation of healthcare information systems in developing countries. Inf. Syst. J. 13(1), 9–16 (2010)

24. Heller, M.: How to Select the Best Self-service BI Tool for Your Business (2017). https://www.cio.com/article/3235394/business-intelligence/how-to-select-the-best-self-service-bi-tool-for-your-business.html#tk.cio_rs

25. Kazim, M., Zhu, S.Y.: A survey on top security threats in cloud computing. Int. J. Appl. Comput. Sci. Appl. 6(3), 10495–10500 (2015)

26. Cloud Security White Paper.: How to Evaluate the Data Security Capabilities of Cloud-Based Services (2011). http://www.carestream.com/WhitePaper_Cloud-Security.pdf

27. Heiser, J.: How to Evaluate Cloud Service Provider Security (2016). https://www.gartner.com/doc/3275117/evaluate-cloud-service-provider-security

28. Agostino, A., Soilen, S.K., Gerritsen, B.: Cloud solution in business intelligence for SMEs – vendor and customer perspectives. J. Intell. Stud. Bus. 3(2013), 5–28 (2013)

29. Vacca, J.R.: Security in the Private Cloud. Taylor and Francis, Denver (2017)

30. Willcocks, L.: Evaluating information technology investments: research findings and reappraisal. J. Inf. Syst. 2(1992), 243–268 (1992)

31. Shimamoto, CD.: How to Evaluate Cloud Security? (2015) https://www.techsoup.org/support/articles-and-how-tos/how-to-evaluate-cloud-security

32. Moghe, P.: 6 Hidden Challenges of using the Cloud for Big Data and How to Overcome Them (2016). https://thenextweb.com/insider/2016/04/12/6-challenges-cloud-overcome

33. Segars, A.H., Grover, V.: Strategic information systems planning success: an investigation of the construct and its measurement. MIS Q. 22(2), 139–163 (1998)

34. Chang, S.J., Van Witteloostuijn, A., Eden, L.: From the editors: common method variance in international business research. Int. J. Bus. Stud. 41(2), 178–184 (2010)

Preventing and Mitigating Ransomware
A Systematic Literature Review

Zandile Manjezi[✉] and Reinhardt A. Botha

Center for Research in Information and Cyber Security, Nelson Mandela University,
Port Elizabeth, South Africa
{Zandile.Manjezi,ReinhardtA.Botha}@mandela.ac.za

Abstract. There has been significant growth in ransomware attacks over the past few years. Many organizations have been affected by a variety of ransomware attacks, leading to a large amount of data becoming inaccessible. In a typical ransomware attack malicious software encrypts electronic data while extorting money from an unexpecting victim. In order to decrypt and restore data, the attacker requests user to pay the ransom amount, typically through crypto-currency such as Bitcoin. There are various ways how ransomware infiltrate a computer, including phishing emails, drive-by downloads or vulnerable websites containing executable files of the malware. Being a new emerging type of attack, limited consolidated information is known by users. Therefore, this paper sets out to perform a systematic literature review to determine what has been published during the previous 3 years in leading academic journals regarding the prevention and mitigation of ransomware. Two hundred and sixty one (261) journal articles dealt with ransomware from four perspectives: prevention and mitigation methods, detection methods, case studies and attack methods. Out of the 261 journal articles, 35 journal articles that resort under the prevention and mitigation category were further analyzed. The papers were coded and a consolidated list of 13 guidelines was constructed. Interestingly, and somewhat concerning, these prevention and mitigation guidelines cover basic cyber-security practices to prevent and mitigate against any kind of cyber-attack, not specifically ransomware. This raises questions regarding the research agenda, but the repetition of established guidelines also raises questions on the effectiveness of security education, training and awareness interventions.

Keywords: Ransomware · Systematic literature review
Ransomware prevention · Cyber-security · Guidelines

1 Introduction

There has been exponential growth in ransomware attacks over the past few years [13]. The WannaCry and Petya families of ransomware brought renewed attention to ransomware attacks during May 2017. WannaCry, for example, wreaked

© Springer Nature Switzerland AG 2019
H. Venter et al. (Eds.): ISSA 2018, CCIS 973, pp. 149–162, 2019.
https://doi.org/10.1007/978-3-030-11407-7_11

havoc as it was reported to have infected 35 000 machines in 150 countries in the first three days of its emergence [8]. This attack caused monetary loss in multiple organizations such as hospitals, schools and gas stations. According to Chen et al. [8] the attackers demanded 300–600 US dollars per attack in exchange for a decryption key.

Ransomware is a type of malware that extorts money from an unsuspecting victim by prohibiting access to computer data or locking functionalities of the computer [8]. There are various ways how ransomware can infiltrate computer systems without being detected. Attackers may use malicious emails, drive-by downloads or malicious advertisements. Brewer [5] provides five phases on how ransomware infects a user's system. Firstly, the attacker will exploit system vulnerabilities by forwarding a phishing email or through a malicious toolkits. Secondly, there will be a delivery of a ransomware executable file to the user's system via encrypted channels. Thirdly, when the file has been executed, the malware will focus on backed up files and other folders on the system. These files will be deleted to prevent user from recovering them. Fourthly, the attacker creates an encryption key by doing a secure key exchange with the command and control server. Lastly, when the encryption process of the files is complete, the user is notified through a list of instructions of the extortion and payment.

Researchers and cybersecurity professionals have made efforts to thwart the appearance of ransomware before causing detrimental effects to organizations and individual users. There has been a proliferation of studies providing mitigation strategies for ransomware attacks. These strategies come in various forms such as tools, guidelines, and frameworks. Some strategies may contradict one another or some may even support one another. Therefore, this study reviews existing literature on ransomware in a systematic manner to produce a consolidated list of preventative guidelines from all relevant sources. The objective of this study is to promote cyber-hygiene in organizations to prevent and mitigate ransomware.

2   Research Design

A systematic literature review is used as a methodology to analyse existing literature on what are the relevant prevention methods used to protect computer users from any types of ransomware. According to Webster and Watson [29] a systematic review ensures that a complete census of relevant literature is collected. This literature review followed a meticulous plan to provide qualitative data on ransomware. This section explains how the literature was sourced and selected (Subsect. 2.1) and analysed to determine the type of contribution to ransomware (Subsect. 2.2). Subsection 2.3 briefly discusses the findings of papers that do not deal with prevention and mitigation.

In Sect. 3 the prevention and mitigation strategies are further analysed, finding that many of them provide guidelines for user to follow. Therefore Sect. 4 combines and enumerates the guidelines found in the papers.

This process is graphically summarised in Fig. 1.

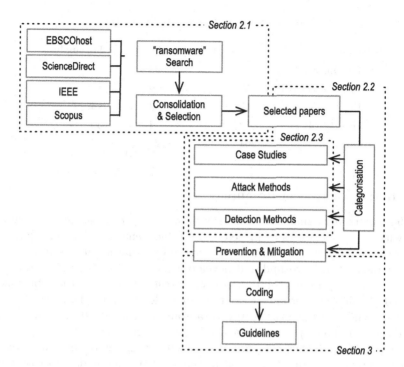

Fig. 1. The research process

2.1 Sourcing Literature for Analysis

The systematic literature review was performed using high-quality online databases as sources to get existing literature on ransomware. These were: EBSCOhost, Science Direct, IEEE and Scopus. These sources were accessible and are known for containing high-quality journals in their respective collections, including a substantial number of papers in the Information Technology, Information Systems and Computer Science disciplines.

Each source was searched using "ransomware" as the search term. The search was limited to return full text journal articles. The set of search results for each source was exported individually. In total 261 results were downloaded.

Since the "ransomware" search term was allowed anywhere in the paper, several papers did not deal with ransomware specifically, but maybe just referred to the term in a general context. Based on the title and abstract a total of 128 papers were judged "Not applicable" to this study.

Some journals are represented in more than one of the queried databases and as such appeared in more than one result set. Twenty-nine (29) such duplicate entries could be removed yielding 94 journal papers that needed to be analysed further.

Table 1 summarises the process followed to select the papers for further analysis.

Table 1. Sources of literature for analysis

Sources	Found	Not appl	Duplicate	For analysis
EBSCOhost (SR1)	71	26	22	23
Science Direct (SR2)	52	16	0	36
IEEE (SR3)	65	59	3	3
Scopus (SR4)	73	37	4	32
Total	261	128	29	94

2.2 Initial Analysis of Resources

The 94 papers were analysed to determine what aspect(s) of ransomware they deal with. Four categories as presented in Table 2 emerged. The categories are indicative of the research efforts to understand the nature of ransomware. The goal for researchers is to find and develop a panacea for this ransomware epidemic. However, finding a solution involves investigating about the attack methods and probing case studies to obtain an understanding about ransomware. Therefore, understanding the nature of ransomware can lead to the development of detection methods, prevention and mitigation strategies.

The papers were thus categorised as dealing with one or more of detection methods, prevention and mitigation methods, attack methods and case study. Table 2 shows the number of articles per category. Please note that a paper may appear in more than one category, and that the numbers do not add to 94.

2.3 Initial Findings

The initial analysis of resources produced four categories of ransomware literature. These categories are attack methods, case studies, detection methods and prevention and mitigation. The following sections provide further explanations of each category.

Studies concentrating on **ransomware attack methods** reveal detailed phases on how the malware infiltrates the machine and the threat to computer data. Zimba et al. [32] present a ransomware attack model aimed at Critical Infrastructure such as power plants, air traffic control and waste treatment plants. The attack model consists of methods on how ransomware attackers

Table 2. Categorization of papers dealing with ransomware

Category	Number of papers
Prevention and mitigation	43
Attack methods	11
Case studies	22
Detection methods	8

deposit the malware through the network. In the initial step in the attack model, the attacker seeks an infiltration sources such as the corporate network. Secondly, the attacker checks if the network has been previously exploited or not. Lastly, the attacker seeks for adjacent networks and vulnerabilities in order to propagate the payload to other networks [32].

Case studies inform readers about the attacks, the severity and the organizations affected. Hospitals have been the main target of ransomware as medical records have been encrypted. The Methodist Hospital in Henderson, Kentucky's patient health records were encrypted, however, the records were recovered from backups [20]. "Poor defences on the part of organisations – in particular, their slowness in patching systems – are making life easier for the cyber-criminals" says Gordon [14]. Such studies provide a wealth of information on how organizations dealt with this crisis. Case studies explore ransomware attacks that occurred on a global scale with the purpose to bring focus to ransomware awareness. Researchers and anti-malware developers will gain substantial information to develop tools to prevent and mitigate ransomware from understanding ransomware through case studies and its attack methods.

Detection methods provide warning signals before an attack occurs in order for the user to act fast. These methods rely on ransomware attacks that reveal behaviors of the attack on computer systems such as the file system or the network system. Cabaj and Mazurczyk [7] proposed a system that employs Software-Defined-Networking based detection that observes the behavior of ransomware attacks. Their observation of the network communication between two ransomware families, CryptoWall and Locky, resulted in detecting the appearance of ransomware based on the HTTP message sequences and their respective content sizes [7]. Monika, Zavarsky and Lindskog [21] analysed different ransomware families on Windows and Android environments to determine a detection method for both operating systems. They concluded that to detect Android ransomware it is crucial to monitor request permissions when downloading an application. In a Windows environment, detection will involve detecting abnormal behaviors on file systems [21]. Researchers need to analyse the different behaviors of ransomware to develop an effective detection method. By doing this, they will know what defence mechanisms to use in detecting ransomware.

The fourth category, **prevention and mitigation strategies**, is the focus of this paper, therefore before discussing the findings further analysis has been done. The next section describes the further analysis.

3   Analysis of Prevention and Mitigation Strategies

Since the outbreak of ransomware attacks cybersecurity professionals have been seeking strategies that could help organizations protect data from being held ransom. Companies that were affected by ransomware had to come up with mitigation plans to alleviate the damaged that has been caused by the attack. While others work on preventions before the attack occurs. Ransomware prevention is a proactive approach, whereas ransomware mitigation is a reactive approach of limiting the damage caused by the attack [1].

Table 3. Number of articles on each guideline

Guidelines	Number of articles
Implement backup strategies	31
Install and update protective software	29
Conduct cyber-security training	11
Implement access control	6
Implement strong and complex passwords	5
Do not open untrusted links or attachments	3
Contact law enforcement	3
Hire cyber-security professionals	2
Implement security policies	2
Switch off machines after infections	1
Block pop-ups	1
Encrypt your own data	1
Update computer hardware	1

Table 2 showed 43 journal articles focusing on prevention and mitigation. These articles were further analysed in terms of the platforms involved, the artefacts created, the research method and paradigm employed. As can be expected, some researchers focus on specific platforms such Windows, Linux, or Android. Some artefacts were in the form of computer-based tools. Eight of the papers concerned themselves with tools used to prevent or mitigate ransomware attacks. For example, Gómez-Hernández [13] proposed a tool named R-Locker as a proof of concept to thwart the appearance of ransomware. Jones [16] presents a prototype software that enables a computer user to prevent ransomware from depositing its payload. Some studies mention cloud-based systems to enhance ransomware prevention [17,31]. Cimitile et al. [9], evaluate a tool named Talos to confirm its effectiveness on Android devices.

Another type of artefact found was guidelines. Thirty-five (35) papers explicitly proposed some guidelines. Some guidelines presented by researchers were contradictory. For example, Yaqoob et al. [30] recommends victims to pay the ransom amount, whereas, Erridge [10] forbids people from paying the ransom. Payment does not guarantee data would be restored, instead it may lead to more extortion attempts. A majority of the studies produced guidelines that were similar. For example, backing up of data has appeared on all journal articles as a fundamental guideline to mitigate ransomware attack [3,10,15].

While none of the guidelines is a panacea for ransomware attacks, a consolidated list of the guidelines proposed by the papers would be useful and interesting. Remember the literature search focused on journal papers in well-regarded online databases, this representing the state-of-the-art thinking around ransomware. Table 3 represents the consolidated list of guidelines from the surveyed literature. It also shows the number of articles that emphasized a particular guideline.

This list of guidelines represents the main findings of this study. The next section therefore visits each of the prevention and mitigation guidelines and discusses its role in the prevention and mitigations of ransomware.

4   Prevention and Mitigation Guidelines

The reviewed literature presented common ground between the guidelines. As a result, a consolidated list of guidelines for ransomware prevention and mitigation was produced from the reviewed journal articles. While not a panacea, implementing these guidelines can assist with preventing and mitigating ransomware attacks. The guidelines can be considered by all computer users, but some are more applicable to business users. Consider each of the guidelines in turn.

4.1   Implement Backup Strategies

Organizations need to be crisis-resilient when disaster strikes by having contingency plans to recover lost data. A number of studies place emphasis on regularly backing up computer data to minimize the damage of the attack. For example, Allen [3] explains the importance of data backups to overcome ransomware. Users should regularly create a clone of their computer data and these clones should be timestamped. Therefore, an organization will not have to worry about the availability of their data once data has been restored. There are specialized programs for backing up data. For example cloud storage such as Dropbox and external storage such as USB flash drives, rewritable optical discs or backup tapes [12]. However, it is important that data is backed up offline as ransomware is capable of infecting data backup tools [10]. This means that backup storage should not be connected to the internet and backups need be done daily in order to recover recent data [18]. Creating data backup is a form of a mitigation strategy. In an event where an organization is affected by ransomware, data can be recovered from backup files. Backup storage is a safe haven for data that is used on a daily basis by an organization, so that when disaster strikes business affairs can carry on as normal.

4.2   Install and Update Protective Software

Technical safeguards should be implemented to prevent and detect ransomware as a first line of defense. Antimalware software should be implemented and updated frequently. Patches for operating systems and web browsers should be automated [22]. Out-dated operating systems and other malware programs tend to be more vulnerable to exploitation [12]. Other antimalware programs include virtual private network software when connected to public wi-fi [12]. Ransomware monitoring software can be used to detect ransomware based on its behaviour or signature [15]. However, antivirus software and other software

are an incomplete solution because ransomware families have different signatures of infiltration [24]. Updating computer software is crucial because each software update released will offer advanced features that will defend the device from constantly evolving ransomware attacks [3].

4.3   Conduct Cyber-Security Training

Human behaviour contributes a lot in cyber security as a whole. Therefore, training users on how to prevent and mitigate ransomware attacks is important. A significant proportion of ransomware attackers employ social engineering by using phishing emails as a payload [20]. Businesses should conducts cyber security awareness programs to educate users about the dangers of ransomware attacks and how to prevent and mitigate an attack. Training and education can enable employees that are aware of cyber crimes to analyze, identify and respond to vulnerabilities [18]. By training new and continuing employees, executive management is a establishing a cyber-security culture that will greatly benefit the organization in future [25].

Cyber-security programs should place an emphasis on phishing messages as they are the most prominent ransomware payload [26]. Cyber-security education is a prevention strategy that will provide people with the knowledge and skills to identify ransomware payloads that need to be avoided. If all employees are conscious about this malware, the organization can be spared from the monetary loss caused by ransomware.

4.4   Implement Access Control

Access control is one the basic practices of cyber "hygiene". In regards to ransomware, it may not the ultimate solution to prevent the attack. However, restricting access based on roles in the organization can work as mitigation strategy. Green [15] mentions that through access control it is difficult for the attacker to access high level data after hacking a normal user through malicious emails and ransomware based on user's credentials. Therefore, even if an organization has been affected by ransomware, access control can prevent additional exploitation of computer data.

4.5   Implement Strong and Complex Passwords

In a good cyber-security culture, a strong password is one of the important factors in data protection. Authentication methods should be made high priority in order to protect devices, networks and other accounts against cyber-crimes [3]. A password is a key that allows access to systems and information. In a house the owner will have a different keys to open different rooms. Similarly, users should not use the same password for different accounts to ensure the safety of information [12]. This will make it difficult for a cyber-attacker to access other information with the same password should he or she gain access to a password.

House keys have different and complex indentations to make the keys unique and difficult to copy. A password should also be made complex and strong with a combination of special characters, numeric and alphabets [25].

Passwords are important as they connect everything that has been said in this paper. For example, passwords are for data encryption, access control and backup applications. This linkage is important as it demonstrates that ransomware cannot be prevented or mitigated without having proper passwords. For instance, if the password of a backup storage is weak, ransomware can easily infiltrate the storage that is meant to mitigate the attack. Without strong passwords there is no proper encryption of data and there is easy access. Users can be educated about passwords through cyber-security education and company policies will reinforce the use of strong passwords.

4.6   Do Not Open Untrusted Links or Attachments

A computer is infected by various attack vectors such as drive-by-downloads, malicious advertisements and phishing attacks [7]. In cyber-security training, users are trained on how to differentiate between trusted and untrusted links or email attachments [4]. Ransomware attackers will often use email attachments and links as payloads to infiltrate computer systems. Users are advised to not open suspicious websites and never click on attachments from unknown senders [11]. Organizations have the responsibility to block all malicious websites and filter all employee emails to avoid malicious messages. This is a prevention strategy that will hinder ransomware from infiltrating the computer system.

4.7   Contact Law Enforcement

Erridge [10] proposes steps which a business should take when affected by an attack. Reporting the ransomware attacks to law enforcement is included in these steps. Sheffield [25] also supports this statement, however, he additionally explains that reporting the cybercrime should done promptly. Reporting the cybercrime to law enforcement does not prevent the damage. However, according to Luo and Liao [19] reporting the matter can cause a widespread outcry which can draw the attention of legislator to create laws against ransomware.

4.8   Hire Cybersecurity Professionals

According to Yaqoob et al. [30], a team of cybersecurity professionals should be employed to perform extensive forensic analysis on the network as a whole periodically. This strategy of preventing ransomware attacks can be adopted by large corporations that can meet the expense of a specialized team of experts. These expert may include ethical hackers and penetration testers that will challenge existing systems to expose vulnerabilities [28]. The services provided by these individuals can be outsourced from external companies such as information security consultancy firms. IS consultants will contribute their skills to deign and implement cyber-security best practices that will assist in combating cyber-crimes. In the case of ransomware skilled cyber-security experts will perform security checks for any appearance of ransomware attack. They will develop countermeasures for mitigation strategies should the organization experience the attack. Cyber-security professionals can also facilitate ransomware awareness programs to bridge the gap in cyber-security.

4.9 Implement Security Policies

In organizations it is important that the board of directors draw up policies to protect the business. This allows executive management to provide direction and guidance in a company, therefore, these directives can be expanded into policies [27]. These policies should protect companies from cybercrimes such as ransomware. Sheffield [25] urges business to develop and maintain actionable policies for employees who fail to adhere to the regulations. In medical institutions such as hospitals, being vigilant about cyber-security best practices will protect patient medical records from being encrypted [4]. However, there is no value in merely having a list of best practices and policies, they should be followed by action reinforced by management. Policies should be written from the perspective of ransomware prevention and mitigation guidelines to adequately protect organizations against the attacks. For example, a backup strategy policy will provide detailed standards on how to implement backup strategies and which backup strategies will be ideal for the company. Other policies will focus on password management and access control features.

4.10 Switch Off Machines After Infections

When ransomware has been deposited in a computer that is connected through a network, the malware has the ability to self-propagate to adjacent computer networks resulting in numerous devices being held ransom [32]. A computer will exhibit visible signs of the infection. These signs include a locked screen or encrypted files [5]. At this moment, users are required to act fast by disconnecting all networks and switching off all devices immediately. This mitigation technique is called drop-and-roll [23]. This will alleviate the damage caused by the attack by hindering the malware from propagating. This will prevent further infections of other computers in the network.

4.11 Block Pop-Ups

Pop-up websites may host malicious advertising websites that contain drive-by-downloads. As part of cybersecurity hygiene, it is important to block pop-ups on web browsers [10,22]. Pop-up website and advertisements may contain ransomware link and drive-by-downloads. It is vital to implement Ad-blockers and script-blockers to prevent the execution of ransomware [10]. Blocking pop-up websites is a preventative measure to protect against ransomware attack before they occur.

4.12   Encrypt Your Own Data

Brody [6] emphasizes that data should be encrypted by the user with purpose of concealment. This means that anyone without the encryption key cannot convert the code back to usable, readable information. In the case of ransomware an attacker may allow someone else to steal the data, however, the data will be inaccessible due to the encryption [6]. It can be argued that encryption is neither a prevention or mitigation strategy for ransomware, but it protects the organization's intellectual property such as sensitive information from being useful if stolen. Nevertheless, users should be cautious of other cyber-attacks that may accompany ransomware and data protection should be the priority in an organization.

4.13   Update Computer Hardware

Computer hardware should be kept up to date, hence, Ali [2] urges users to purchase new computers. Old computer hardware tends to be too slow and the latest software cannot run on old computers. Therefore, ransomware attackers will find it easy to exploit system vulnerabilities. It is essential that organizations renew computer hardware in order to run the latest versions of software. Ransomware attacks can be prevented by running the latest software such as anti-malware programs on computers.

5   Conclusion

We live in an era that is information-centric. Information, including some high-value and confidential information, are kept in digital format. Cybercrime syndicates work tirelessly to obtain this information illegally for financial gain. Cyber-crimes such as ransomware attacks have brought large companies to their knees through cyber extortion. Ransomware has evolved in this past few years to be one of the most prominent and dangerous attacks.

Researchers and cyber-security experts have been seeking to find a panacea to this type of cyber-attack, but organizations continue to suffer. Research efforts led to the development of detection techniques and the discovery of ransomware attack methods. Several case studies of recent attacks have been documented. This paper set out to investigate current thinking regarding the prevention and mitigation of ransomware attacks.

To identify state-of-the-art papers were selected from journal papers published since 2015. Studying and coding of the literature were done by a single coder. This may affect the exact reproducibility of the data, but given the granularity of coding and the ultimate goal to find prevention and mitigation methods for results are still interesting and trustworthy enough. Particularly insightful is the consolidated list of guidelines to prevent and mitigate ransomware attacks.

The thirteen guidelines collected all contribute in some way or another to the prevention or mitigation of ransomware attacks. None, however represents a panacea. Somewhat shockingly all of these prevention and mitigation guidelines are basic cyber-security guidelines that should have been adopted by organizations and companies by now. According to the authors there is nothing "unexpected" in the prevention and mitigation guidelines; any cyber-security expert could have listed these guidelines. This observation warrants further reflection.

Firstly, this list of guidelines demonstrates that it is believed that a relatively new, constantly evolving type of cyber-attack, such as ransomware, can be conquered by old cyber-security strategies. However, secondly, that it is even necessary to mention such basic guidelines is concerning as it speaks to the level of security awareness within businesses. This, thirdly, may critique the effectiveness of current security awareness and training efforts (which ironically is one of the guidelines). Fourthly, it also shows that cyber-security researchers are not creating new techniques or strategies to prevent and mitigate ransomware attacks. Not only does this speak to the reactiveness of research, but demonstrates an important gap in the security research agenda.

How should this impact researchers in information security? What is clear is that the work around specific attacks is reactive, more than pro-active. While it is impossible to predict the next generation of attacks, researchers should nevertheless continue their search for new approaches, techniques and tools to combat attacks. We saw little research regarding ransomware going this direction.

A significant portion of the sampled ransomware research focused on the prevention and mitigation of attacks. Alarming though is the fact that there seem to be a significant portion of the research discussing well-matured guidelines. Researchers should reflect on why awareness and training exercises of the past is so ineffective. Clearly research does not reach the required audiences.

What do these findings mean to the business world? Of course, there is no organization that is completely safe from cyber-attacks. However, ignoring the basics, such as encapsulated in these guidelines, increases the risk of falling prey to ransomware attacks, or whatever the next flavour of attack will be. Although attacks cannot always be prevented, good practices could help limit the impact of a ransomware attack should it occur.

Businesses should therefore implement technical security measures as best they can. Furthermore they should institutionalize certain best practices by encapsulating them in policies, thus directing the users of the organization along a certain way. Business users should act responsibly and as such it is necessary that business inculcates a culture that encourages good behaviour. Security awareness programmes should form part of this. However, these should not be once offs, but incorporate continual interventions.

Individual users are reminded that ransomware, like many other security attacks, can be compared to an influenza virus in the human body. In order for one to prevent the illness, it is important to practice basic hygiene such as washing of hands to kill influenza-causing germs. Ransomware is similar in that one cannot fight the attack without practicing basic cyber-hygiene such as suggested by the 13 guidelines derived from literature. Remember, therefore, *Good cyber hygiene promotes good cyber health.*

Acknowledgements. This work is based upon research partially supported by the National Research Foundation, and partially through a CSIR-DST Inter-Programme Bursary. Any opinion, findings and conclusions or recommendations expressed in this material are those of the author(s) and not of the respective funders.

References

1. Al-Rimy, B.A.S., Maarof, M.A., Mohd Shaid, S.Z.: Ransomware threat success factors, taxonomy, and countermeasures: a survey and research directions. Comput. Secur. **74**, 144–166 (2018). https://doi.org/10.1016/j.cose.2018.01.001
2. Ali, A.: Ransomware: a research and a personal case study of dealing with this nasty Malware. J. Issues Inform. Sci. Inf. Technol. **14**, 87–99 (2017). http://www.informingscience.org/Publications/3707
3. Allen, J.: Surviving ransomware. Am. J. Fam. Law **31**(2), 65–68 (2017)
4. van Alstin, C.M.: Ransomware: it's as scary as it sounds. Health Manag. Technol. **37**(4), 26–27 (2016)
5. Brewer, R.: Ransomware attacks: detection, prevention and cure. Netw. Secur. **2016**(9), 5–9 (2016). https://doi.org/10.1016/S1353-4858(16)30086-1
6. Brody, M.L.: Protecting yourself from ransomware and should you become a victim, here's how to recover. Podiatry Manag. **36**(6), 39–40 (2017)
7. Cabaj, K., Mazurczyk, W.: Using software-defined networking for ransomware mitigation: the case of CryptoWall. IEEE Netw. **30**(6), 14–20 (2016). https://doi.org/10.1109/MNET.2016.1600110NM
8. Chen, J., et al.: Uncovering the face of Android ransomware: characterization and real-time detection. IEEE Trans. Inf. Forensics Secur. **13**(5), 1289–1300 (2018). https://doi.org/10.1109/TIFS.2017.2787905. http://ieeexplore.ieee.org
9. Cimitile, A., Mercaldo, F., Nardone, V., Santone, A., Visaggio, C.A.: Talos: no more ransomware victims with formal methods. Int. J. Inf. Secur. (2017). https://doi.org/10.1007/s10207-017-0398-5
10. Erridge, T.: Ransomware: threat and response. Netw. Secur. **2016**(10), 17–19 (2016). https://doi.org/10.1016/S1353-4858(16)30097-6
11. Goldsborough, R.: Protecting yourself from ransomware. Teacher Librarian **43**(4), 70–71 (2016)
12. Goldsborough, R.: The increasing threat of ransomware. Teacher Librarian **45**(1), 61 (2017)
13. Gómez-Hernández, J.A., Álvarez-González, L., García-Teodoro, P.: R-Locker: thwarting ransomware action through a honeyfile-based approach. Comput. Secur. **73**, 389–398 (2018). https://doi.org/10.1016/j.cose.2017.11.019
14. Gordon, S.: Ransomware menace grows as new threats emerge. Netw. Secur. **2016**(8), 1–2 (2016). https://doi.org/10.1016/S1353-4858(16)30072-1
15. Green, A.: Ransomware and the GDPR. Netw. Secur. **2017**(3), 18–19 (2017). https://doi.org/10.1016/S1353-4858(17)30030-2
16. Jones, J., Shashidhar, N.: Ransomware analysis and defense WannaCry and the Win32 environment. Int. J. Inf. Secur. Sci. **6**(4), 57–69 (2017)
17. Lee, J.K., Moon, S.Y., Park, J.H.: CloudRPS: a cloud analysisbased enhancedransomware prevention system. J. Supercomput. **2017**(73), 3065–3084 (2017). https://doi.org/10.1007/s11227-016-1825-5
18. Lee, S.y.: Guarding against ransomware. Internal Auditor **74**(4), 13 (2017)
19. Luo, X., Liao, Q.: Awareness education as the key to ransomware prevention. **16**(4), 195–202 (2007). https://doi.org/10.1080/10658980701576412

20. Mansfield-Devine, S.: Hospitals become major target for ransomware. Netw. Secur. **2016**(4), 1–2 (2016). https://doi.org/10.1016/S1353-4858(16)30031-9
21. Monika, Zavarsky, P., Lindskog, D.: Experimental analysis of ransomware on windows and android platforms: evolution and characterization. In: Shakshuki, E. (ed.) The 2nd International Workshop on Future Information Security, Privacy & Forensics for Complex Systems, pp. 465–472. Procedia Computer Science, Edmonton (2016). https://doi.org/10.1016/j.procs.2016.08.072
22. Pope, J.: Ransomware: minimizing the risks. Innov. Clin. Neurosci. **13**(11–12), 37–40 (2016)
23. Richardson, R., North, M.: Ransomware: evolution, mitigation and prevention. Int. Manag. Rev. **13**(1), 10–21 (2017)
24. Scaife, N., Traynor, P., Butler, K.: Making sense of the ransomware mess (and planning a sensible path forward). IEEE Potentials **36**(6), 28–31 (2017). https://doi.org/10.1109/MPOT.2017.2737201
25. Sheffield, J.: Pirates of the PHI: identifying and responding to a ransomware attack according to HIPAA best practices. Benefits Law J. **30**(4), 36–54 (2017)
26. Solander, A.C., Forman, A.S., Glasser, N.M.: Ransomware-give me back my files! Empl. Relat. Law J. **42**(2), 53–55 (2016)
27. von Solms, R., von Solms, S.H.: Information security governance: a model based on the direct-control cycle. Comput. Secur. **25**(6), 408–412 (2006). https://doi.org/10.1016/j.cose.2006.07.005
28. Srinivasan, C.R.: Hobby hackers to billion-dollar industry: the evolution of ransomware. Comput. Fraud Secur. **2017**(11), 7–9 (2017). https://doi.org/10.1016/S1361-3723(17)30081-7
29. Webster, J., Watson, R.T.: Analyzing the past to prepare for the future: writing a literature review. MIS Q. **26**(2), xiii–xxiii (2002). http://www.misq.org/misreview/announce.html
30. Yaqoob, I., Ahmed, E., ur Rehman, M.H., Ahmed, A.I.A., Al-Garadi, M.A., Imran, M., Guizani, M.: The rise of ransomware and emerging security challenges in the Internet of Things. Comput. Netw. **129**(Part 2), 444–458 (2017). https://doi.org/10.1016/j.comnet.2017.09.003
31. Yun, J., Hur, J., Shin, Y., Koo, D.: CLDSafe: an efficient file backup system in cloud storage against ransomware. IEICE Trans. Inf. Syst. **100**(9), 2228–2231 (2017). https://doi.org/10.1587/transinf.2017EDL8052
32. Zimba, A., Wang, Z., Chen, H.: Multi-stage crypto ransomware attacks: a new emerging cyber threat to critical infrastructure and industrial control systems. ICT Express **4**(1), 14–18 (2018). https://doi.org/10.1016/j.icte.2017.12.007

Mitigating the Ransomware Threat:
A Protection Motivation Theory Approach

Jacques Ophoff[(✉)] [ID] and Mcguigan Lakay

University of Cape Town, Cape Town, South Africa
{jacques.ophoff,mcguigan.lakay}@uct.ac.za

Abstract. Ransomware has emerged as one of the biggest security threats to organizations and individuals alike. As technical solutions are developed the creators of ransomware are also improving the sophistication of such attacks. A combination of technical and behavioral measures is required to deal with this problem. This study investigates computer users' motivation to adopt security measures against ransomware, using protection motivation theory (PMT) as a theoretical foundation. We conducted empirical research, using a survey methodology, collecting data from 118 respondents. Using partial least squares structural equation modelling our analysis provides support for several factors influencing protection motivation in this context. These include perceived threat severity and perceived threat vulnerability, mediated by fear. Self-efficacy is shown as a significant coping factor. Maladaptive rewards and response costs both have a significant negative influence on protection motivation. The results provide support for the use of fear appeals and PMT to influence protection motivation in the context of ransomware threats.

Keywords: Ransomware · Malware · Cybersecurity
Protection motivation theory · Fear appeal

1 Introduction

Data is one of the most valuable assets in any organization. Ensuring the availability of data is a main objective of information security [1]. There are numerous threats to the availability of data, but one of the fastest growing in recent years is ransomware. Ransomware is a type of malware which makes data inaccessible until the victim pays a ransom to the attacker [2].

Ransomware has impacted organizations worldwide and across industries. Since 2014 there has been significant growth in the number of reported attacks [2]. There have been several high-profile attacks, including major incidents in the healthcare industry [3]. Attacks have also targeted users and their personal data, increasingly through mobile devices [4, 5]. Considering the bring your own device (BYOD) trend this presents another attack vector for organizations to manage. While detection and recovery tools have improved, there are indications that ransomware attacks are becoming more sophisticated and will continue to be a threat to organizations and individuals [5, 6].

© Springer Nature Switzerland AG 2019
H. Venter et al. (Eds.): ISSA 2018, CCIS 973, pp. 163–175, 2019.
https://doi.org/10.1007/978-3-030-11407-7_12

Mitigating ransomware is as much a behavioral as a technical problem. From a behavioral information security perspective the focus is on users and their performance of important security measures [7, 8]. Several measures are advised in response to the increasing number of ransomware attacks, such as backing up critical data and not opening suspicious (phishing) email links or files. However, there is evidence that technically unsophisticated users do not implement such measures [4].

In this paper we investigate computer users' motivation to adopt security measures against ransomware from a behavioral information security perspective. We use the term computer user broadly to include both employees using organizational systems as well as individual users of personal devices. We address the following research question: *Which factors influence user motivation to adopt security measures against ransomware attacks?* To answer this question, both theoretically and empirically, we base our research on protection motivation theory (PMT). We use PMT because of its ability to explain voluntary security-related actions, for instance the adoption of anti-spyware [9] and backing up data [10].

The remainder of this paper is organized as follows. First, the conceptual and theoretical background will be presented. This includes our research hypotheses and conceptual model. Next, we discuss the research methodology that was used. This is followed by data analysis and a discussion of the results. Lastly, the conclusion summarizes the research contributions.

2 Background

In the following subsections we first provide some context around ransomware and end-users' behavioral security issues. Then we discuss PMT as theoretical foundation for the study. This is followed by the hypotheses for the study.

2.1 Ransomware

Ransomware is a type of malware that threatens the availability of data, with the intention of gaining a financial reward. To gain access to a system social engineering tactics are frequently used to exploit a potential victim [11]. Once ransomware is installed on a system it encrypts data files and demands payment in return for a decryption key [5]. The typical method of ransom payment is in a digital currency, such as Bitcoin, as it provides anonymity and can be used globally [12]. This also means that there is no guarantee of receiving a valid decryption key even if the ransom payment is made.

Ransomware can have a severe impact on organizations, potentially halting all operations. This often damages the organizations reputation, leading to further financial losses [5]. Small and under resourced organizations are prone to being targeted, especially if it is known that they are willing to pay the ransom [13]. Although there are technical measures to mitigate ransomware, such as anti-malware software, these are often temporary as ransomware is continuously evolving [4]. Due to the lack of a permanent technical solution to ransomware, only awareness and protective behaviors of users can help to reduce the impact of ransomware attacks [8].

The central idea behind ransomware is to leverage the victim's fear of data loss. The current problem is that users do not necessarily put in effort and time to secure their information assets [14]. Conceivably users are not aware of how vulnerable they are or how severe ransomware can be. From a protection motivation perspective, manipulating individuals' fear has been shown to lead to change in behavioral intentions [9]. In this regard the intention is to get users to adopt security measures when interacting with their information assets, to avoid falling victim to ransomware attacks. This notion of using fear to modify security behavior is one of the main research areas in behavioral information security and forms the foundation of PMT.

2.2 Protection Motivation Theory

PMT was developed by Rogers [15] with the objective of promoting healthy behaviors. It is applicable to any threat-related study for which there is a practical recommended action that can be carried out. The theory conceptualized that persuasive communication, using a fear appeal, initiates a cognitive appraisal process involving the threat and a coping response [15].

The threat-appraisal process is triggered by a fear appeal message which may, or may not, induce fear. Threat-appraisal consists of the perceived threat vulnerability and perceived threat severity constructs [10, 15]. PMT suggests that fear could be predicted as it is an emotion in response to a threat. Fear as a stimulus can influence an individual's intention to take recommended protective actions.

The coping-appraisal evaluates the belief that a recommended response can prevent the threat [15]. Coping-appraisal consists of the response efficacy, self-efficacy, and response costs constructs [10]. A user will engage in protection motivation if response efficacy and self-efficacy outweigh the response costs.

In behavioral information security research PMT has been used and extended [e.g. 16] to motivate employees and individuals to adopt security measures. Boss et al. [10] identifies two versions of PMT: the core model in its fundamental form and the full model (nomology). The core model consists of perceived threat severity, perceived threat vulnerability, response efficacy, self-efficacy, response costs, and protection motivation. This model is partially supported by a number of information security studies [e.g. 17, 18], but contains little or no emphasis on fear appeal manipulations. The full model includes fear, as a partial mediator between perceived threat severity, perceived threat vulnerability and protection motivation, as well as maladaptive rewards. The full model was used in this study.

2.3 Hypotheses Development and Conceptual Model

The threat of ransomware is used in combination with PMT in this study. Protection motivation includes the intention to adopt security measures aimed at mitigating data loss caused by ransomware. Measures could include backing up data, changing default passwords, updating the operating system and software applications, using an anti-virus tool to scan the device for malware, setting user access controls, using a firewall, and using popup blockers in web browsers [14]. This study will consider two of these measures: using anti-malware software and backing up data.

Threat-Appraisal. In the full PMT model the threat-appraisal process consists of perceived threat severity, perceived threat vulnerability, and maladaptive rewards. Perceived threat severity refers to the degree of the consequences if the threat causes harm [19]. In the ransomware context the loss of data can lead to severe organizational consequences, such as halting of business operations and reputational damage. Perceived threat vulnerability refers to users' judgment of the probability of being exposed to the threat [19]. In our research context this refers to users' assessment of the probability of their devices being exposed to ransomware. We hypothesize that:

> *H1a: An increase in perceived severity of ransomware threats increases protection motivation.*
> *H1b: An increase in perceived vulnerability to ransomware threats increases protection motivation.*

Fear is a negative emotion that can be triggered if the perceived threat is relative to the individual [20]. A ransomware fear appeal is a stimulus designed to trigger the threat-appraisal and coping-appraisal processes [19]. This could be achieved by informing users of the consequences of ransomware and appropriate security measures. Fear influences both protection motivation and acts as a mediator between the threat and protection motivation [10]. With respect to fear we hypothesize that:

> *H2a: An increase in perceived severity of ransomware threats increases perceived fear.*
> *H2b: An increase in perceived vulnerability to ransomware threats increases perceived fear.*
> *H3: An increase in fear increases protection motivation.*

Maladaptive rewards can influence the threat appraisal process depending on the user's assessment of the reward if the recommended action is ignored. The user may opt for the maladaptive reward if it holds more weight than the perceived threat [10]. An example is when a user chooses to install software from an unknown source, even though it may contain hidden ransomware. Therefore, we hypothesize:

> *H4: An increase in maladaptive rewards decreases protection motivation.*

Coping-Appraisal. The coping-appraisal process consist of the response efficacy, self-efficacy, and response costs. Response efficacy is the confidence users have in the effectiveness of the recommendation provided in the fear appeal. Self-efficacy is the confidence or belief of users that they can perform the recommendation. Response costs are the expenses users experience to implement the recommendation, such as time and effort [10]. Belief in the effectiveness of security recommendations and the user's ability to perform them is required for a positive appraisal [19]. In the context of preventative measures against ransomware, if users believe that making regular backups of their data and using anti-malware software will be useful to minimize the severity of ransomware, there will be a greater chance of protection motivation. We hypothesize that:

H5a: An increase in response efficacy increases protection motivation.
H5b: An increase in self-efficacy increases protection motivation.
H5c: An increase in response costs decreases protection motivation.

Based on the above discussion, Fig. 1 presents our conceptual research model. Based on the constructs from PMT the model predicts several factors which influence users' protection motivation in the context of ransomware.

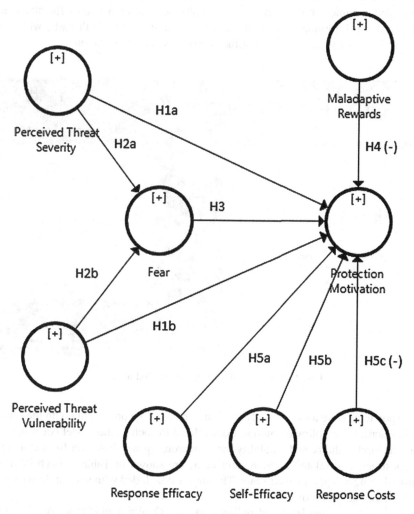

Fig. 1. Conceptual model (based on Boss et al. [10]).

3 Methodology

We evaluated our conceptual model empirically, using a cross-sectional survey. Data was collected from a random sample of staff and students at a large research university. The university was deemed an appropriate organization as it had faced regular ransomware attacks, targeting both staff and students.

We developed a fear appeal for the survey, which is shown in Fig. 2. The fear appeal is a combination of ransomware communications (previously sent by the university) and a typical ransom message (usually seen after a successful attack has encrypted data). Information about the threat was conveyed by both parts, while recommended actions were contained in the (university) communication.

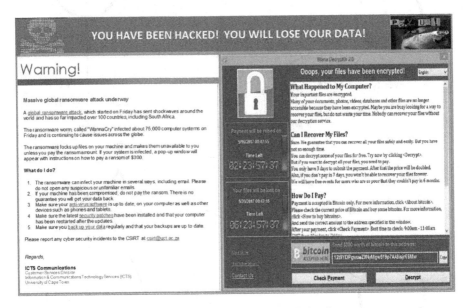

Fig. 2. Fear appeal with recommended actions.

Respondents were asked to study the fear appeal before proceeding with the survey. The fear appeal was followed by questions related to each of the model constructs. To ensure research validity and reliability the item wording was based on Boss et al. [10]. The constructs and related measurement items are shown in Table 1. Each item was measured using a 7-point Likert scale. The survey concluded with several demographic and device usage questions.

The survey was implemented online using the Qualtrics platform.[1] A pilot study was conducted to pretest the survey fear appeal, item wording, and flow. After minor modifications a survey link was distributed via email.

---

[1] https://www.qualtrics.com/.

Table 1. Study measurement items.

Construct	Code	Items (R = reverse coded)
Perceived threat severity (PTS)	PTS1	If I were to lose data from my hard drive, I would suffer a lot of pain
	PTS2	Losing data would be unlikely to cause me major problems. (R)
	PTS3	If my computer were infected by ransomware, it would be severe
Perceived threat vulnerability (PTV)	PTV1	I am unlikely to lose data in the future. (R)
	PTV2	My chances of losing data in the future are less likely. (R)
	PTV3	It is likely that my computer will become infected with ransomware
Maladaptive rewards (MR)	MR1	Not using an anti-malware application saves me time
	MR2	Not using an anti-malware application saves me money
	MR3	Not using an anti-malware application keeps me from being confused
Fear (F)	F1	I am afraid of ransomware
	F2	My computer might be seriously infected with ransomware
	F3	My computer might become unusable due to ransomware
	F4	I am frightened about the prospect of losing data from my computing device
	F5	I am worried about the prospect of losing data from my computing device
Response efficacy (RE)	RE1	Backing up my hard drive is a good way to reduce the risk of losing data
	RE2	If I were to back up my data at least once a week, I would lessen my chances of data loss
	RE3	When using anti-malware software, a computers data is more likely to be protected
Self-efficacy (SE)	SE1	Anti-malware software is easy to use
	SE2	Anti-malware software is convenient to use
	SE3	I am able to use anti-malware software without much effort
Response costs (RC)	RC1	The benefits of backing up my hard drive at least once a week outweigh the costs. (R)
	RC2	I would be discouraged from backing up my data during the next week because it would take too much time
	RC3	Taking the time to back up my data during the next week would cause me too many problems
Protection motivation (PM)	PM1	I intend to back up my hard drive during the next week
	PM2	I do not wish to back up my data during the next week. (R)
	PM3	I intend to use anti-malware software in the next three months
	PM4	I predict I will use anti-malware software in the next three months
	PM5	I plan to use anti-malware software in the next three months

4 Data Analysis and Results

A total of 234 responses were collected. From these 94 incomplete responses were removed. A further 22 responses were removed due to not answering a control question correctly, leaving a final dataset of 118 responses for analysis. There were many responses in which no questions were answered, which could be due to a reluctance to read the fear appeal and no incentives being offered.

The demographic data indicates a younger (59% aged below 25) and slightly more female (52%) sample. Most of the respondents were regular users of computing devices. A summary of the demographic data is provided in Table 2.

Table 2. Demographic data

Demographic	Items	Count	Percentage
Gender	Male	55	47%
	Female	62	52%
	Prefer not to answer	1	1%
Age	Under 18 years	0	-
	18–24 years old	70	59%
	25–34 years old	27	23%
	35–44 years old	13	11%
	45–54 years old	6	5%
	55–64 years old	2	2%
	65 years or older	0	-
Primary role	I am an undergrad student	65	55%
	I am a post-grad student	33	28%
	I am an academic staff member	2	2%
	I am an admin staff member (Non-IT)	7	6%
	I am an IT staff member	11	9%
Primary device	Smartphone/mobile phone	22	19%
	Tablet	2	2%
	Personal Computer	16	14%
	Laptop	78	66%
Device experience	Less than 1 year	5	4%
	1–2 years	11	9%
	3–5 years	12	10%
	6–10 years	28	24%
	More than 10 years	62	53%
Device use	Less than 1 h a day	0	-
	1–2 h a day	6	5%
	3–5 h a day	35	30%
	More than 5 h a day	77	65%

Data analysis was performed using partial least squares structural equation modelling (PLS-SEM). PLS-SEM focuses on explaining the variance in dependent variables [21]. The approach is suitable for validating predictive models and can be used with small sample sizes [22]. The tool used for analysis was SmartPLS [23]. In analyzing our data we followed the recommended multi-stage process [22], which starts with estimating the path model and assessing the reflective measurement model.

4.1   Analysis of the Measurement Model

A model is said to be reflective if the indicators are highly correlated and interchangeable [21]. Due to the high correlations their reliability and validity should be thoroughly examined. The first criterion to be evaluated is internal consistency reliability (CR). In this regard we examined composite reliability, with all constructs above the recommended threshold (0.70). Next we examined convergent validity, during which three indicators with weak outer loadings (F2 and F3 < 0.40; RE2 < 0.70) were removed. The remaining indicators' loadings were acceptable. The average variance extracted (AVE) for all constructs were above the recommended threshold (0.50). Finally, discriminant validity was assessed using the Fornell-Larcker criterion. This showed that all constructs were within acceptable ranges. The above results are summarized in Table 3. All model evaluation criteria were met, providing support for the measures' reliability and validity.

Table 3. Reliability and validity assessment results.

Cons.	CR	AVE	Fornell-Larcker Correlations						
			F	MR	PTS	PTV	PM	RC	RE	SE
F	0.896	0.742	0.861							
MR	0.818	0.601	-0.065	0.775						
PTS	0.808	0.585	0.666	-0.139	0.765					
PTV	0.85	0.658	0.338	0.087	0.218	0.811				
PM	0.89	0.627	0.29	-0.599	0.234	-0.036	0.792			
RC	0.849	0.652	-0.096	0.235	-0.045	-0.014	-0.482	0.808		
RE	0.759	0.615	0.201	-0.28	0.198	-0.144	0.415	-0.152	0.784	
SE	0.877	0.705	0.103	-0.581	0.052	-0.226	0.582	-0.293	0.418	0.839

4.2   Analysis of the Structural Model

The structural model was tested to estimate the path coefficients, which calculates the strength of the relationships between constructs. The coefficients of determination (R^2) values indicate that the model explains approximately 48% of the variance for fear, and 59% for protection motivation. Compared to previous information security studies using PMT, the values show a medium to high effect size [10]. In addition, the f^2 effect size showed a medium effect of maladaptive rewards (0.195) and response costs (0.196) on protection motivation, as well as a large effect of perceived threat severity on fear (0.711).

Bootstrapping with 5,000 samples [21] was used to test the significance of the structural paths (hypotheses). The results indicate that only H1a, H1b, and H5a are not significant. The PLS path modelling estimation, including path coefficients and p-values, is shown in Fig. 3. The results of hypothesis testing are summarized in Table 4.

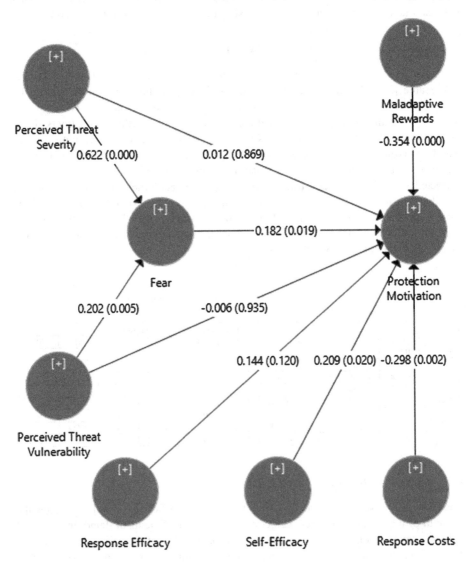

Fig. 3. Structural model analysis.

Table 4. Overview of findings.

Hypothesis	Path Coefficient	T Value	P Value	Supported?
H1a: PTS => PM	0.012	0.165	$p > 0.1$	Not supported
H1b: PTV => PM	−0.006	0.082	$p > 0.1$	Not supported
H2a: PTS => F	0.622	9.663	$p < 0.001***$	Supported
H2b: PTV => F	0.202	2.813	$p < 0.01**$	Supported
H3: F => PM	0.182	2.353	$p < 0.05*$	Supported
H4: MR => PM	−0.354	3.535	$p < 0.001***$	Supported
H5a: RE => PM	0.144	1.557	$p > 0.1$	Not supported
H5b: SE => PM	0.209	2.33	$p < 0.05*$	Supported
H5c: RC => PM	−0.298	3.089	$p < 0.01**$	Supported

4.3   Discussion

The results show strong support for the application of PMT in the context of a ransomware threat. The perceived threat severity and vulnerability seems to have no direct influence on protection motivation, but does strongly influence fear as an emotional response. From our results there is evidence that fear acts as a mediator between the threat and protection motivation [10]. H2a and H2b explain that a user's perception of fear of a threat must be high to motivate the user to perform a recommended behavior as provided in the fear appeal message. The findings demonstrate that that fear is an independent and dependent multi-dimensional construct [7] which is affected significantly by perceived threat severity and perceived threat vulnerability.

It is interesting to note the significant influence of maladaptive rewards and response costs on protection motivation. This indicates that there are significant barriers to overcome to influence users. We investigated this further using multigroup analysis [21], looking at the influence of the users primary device. When comparing smartphones and laptops there is a significant difference ($p < 0.05$) in the effect of maladaptive rewards (for smartphones) and perceived threat severity, where the perception of a threat is less on smartphones.

In terms of coping-appraisal response efficacy was not significant, which could indicate that respondents did not fully understand the recommendations. Due to the coping responses being backing up data and using anti-malware software, a user's perception could be negatively impacted as there have been recent reports on ransomware attacks [5].

A fear appeal with recommended behaviors to protect oneself from ransomware was introduced to influence users towards protection motivation. The fear appeal may have induced fear which triggered the processes in PMT. However, the fear appeal message could have been ignored by the user. Respondents' answers would then be based on their personal experiences with similar threats and their means of dealing with those threats.

Protection motivation is a dependent variable which is significantly affected by fear as well as some of the other constructs, as seen in the analysis section. In this study perceived threat severity, perceived threat vulnerability, and response efficacy did not play a significant role in influencing protection motivation.

5   Conclusion

This study examined the threat of ransomware, analyzing the factors that could influence protection motivation in users. This is motivated by the fact that the mitigation of ransomware requires both technical solutions as well as behavioral changes. The study used PMT as a theoretical basis. Based on our empirical results it was shown that PMT is a good foundation in this context.

Several factors were shown to significantly influence user motivation to adopt security measures against ransomware attacks. These include perceived threat severity and perceived threat vulnerability, mediated by fear, as part of the threat-appraisal process. Self-efficacy was shown as a significant factor in the coping-appraisal process. Maladaptive rewards and response costs both had a significant negative influence on protection motivation.

This study has several limitations which present promising directions for future research. It could be argued that the research sample was limited and too homogenous, consisting only of university staff and students. However, within university environments ransomware threats have been a problem and thus it is argued as a valid organizational context. Future research could expand the study using a larger and more heterogenous sample.

We created a custom fear appeal, but did not extensively test differences in the design of this message. Future research could examine this aspect of PMT in more detail, potentially using an experiment to test differences in fear appeal designs. A theoretical basis for the design which ties in with PMT would add credibility and extend existing behavioral information security research.

In literature numerous recommended actions are given to mitigate ransomware. We only focused on two such recommendation, the use of anti-malware software and backing up data. Future studies could expand this with questions related to phishing emails, installing operating system and software updates, etc. In this way protection motivation can be formalized as a formative construct.

Acknowledgement. This work is based on the research supported wholly/in part by the National Research Foundation of South Africa (Grant Numbers 114838).

References

1. Whitman, M.E., Mattord, H.J.: Principles of Information Security. Cengage Learning, Boston (2011)
2. Al-rimy, B.A.S., Maarof, M.A., Shaid, S.Z.M.: Ransomware threat success factors, taxonomy, and countermeasures: a survey and research directions. Comput. Secur. **74**, 144–166 (2018)

3. Investigation: WannaCry cyber attack and the NHS - National Audit Office (NAO). https://www.nao.org.uk/report/investigation-wannacry-cyber-attack-and-the-nhs/
4. Kharraz, A., Robertson, W., Kirda, E.: Protecting against ransomware: a new line of research or restating classic ideas? IEEE Secur. Priv. **16**, 103–107 (2018)
5. Mansfield-Devine, S.: Ransomware: taking businesses hostage. Netw. Secur. **2016**, 8–17 (2016)
6. Nadeau, M.: 11 ransomware trends for 2018. https://www.csoonline.com/article/3267544/ransomware/11-ways-ransomware-is-evolving.html
7. Crossler, R.E., Johnston, A.C., Lowry, P.B., Hu, Q., Warkentin, M., Baskerville, R.: Future directions for behavioral information security research. Comput. Secur. **32**, 90–101 (2013)
8. Fimin, M.: Are employees part of the ransomware problem? Comput. Fraud Secur. **2017**, 15–17 (2017)
9. Johnston, A.C., Warkentin, M.: Fear appeals and information security behaviors: an empirical study. MIS Q. **34**, 549-A4 (2010)
10. Boss, S.R., Galletta, D.F., Benjamin Lowry, P., Moody, G.D., Polak, P.: What do systems users have to fear? Using fear appeals to engender threats and fear that motivate protective security behaviors. MIS Q. **39**, 837–864 (2015)
11. Gallegos-Segovia, P.L., Bravo-Torres, J.F., Larios-Rosillo, V.M., Vintimilla-Tapia, P.E., Yuquilima-Albarado, I.F., Jara-Saltos, J.D.: Social engineering as an attack vector for ransomware. In: 2017 CHILEAN Conference on Electrical, Electronics Engineering, Information and Communication Technologies (CHILECON), pp. 1–6 (2017)
12. Brewer, R.: Ransomware attacks: detection, prevention and cure. Netw. Secur. **2016**, 5–9 (2016)
13. Simmonds, M.: How businesses can navigate the growing tide of ransomware attacks. Comput. Fraud Secur. **2017**, 9–12 (2017)
14. Crossler, R.E., Bélanger, F., Ormond, D.: The quest for complete security: an empirical analysis of users' multi-layered protection from security threats. Inf. Syst. Front., 1–15 (2017)
15. Rogers, R.W.: A protection motivation theory of fear appeals and attitude change. J. Psychol. **91**, 93–114 (1975)
16. Aurigemma, S., Mattson, T.: Exploring the effect of uncertainty avoidance on taking voluntary protective security actions. Comput. Secur. **73**, 219–234 (2018)
17. Herath, T., Rao, H.R.: Protection motivation and deterrence: a framework for security policy compliance in organisations. Eur. J. Inf. Syst. **18**, 106–125 (2009)
18. Vance, A., Siponen, M., Pahnila, S.: Motivating IS security compliance: insights from habit and protection motivation theory. Inf. Manag. **49**, 190–198 (2012)
19. Rogers, R.W.: Cognitive and physiological processes in fear appeals and attitude change: a revised theory of protection motivation. Soc. Psychophysiol., 153–176 (1983)
20. Witte, K.: Fear control and danger control: a test of the extended parallel process model (EPPM). Commun. Monogr. **61**, 113–134 (1994)
21. Hair Jr., J.F., Hult, G.T.M., Ringle, C.M., Sarstedt, M.: A primer on partial least squares structural equation modeling. SAGE Publications Inc., Los Angeles (2016)
22. Hair Jr., J.F., Sarstedt, M., Hopkins, L., Kuppelwieser, V.G.: Partial least squares structural equation modeling (PLS-SEM): an emerging tool in business research. Eur. Bus. Rev. **26**, 106–121 (2014)
23. Ringle, C.M., Wende, S., Becker, J.-M.: SmartPLS 3. SmartPLS GmbH (2015)

Skills Requirements for Cyber Security Professionals: A Content Analysis of Job Descriptions in South Africa

Amaanullah Parker[(⊠)] and Irwin Brown[(⊠)]

Department of Information Systems,
University of Cape Town, Cape Town, South Africa
prkama003@myuct.ac.za, Irwin.Brown@uct.ac.za

Abstract. With cybercrime increasing at a rapid rate due to the improvement in technologies, cyber security has become a global matter of interest. Cyber security professionals protect organisations from cybercrime and other cyber threats. A shortage of skills has increased the demand for cyber security professionals. This research study examines the skills, knowledge and qualification requirements that are required of a cyber security professional in South Africa. 196 unique job advertisements from 5 job portal websites were collected. A content analysis of the advertisements show that cyber security professionals require technical and interpersonal skills amongst others. Organisations looking to employ cyber security professionals require most professionals to have a Bachelor degree in either Computer Science, Information Systems or Engineering as a minimum qualification along with industry certifications. This paper is an initial exploratory study that can serve as a basis for more specific studies in future.

Keywords: Cyber-security · Qualifications · Skills · Roles
Cyber-security South Africa

1 Introduction

Over the last few years, cybersecurity has "become a matter of global interest and importance" [1, pp. 1–2] with cybercrime increasing at a rapid rate due to the betterment of technologies and connectivity [2]. Many organisations are experiencing higher levels of cyber-attacks and threats, and this, in turn, has made cybersecurity a feature that needs to be implemented in an organisation's daily activities and operations [2]. Thus far, insufficient attention has been paid to cyber security by organisations [3]. Increases in incidences of cybercrime and security breaches suggest that there is a skills shortage within the technology industry [4]. The increase in cybercrime combined with the skills shortages, have led to an increased demand for cyber security professionals. The shortage of trained cyber security professionals and a shortage of academic programs to address these threats is considered a crisis in the world of cyber security [3]. "While supply and demand are factors in the recruitment process for any position, in order to secure the best people in the security field we need to know what skills are required to be a security professional in the current cyber security environment"

© Springer Nature Switzerland AG 2019
H. Venter et al. (Eds.): ISSA 2018, CCIS 973, pp. 176–192, 2019.
https://doi.org/10.1007/978-3-030-11407-7_13

[4, p. 67]. Overall, these factors raise the need for research in the field of cyber security as well as research into the skills and competencies that are required to be a cyber security professional.

The primary purpose of this research study was to determine through job advertisement analysis a descriptive set of skill requirements that are needed to work as a cyber security professional in South Africa. This paper is an initial exploratory study that can serve as a basis for more specific studies in future. Studies have been conducted in the area of cyber security and a recent review of literature in this context revealed a skills study that was conducted in Australia [4] as well as the National Initiative for Cybersecurity Education (NICE) framework [5]. No South African studies could be found in relation to the determining of skills requirements for cyber security professionals, thus identifying an opportunity to contribute and fill this knowledge gap.

2 Literature Review

Security can be defined as referring to the state of being safe and protected from hazards such as loss, damage and unauthorised alterations [6]. Computer security is not a product but rather a process that involves the protection of assets such as information, hardware and software, against unauthorised misuse or abuse, with the intention of reducing or mitigating the consequences should misuse or abuse occur [6, 7].

Cyber security is defined as the governance, development, management and use of information security, operational technology (OT) security, and information technology (IT) security tools, concepts, practices and strategies to protect the cyber environment as well as the assets of an organisation or user [1]. Information security is defined as the preservation of the Confidentiality, Integrity and Availability of information and is known as the CIA triad [8, 9]. Information is considered to form part of an organisation's assets, and any vulnerabilities related to its Information and Communication Technologies in which the information is stored on, is referred to as an information security vulnerability [1]. The term cyber security is commonly interchanged with information security, with the former, accounting for the roles of humans in the security process [1].

Information Technology Security also referred to as Information and Communication Technology (ICT) security, outlines the protection of the technology systems where information is stored and transferred [1]. IT security is considered a sub-component of information security [1, 10, 11]. Bai and Wang [12] define offensive security as a proactive defence strategy which can be used by managers to prevent security incidents. An example of a proactive defence strategy is penetration testing [13]. Penetration testing is a legal and authorised manner in which an individual attempts to exploit computer systems with the goal of improving on the flaws and making the system more secure [13, 14]. According to Timchenko and Starobinski [15], offensive security is used to mitigate possible cyber-attacks.

2.1 Cyber Security Research in South Africa

"Africa has recently seen explosive growth in information and communication technologies, making cybercrime a reality in this part of the world" [16, p. 1]. In 2009, President Zuma announced that one of the key initiatives for South Africa would be to intensify its efforts against identity theft and cybercrime [16], indicating the importance of cyber security research in South Africa. The internet continues to expand, offering opportunities to both small and large organisations, to forge international relationships with customers and vendors [17].

Small, and Medium Enterprises (SME), play an important role in South Africa's economy and tend to have most of their electronic systems either hosted locally or in the cloud [17]. Small organisations are classified as having 1–49 employees, medium organisations 50–249 employees and large organisations 250 or more employees [18]. Kent, Tanner and Kabanda [17], found that SME's in South Africa lacked the relevant skills and budget to secure their organisations against cyber threats.

Studies related to South African Banks found that banks are at an increased risk of cybercrime as their reliance and integration with third party systems (such as PayPal), which they have no control over have increased [19]. The study found that the banks were vulnerable due to having inadequate audit logs, insufficient response capabilities and having poor or no policy and standard management in place [19]. It could be argued that compared to SME's, banks have sufficient funds to ensure that relevant controls are implemented. However, this lack of controls could be due to the shortage of skilled cyber security professionals available locally as well as globally.

Irons and Ophoff [20] highlight the growing threats of cybercrime and argue that there is a lack of digital forensics skills to investigate these crimes and threats. As a result, there is a need to increase the skill base of the country's digital forensics professionals, and that this should be aided by the development of full-time university forensics programs [20].

Kritzinger [21] investigated the aspect of cyber safety awareness in South African schools. The increased availability and decrease in cost of ICT devices has resulted in users using ICT in their daily lives for information gathering, education and socialising. This in turn exposes school kids to digital risks and threats, such as phishing scams and identity theft [21].

2.2 Cyber Security Professionals

The key responsibility of a cyber security professional is to protect the network and cyber environment from harm [22]. Advances in technological tools in information and network security has automated the task of monitoring and detection of threats. However, some cyber security tasks cannot be completely automated and still require the analytical capabilities of a human decision maker [22].

Existing studies examine and assess the skills required for broader technology professions such as business analysis and software development [4, 23, 24] and business intelligence [25] however, "studies specific to the skills required by a modern security professional are sparse" [4, p. 67].

One of the roles that have been on the increase is that of the Chief Information Security Officer (CISO) [26]. The CISO forms part of the executive suite, and their job is to keep the enterprise safe from threats and vulnerabilities, through the management of various teams and cyber security professionals [26]. The skills required to perform the role of a CISO comprise of technical skills in combination with business management skills, with the focus on the latter [26].

Caldwell [27] argues that 85% of organisations fail to hire new cyber security professionals, as not enough candidates have the right cyber-security skills. A survey conducted with 40 CISO's, who manage about 6100 cybersecurity employees, indicated that the top three in-demand skill areas [27] are "information security architecture; risk management and compliance; and intelligence/threat analysis [27, p. 6].

Potter and Vickers [4], conducted a study in 2015 to identify the skills required to work in the Australian cyber security industry. The study examined 33 job advertisements that covered a broad range of jobs and job titles [4]. The advertisement study was combined with a questionnaire which asked a group of cyber security professionals (who manage large complex organisations) what they deemed to be the skills required to work in the cyber security field [4]. The results of the study identified skills which fell into six cyber security roles/categories. A short description of each role is provided in Table 1 below.

Table 1. Cyber Security roles as identified by Potter and Vickers [4].

Role	Description
Analyst	Described as a position or role that provides expert advice and subject matter to stakeholders while supporting the team with cyber security incidents. The Analyst is also involved in risk management activities and security-related support services. Skill identified as being needed to fulfil the role include Team Work, Process Creation, Analysis, Innovation, Motivation and able to work able to work independently [4]
Consultant	Consultants are independent workers who aid teams, through analysis and complex technical investigations. They also aid in the identification, development, and management of customer relationships and development of solutions [4]. Skills associated with the role relate to leadership, presentation skills, time management, process skills, technical expertise, risk management and ability to work independently [4]
Security Engineer	The position of Security Engineer has a technical focus dealing with network security, incident response, intrusion detection, and vulnerability assessment" [4, p. 69]. Skills required to perform the role of a security engineer include technical expertise, analytical skills [4]
Security Assessor	Advisors are primarily involved in conducting security assessments, penetration testing, vulnerability assessments and design tasks [4]. Skills identified for this category include analysis, process skills, relationship management, consulting, and presentation skills amongst others [4]

(continued)

Table 1. (*continued*)

Role	Description
Manager	Managerial positions included executive manager, cyber security manager and Operations managers and are involved in the management of teams, units and security centres [4]. Skills required for managerial roles included leadership, risk management, project management, process creation, process management and presentation skills to name a few
Sales	Sales positions were described as fulfilling the position of a Business Development Manager, which is responsible for growing a range of key Enterprise accounts in the cyber security area. Skills needed, ranging from technical expertise, Innovation, presentations skills, relationship management to communication [4]

Other cyber security roles found in the literature, outside of these six key categories, is that of the professionals in digital computer forensics. Irons and Ophoff [20] note that in South Africa there is a critical gap in skills with regards to digital forensics. The role of digital forensics in South Africa is vital given the "numerous challenges related to cybercrime and cyber threats, thus making the ability to investigate such incidents essential" [20, p. 1].

Studies aimed at finding the requisite skills for specific professions have been found in other disciplines, and feature studies such as cataloguing professionals in digital environments [28]. In South Africa, a study conducted by De Jager and Brown [25] assessed the required skill set for Business Intelligence professionals, while on the contrary no similar studies could be found in regards to the requisite skills for cyber security professionals.

3 Research Methodology

The research approach applied to this study consisted of a mixed approach as it was both deductive and inductive. The deductive approach relates to using existing cyber security roles and skills that were identified by Potter and Vickers [4] in their Australian study as well as contained in other sections of the literature. The inductive approach refers to having determined themes and categories relating to skills and knowledge areas from job advertisements as well establishing relationships between these categories and themes. An example of this would be, determining which job roles require which skills.

The initial phase of the study consisted of finding and reviewing existing literature on skills requirements for cyber security professionals. The findings from this review were then used to compile a list of categories pertaining to roles, skills and titles, that could be used in part to analyse the South African job advertisements. Similar approaches have been used by De Jager and Brown [25] in their business intelligence (BI) requisite skills study as well as Potter and Vickers [4] in their cyber security skills assessment study. The second phase involved collecting adverts over a two-month period and checking these adverts for duplicates in order to yield a unique set of 196 adverts. Adverts were collected from various major internet-based job sites [29]. The third phase involved analysing the adverts using content analysis to determine categories of job roles and required skills. Once this was process was completed qualitative and quantitative methods (mixed methods) were used to summarise the frequency of the skill themes and categories to produce a set of descriptive statistics.

3.1   Data Collection

The researcher aimed to collect 200 unique job advertisements to conduct the study. Similar studies [4, 29] used a sample of less than 50 unique job adverts to conduct their research. For this study a sample of size at least four times the size allowed for better results. It has been assumed that the human resources department does not operate in isolation but works with the field specialists and managers in the firm to ensure they attract the skills that they need, when constructing the required job advertisements.

The data sources from which the adverts were collected from, consisted of five job portal websites. The five were considered to be "widely used in South Africa by various organisations and agencies to advertise job vacancies in the country" [29, p. 215] and also used by Ndwandwe and Onyancha [29] to conduct their South African job advertisement study. LinkedIn.com is a popular social networking platform that aims to help business professionals and individuals meet and inquire about jobs and is also used by prospective recruits to find prospective employers [30]. A large proportion of the sample was obtained from LinkedIn.com as the adverts listed on the platform offered greater depth of information as compared to the other websites.

A sample of 280 advertisements were downloaded from the websites. The search phrases "Cyber Security" and "IT Security" were used to search for relevant adverts. Search terms such as Computer Security, Network Security, Information Security were also used, however, as these mainly yielded duplicate adverts, it was decided that "Cyber Security" and "IT Security would be sufficient in collecting the relevant adverts. Adverts containing the word "Security" in the job title were selected and where adverts did not contain the word "Security" in the job title, but made a clear reference to cyber or IT security in its job description, they were also selected.

Adverts were collected on a weekly basis over a two-month period. With each collection instance the collected adverts were checked for any possible duplicates (with the already collected adverts) and the duplicates were removed. Adverts that did not provide sufficient information or seemed to have been posted by more than one recruiter were also removed from the sample. Each advert found was exported in a . PDF format and adverts that were not exported with all the information intact were removed from the sample. After performing the above steps, the researcher was left with 196 unique adverts. Each advert was assigned an advert number ranging from "Advert 001" to "Advert 196". The assigning of an advert number made it possible to check for duplications as well to refer to the advert within the research. Table 2 lists the relevant website sources along with the respective unique advert counts that was used to construct the sample of 196 unique job advertisements.

Table 2. Data sources: Job advertisements

Website/Job portal	Number of adverts	Percentage of sample
www.linkedin.com	106	54.1%
www.pnet.com	49	25.0%
www.careerjunction.co.za	21	10.7%
www.indeed.co.za	16	8.2%
www.careers24.co.za	4	2.0%
Total	**196**	**100.0%**

3.2 Data Analysis

Microsoft Excel and Nvivo 11 were used to analyse the 196 job adverts. Nvivo 11 was used to conduct the first pass through of the data and code the text found in the adverts to initial themes (called Nodes in Nvivo) and categories relating to skills, experience and qualifications required for cyber security jobs. A second pass through of the data was made this time capturing in Excel. The second data pass through assisted in validating the coding frequency listed in NVivo. Once the data had been coded and categorised into NVivo and Excel, quantitative methods were applied to calculate frequencies for the values captured and to produce a set of descriptive statistics.

4 Results and Analysis

The results are presented using various tables that summarise the frequency counts of categories as well as discovered themes. Where possible tables in this section have noted the frequency counts and the counts as a percentage of the total number of adverts (196 Adverts).

4.1 Industries

Table 3 presents the industries that were looking to recruit cyber security professionals. A total of 20 industries were identified in the 196 adverts, with Financial services accounting for 27% of the demand, followed by the Information Technology and Services sector which accounted for 24% of the demand. Other industries of interest such as aviation and agriculture had at least one job and this illustrates the need for cyber security professionals in other sectors. Companies and recruiters used phrases and statements such as "One of the leading big four financial services providers in South Africa, with a massive footprint is currently seeking the expertise of a Cyber Security...", "My client is one of Africa's trusted provider of Managed Security Services" and "Our client is a dynamic agricultural company in the Free State and Limpopo". These statements were used to identify the industry that the job was being offered in.

Table 3. Industries requiring cyber security professionals.

Industry	Frequency	Frequency %
Financial services	53	27.0%
Information Technology and Services	47	24.0%
Not Specified	37	18.9%
Management consulting	11	5.5%
Telecommunications	7	3.6%
Government Parastatals	6	3.1%
Insurance	6	3.1%
Manufacturing	5	2.6%
Other	24	12.2%

4.2 Job Locations

South Africa consist of nine provinces [31]. Five provinces were identified in which cyber security jobs were being offered. Table 4 illustrates this along with their respective frequencies. The Gauteng province accounted for the majority (64.8%) of cyber security jobs being offered, followed by the Western Cape province which accounts for 22.5%. Adverts where the location was not disclosed or could not be identified accounted for 7.6% of the sample. Where the province was not explicitly specified, but a city name provided, the researcher traced the province that the city was in and then made the appropriate classification.

Table 4. Cyber security jobs by province.

Province	Frequency	Frequency %
Gauteng	127	64.8%
Western Cape	44	22.5%
KwaZulu-Natal	7	3.6%
Eastern Cape	2	1.0%
Limpopo	1	0.5%
Not Specified	15	7.6%

4.3 Job Levels

Each advert was categorised according to a job level (seniority). The list comprised of the following: Entry or Junior Level, Mid-Level, Senior Level, Executive Level and Not Specified. The job level was determined by observing the job title as it contained key identifiers such as "Senior Cyber Threat Intelligence" and "Head of Cyber Security". Other areas where the job level could be determined was in the body of the advert, which referred to descriptions such as "Experienced Mid-Senior level" in the job description text or where the advert body specified reporting lines such as "Reporting to: Sales manager", "Reporting directly to the Vice-Chancellor" and "Reporting to the Chief Information Officer".

The mid- level positions and senior level positions made up approximately 70% of the sample adverts, with each category respectively accounting for approximately 35% each. Executive level positions accounted for 5.1% of the sample, and "Entry or Junior Level" positions being the lowest with 15.8%. Table 5 summarises the job levels along with their observed frequency obtained from the adverts. 8.2% of the adverts were not able to be classified and therefore listed under "Not Specified".

Table 5. Adverts classified in terms of job level (Seniority).

Job level	Frequency	Frequency %
Entry or Junior Level	31	15.8%
Mid-Level	69	35.2%
Senior Level	70	35.7%
Executive Level	10	5.1%
Not Specified	16	8.2%

4.4   Job Titles

As discussed in the previous section, keywords in the job titles were used in identifying the job level of cyber security positions being offered. As titles vary from one organisation to the next, the researcher intended on determining which words frequently occurred in the job titles. Figure 1 depicts a word cloud diagram that was constructed to visually illustrate the frequently reoccurring words used in cyber security job titles.

Fig. 1. Frequently reoccurring words used in cyber security job titles.

Using the word cloud diagram, the word "Security" was identified as being frequently used in the job title, followed by "Information", "Specialist and "Cyber". Titles such as "Information Security Officer", "Cyber Security Assistant Manager", "Cyber Associate Partner", "Information Security Information and Event Management (SIEM)", "Information Security and Governance Specialist" and "Information Security and Infrastructure Specialist" illustrate the use of these reoccurring words in the sample of job adverts.

4.5   Job Roles

The job description text and titles of each advert was analysed to identify a job's primary role. Roles used by Potter and Vickers [4] were used as an initial categorical list to identify some of the roles. The list of roles was updated as new roles were identified. Text relating to the descriptions of these roles within the adverts comprised of descriptions, sentences and explanations such as "As an information security consultant, you will lead the implementation of security solutions for our clients and support the clients in their desire to protect the business.", "The Information Security Officer (ISO) is responsible for establishing and maintaining the enterprise vision, strategy, and program", "As an Information Security Consultant, you'll contribute technical insights to client engagements and internal projects." and "Role Purpose: To manage and lead a team of professionals to ensure that independent assurance of the control environment and effective risk management practices".

In total, 46 descriptive roles were identified from the adverts. The 46 role descriptions were then generalised to a set of 14 roles as presented in Table 6. The top five roles that most organisations were seeking to employ were that of a "Specialist" (28.1%), followed by the role of an "Engineer" (13.8%), "Manager" (10.7%), "Analyst" (10.7%) and "Penetration Tester" (6.6%). The roles with lowest demand were that of an "Ethical Hacker", "Expert", and a role in "Operations" each accounting for less than 1% of the sample of adverts. The "Expert" role can see be as an exception as the advert (LinkedIn Advert (39)), was specifically looking for a cyber security professional that was a mining expert, which indicates the need for cyber security in many industries.

4.6   Required Experience (Years)

For each advert in the sample, the minimum required experience (years) was noted and captured. Where an advert noted multiple experience requirements, the average for the overall set was calculated and taken as the minimum (rounded to the nearest whole number). Experience in this study refers to experience working in a cyber or security role.

Table 7 illustrates the categories of the "minimum number of cyber security experience" in years that was identified in the sample of adverts. The category of "5 Years" (24.5%) was identified as being needed by most adverts followed by "3 years" (17.9%) and then 8 years (9.7%). 16.8% of the adverts had not listed any reference to required experience.

Table 6. Generalised list of cyber security roles.

Role category	Frequency	Percentage
Specialist	55	28.1%
Engineer	27	13.8%
Manager	21	10.7%
Analyst	21	10.7%
Penetration Tester	13	6.6%
Sales	13	6.6%
Architect	12	6.1%
Consultant	11	5.6%
Leadership	10	5.1%
Officer	6	3.1%
Auditing	4	2.0%
Operations	1	0.5%
Ethical Hacker	1	0.5%
Expert	1	0.5%

Table 7. Minimum required experience (Years)

Minimum years experience	Frequency	Percentage
2 Years	14	7.1%
3 years	35	17.9%
4 years	16	8.2%
5 Years	46	23.5%
6 Years	9	4.6%
7 Years	8	4.1%
8 Years	19	9.7%
10 Years	11	5.6%
10+Years	2	1.0%
15 Years	3	1.5%
Not Specified	33	16.8%

4.7   Qualifications and Certifications

The minimum required qualification was extracted for each advert and classified into one of the categories represented in Table 8. The categories represented in Table 8, were identified through determining qualification themes in relation to the sample of adverts.

More than half (52.0%) of the adverts required a Bachelors Degree in either Computer Science, Information Systems or Engineering as a minimum qualification. 9.2% of the adverts cited industry certifications as the minimum requirement for the job, followed by 8.7% which cited any "Relevant tertiary qualification" in computer studies. 2.0% noted needing matric as a minimum for a job, while 1.5% of the sample, required a Masters degree as a minimum.

Table 8. Minimum qualifications required.

Minimum qualification	Frequency	Frequency %
Bachelor's Degree	102	52.0%
Not Specified	26	13.3%
Certifications	18	9.2%
Relevant tertiary qualification	17	8.7%
Diploma	10	5.1%
Bachelor's Degree or Postgraduate Degree	7	3.6%
Postgraduate Degree	6	3.1%
Matric	4	2.0%
IT Related	3	1.5%
Master's Degree	3	1.5%

A total of 49.5% of the advert sample (97 adverts) specified that in addition to a minimum qualification the candidate also required industry certification. 33 Adverts or 16,84% of the sample, specified that having an industry certification would be considered advantageous. Table 9 provides a summary of the relationship between requiring an industry certification along with a minimum qualification.

Table 9. Minimum qualification and industry certification.

Minimum qualification	And industry certification required	
	Frequency	Percentage
Bachelor's Degree	72	36.7%
Relevant tertiary qualification	15	7.7%
Postgraduate Degree	3	1.5%
Diploma	2	1.0%
Bachelor's Degree or Postgraduate Degree	1	0.5%
Master's Degree	1	0.5%
Matric	1	0.5%
Not Specified	1	0.5%

The industry certifications that were noted as being required by most professionals, were Certified Information Systems Security Professional (CISSP), Certified Information Security Manager (CISM), Certified Information Systems Auditor (CISA) as well as certifications related to cyber security standards such as International Organization for Standardization (ISO) and the National Institute of Standards and Technology (NIST). Other certifications that reoccurred as themes were Information Technology Infrastructure Library (ITIL) and Cisco Certified Network Associate.

Many of the adverts, in relation to certifications, indicated certification needs through sentences such as "Industry related certification required (e.g. CISSP, CISM, CISA)", "CISSP or CCISO Certification or current studies towards certification would

be greatly advantageous", "Industry related technical certifications will be advantageous", "methodologies Certification in ITIL and ISO 27002 preferred" and "Related
certifications are a plus e.g., CISSP, CISA, CCNA".

4.8 Skills Requirements

Skill categories were based on the categories described by Potter and Vickers [4] as
well as the competencies described by Sonteya and Seymour [23].

Technical skills comprised of the largest skill area with 41.4%, followed by
interpersonal skills with 20.8% and business skills with 15.6%. Leadership skills and
analytical skills were observed as the lowest with 2.7% and 5.9% respectively.
Table 10 provides a list of the major descriptive skills, classified under each general
category. Phrases and sentences such as "strong analytical and problem-solving skills
to develop acceptable solutions for the business", "client relationship management and
business development skills", "Performing in-depth response triage, analysis, and
remediation of security incidents" and "Analyse advanced external attacks to reduce
cyber risk" were used to identify the descriptive list of skills. The frequencies in
Table 10 were computed by noting the number of times a skill appeared in an advert.

Table 10. List of descriptive skills observed in the sample adverts.

Skills Area	Frequency	Percent
Analytical Skills	**55**	**5,9%**
Evaluate, Analyse, Assess Requirements	35	3,77%
Problem Solving	20	2,16%
Business Skills	**145**	**15,6%**
Reporting, Monitor Budgets,	50	4,53%
Research, IT Operations, Consulting	78	23,78%
Sales	17	1,83%
Interpersonal skills	**193**	**20,8%**
Communication (Written and Verbal)	62	6,68%
Client Services (Support, Liaise, Engagement)	38	4,09%
Presentations	21	2,26%
Interpersonal	17	1,83%
Multi-Tasking	13	1,40%
Other (Team work, Managing Personal, Mentoring)	42	1,29%
Leadership Skills	**25**	**2,7%**
Vendor Relationship management	15	1,62%
Team Management, Talent Acquisitions	10	0,97%
Management Skills	**126**	**13,6%**
Development of Security Policies and Procedures	24	2,59%
Project Management	20	2,16%

(continued)

Table 10. (*continued*)

Skills Area	Frequency	Percent
Auditing	18	1,94%
Risk Management	14	1,51%
IT Governance Implementation	13	1,40%
Other (Develop Security Awareness, Process Management)	37	3,99%
Technical Skills	**384**	**41,4%**
Technical Writing	37	3,99%
Design Technical Solutions and Systems	34	3,66%
Vulnerability Management	33	3,56%
Perform Penetration Testing	30	3,23%
Threat Intelligence Gathering	19	2,05%
Firewall Administration	18	1,94%
Implement Security Solutions	15	1,62%
Manage SIEM Products	14	1,51%
Network Administration	14	1,51%
Systems Administration	14	1,51%
Network Architecture & Security design, Troubleshooting	25	1,51%
Programming or Scripting	12	1,29%
Review Source Code	11	1,19%
Other (i.e. IoT, Log Analyses, Data Migration, Disaster Recovery)	108	11,64%
Total	928	100%

5 Discussion and Implications

The Financial Services industry was observed to be the largest industry requiring cybersecurity skills, followed by the Information Technology and Services industry. Most of the organisations seeking to employ cyber security professional fell into the "Large" organisation category. Gauteng was identified as the province offering the most jobs, especially in the city of Johannesburg. At least 10% of the jobs analysed required travelling.

Most jobs being offered could be classified in the mid and senior level categories. The words identified as being most frequently used in cyber security job titles, were "Security", "Information" and "Specialist". The role most sought after was that of a cyber-security specialist. Most roles noted by Potter and Vickers [4] were identified in the study.

On average mid and senior level jobs required a minimum of 3 or 5 years work experience, whilst executive level jobs required a minimum of 8 years or more. Organisations wanted cyber security specialists who had a Bachelor's degree in Computer Science, Information Systems or Engineering along with one or more industry certifications. At least 16% of the sample noted that an industry certification would be advantageous. Technical skills and interpersonal skills were identified as the top two skills being required by cyber security professionals. Given that almost 80% of the sample could not be classified into a remuneration category, no significant observations could be made about salaries.

6 Conclusion

Cyber security professionals are required in more than 20 industries in South Africa. Most jobs to be filled are needed in the Gauteng province, by large organisations in the Financial and Information Technology and Communications industries. Most jobs are located in the mid-senior levels and are required to fulfil the role of a specialist. Overall many of the roles identified in the Australian study were also identified in this study.

Organisations prefer cyber security professionals to have a Bachelor's degree in Computer Science, Information Systems or Engineering along with one or more industry certifications. Certifications were also to be advantages if not deemed to be required.

Five skill requirements categories were determined and comprised of Analytical Skills, Business Skills, Interpersonal skills, Leadership Skills, Management Skills and Technical Skills. Technical skills and Interpersonal skills were observed as the top two categories required by cyber security professionals.

This research study provides insights into the various aspects (Industries, organisational size etc.) of cyber security jobs in South African as well as identifying the skills requirements that professionals need to possess.

Organisations or individuals can use the information in this research study to better understand the requirements needed of a cyber-security professional. Furthermore, educational institutions can identify how curricula might need to be updated in order to equip cyber security professionals with the relevant skills and knowledge. As no studies like this have been done in South Africa, this study makes a small contribution towards this gap in research.

The unstructured nature of job advertisements presented limitations as to what data could be collected and analysed. This limitation directly impacts on the accuracy, insights and observations that can be made using qualitative methods of analyses.

References

1. Von Solms, R., Van Niekerk, J.: From information security to cyber security. Comput. Secur. **38**, 97–102 (2013)
2. Patrick, H., Fields, Z.: A need for cyber security creativity. In: Collective Creativity for Responsible and Sustainable Business Practice, pp. 42–61. IGI Global (2017)
3. Fourie, L., Sarrafzadeh, A., Pang, S., Kingston, T., Watters, P.: The global cyber security workforce - an ongoing human capital crisis. In: Global Business and Technology Association Conference, pp. 173–184 (2014)
4. Potter, L.E., Vickers, G.: What skills do you need to work in cyber security? In: Proceedings of the 2015 ACM SIGMIS Conference on Computers and People Research - SIGMIS-CPR 2015, pp. 67–72 (2015)
5. Newhouse, W., Keith, S., Scribner, B., Witte, G.: National Initiative for Cybersecurity Education (NICE) Cybersecurity Workforce Framework (2017)

6. Hsiao, D.R., Kerr, D.S., Madnick, S.E.: Computer Security. Academic Press, New York (2014)
7. Mitnick, K.D., Simon, W.L.: The Art of Deception: Controlling the Human Element of Security. Wiley, New York (2011)
8. Andress, J.: The Basics of Information Security Understanding the Fundamentals of InfoSec in Theory and Practice, 2nd edn. Elsevier Inc., Amsterdam (2014)
9. Disterer, G.: ISO/IEC 27000, 27001 and 27002 for information security management. J. Inf. Secur. **4**, 92–100 (2013)
10. Cherdantseva, Y., Hilton, J.: A reference model of information assurance & security. In: 2013 International Conference on Availability, Reliability and Security, pp. 546–555, September 2013
11. Walls, A., Perkins, E., Weiss, J.: Definition: Cybersecurity, Gartner, pp. 1–5, June 2013
12. Bai, Y., Wang, X.: Teaching offensive security in a virtual environment. J. Comput. Sci. Coll. **31**(1), 140–142 (2015)
13. Engebreston, P.: The Basics of Hacking and Penetration Testing, 2nd edn. Syngress, USA (2013)
14. Yeo, J.: Using penetration testing to enhance your company's security. Comput. Fraud Secur. **2013**(4), 17–20 (2013)
15. Timchenko, M., Starobinski, D.: A simple laboratory environment for real-world offensive security education. In: SIGCSE 2015 – Proceedings of the 46th ACM Technical Symposium on Computer Science Education, pp. 657–662 (2015)
16. Grobler, M., Van Vuuren, J.J.: Broadband broadens scope for cyber crime in Africa. In: Proceedings of the 2010 Information Security South Africa Conference, ISSA 2010 (2010)
17. Kent, C., Tanner, M., Kabanda, S.: How South African SMEs address cyber security: the case of web server logs and intrusion detection. In: 2016 International Conference on Emerging Technologies and Innovative Business Practices for the Transformation of Societies, EmergiTech 2016, pp. 100–105 (2016)
18. Flynn, A., Davis, P.: Investigating the effect of tendering capabilities on SME activity and performance in public contract competitions. Int. Small Bus. J. **35**(4), 449–469 (2017)
19. Mbelli, T., Dwolatzky, B.: Cyber security, a threat to cyber banking in South Africa: an approach to network and application security. In: 2016 IEEE 3rd International, pp. 1–6 (2016)
20. Irons, A., Ophoff, J.: Aspects of digital forensics in South Africa. Interdiscip. J. Inf. Knowl. Manag. **11**(2014), 273–283 (2016)
21. Kritzinger, E.: Short-term initiatives for enhancing cyber-safety within South African schools. South African Comput. J. **28**(1), 1–17 (2016)
22. Ben-Asher, N., Gonzalez, C.: Effects of cyber security knowledge on attack detection. Comput. Hum. Behav. **48**, 51–61 (2015)
23. Sonteya, T., Seymour, L.: Towards an understanding of the business process analyst: an analysis of competencies. J. Inf. Technol. Educ. Res. **11**, 43–63 (2012)
24. Tanner, M., Seymour, L.: The range and level of software development skills needed in the Western Cape, South Africa. In: Proceedings of the e-Skills for Knowledge Production and Innovation Conference 2014, pp. 487–505 (2014)
25. De Jager, T., Brown, I.: A descriptive categorized typology of requisite skills for business intelligence professionals. In: ACM International Conference Proceeding Series, 26–28 September (2016)
26. Alexander, A., Cummings, J.: The rise of the chief information security officer. People Strateg. **39**(1), 10–13 (2016)
27. Caldwell, T.: Plugging the cyber-security skills gap. Comput. Fraud Secur. **2013**(7), 5–10 (2013)

28. Park, J., Lu, C., Mario, L.: Cataloging professionals in the digital environment: a content analysis of job descriptions. J. Am. Soc. Inf. Sci. Technol. **60**(4), 844–857 (2009)
29. Ndwandwe, S.C., Onyancha, O.B.: Job functions and requirements for knowledge managers: lessons for Library and Information Science (LIS) schools in South Africa. Mousaion **2**(29), 211–226 (2011)
30. Parez, M., Silva, K., Harvey, D., Bosco, S.: Linked into a job? the ethical considerations of recruiting through linkedin. In: Proceedings for the Northeast Region Decision Sciences Institute, pp. 953–961 (2013)
31. Labadarios, D., et al.: The National Food Consumption Survey (NFCS): South Africa, 1999. Public Health Nutr. **8**(05), 533–543 (2005)

Author Index

Printed in the United States
By Bookmasters